To Jenni and Riccardo

ETHICS AND THE ENGLISH NOVEL
FROM AUSTEN TO FORSTER

Ethics and the English Novel from Austen to Forster

VALERIE WAINWRIGHT
University of Florence, Italy

ASHGATE

© Valerie Wainwright 2007

All rights reserved. No part of this publication may be reproduced, stored in a retrieval system or transmitted in any form or by any means, electronic, mechanical, photocopying, recording or otherwise without the prior permission of the publisher.

Valerie Wainwright has asserted her moral right under the Copyright, Designs and Patents Act, 1988, to be identified as the author of this work.

Published by
Ashgate Publishing Limited
Gower House
Croft Road
Aldershot
Hampshire GU11 3HR
England

Ashgate Publishing Company
Suite 420
101 Cherry Street
Burlington, VT 05401-4405
USA

Ashgate website: http://www.ashgate.com

British Library Cataloguing in Publication Data
Wainwright, Valerie
Ethics and the English novel from Austen to Forster
   1. Ethics in literature 2. English fiction – 19th century – History and criticism
   I. Title
   823'.8'09353

Library of Congress Cataloging-in-Publication Data
Wainwright, Valerie, 1951-
   Ethics and the English novel from Austen to Forster / by Valerie Wainwright.
     p. cm.
   Includes bibliographical references and index.
   ISBN-13: 978-0-7546-5432-2 (alk. paper)
   1. Ethics in literature. 2. English fiction—19th century—History and criticism. 3. English fiction—20th century—History and criticism. I. Title.

PR868.E67W35 2007
823'.809384—dc22

2006031680

ISBN: 978-0-7546-5432-2

Printed and bound in Great Britain by MPG Books Ltd, Bodmin, Cornwall.

Contents

Acknowledgements   vi

Introduction   1

PART 1: WHAT MATTERS (MOST)

1   Modes and Sensibilities: Varieties of Ethical Thought   21

2   Narrative Perspectives   45

PART 2: ETHICAL DESIGNS

3   On Being Un/reasonable: *Mansfield Park* and the Limits of Persuasion   59

4   Discovering Autonomy and Authenticity in *North and South*: Elizabeth Gaskell, John Stuart Mill, and the Liberal Ethic   85

5   On Goods, Virtues and *Hard Times*   105

6   Anatomizing Excellence: *Middlemarch*, Moral Saints and the Languages of Belief   123

7   The Magic in *Mentalité*: Hardy's Native Returns   143

8   *Howards End* and the Confession of Imperfection   161

Afterword: *Utz*   183

Bibliography   *197*
Index   *209*

Acknowledgements

This book has taken shape over the years and thanks are due to editors who have allowed me to publish here parts of studies that first appeared in the pages of their journals. An earlier version of 'Discovering Autonomy and Authenticity in North and South: Elizabeth Gaskell, John Stuart Mill and the Liberal Ethic' came out in Clio, 23 (1994), while chapter 5 has developed out of 'On Goods, Virtues and Hard Times', Dickens Studies Annual 26 (1998). Thanks are also due to the editors of English and the English Association for permission to reprint parts of two articles, 'Anatomizing Excellence: Middlemarch, Moral Saints and the Languages of Belief' 49 (2000), and 'Un Being Un/reasonable: Mansfield Park and the Limits of Persuasion' 53 (2004).

For helpful comments on my study of Middlemarch, I should like to thank Ken Newton and Stan Smith. The careful response of Ashgate's external reader was invaluable. His detailed and insightful comments have enabled me to recognize problems and considerably improve the text; though I doubt not that there are still points that require clarifying, qualifying or developing.

Special thanks for comments, discussions and encouragement go to Paul and Marianne Joannides. My warmest thanks also to Jennie Osborn for making periods of research in London such a pleasure.

For their patience and skills during the editorial processes I should like to thank Ann Donahue, Meredith Coeyman and Pat FitzGerald.

For granting me a sabbatical and research grants with which to complete this work, I thank the Dipartimento di Filologia Moderna of the University of Florence.

Introduction

It is difficult to dissent when Terry Eagleton remarks that in pre-Theory decades literary studies could well be described as marked by an 'almighty fetishizing' of value.[1] Often the influence of F.R. Leavis translated into readings deeply concerned with the 'moral intelligence' or the 'moral intensity' manifest in a text. Thought-provoking and inspiring his work has proved to be for many a critic, but over the decades other scholars have adopted distinctly feminist, historicist or Marxist approaches to works of literature. As with studies investigating the politics of culture, despite the obvious shift in emphasis, such lines of inquiry tend to revisit sooner or later the variegated domain of ethics. But a more complex challenge to an ethically-focussed form of criticism emerged with the impact of postmodernist critique, which for a time evinced in the evocative words of one critic 'a rival swallowing mastery'.[2] A succinct account of the repercussions of postmodernism would note that certain issues, some very old, have become as compelling as they are divisive for critics who have taken 'the turn to ethics'.[3] The on-going debate on the nature of the moral subject, on the possibility of achieving (moral) truth and knowledge, has been animated and at times even 'embattled'. It is a debate about the best ways of conceiving of both moral philosophy and ethical criticism. Prominent amongst the ever increasing number of participants are philosophers, such as Martha Nussbaum, Richard Eldridge and Daniel Brudney, who have focussed on literary texts in order to articulate arguments on traditional moral concerns.[4] By contrast, the philosophy of Emmanuel Levinas, and in particular his key concept of 'ethical alterity', has shaped many a postmodernist critical reading. Such readings typically attach immense significance to the intersubjective encounter. Indeed, Levinas has insisted on a radical redefining of ethics.[5]

---

[1] Terry Eagleton, *The Illusions of Postmodernism* (Oxford: Blackwell, 1996), p. 94.

[2] David Parker, *Ethics, Theory and the Novel* (Cambridge: Cambridge University Press, 1994), p. 5.

[3] See Lawrence Buell, 'What We Talk About When We Talk About Ethics', in Marjorie Garber, Beatrice Hanssen and Rebecca L. Walkowitz (eds), *The Turn to Ethics* (New York and London: Routledge, 2000), pp. 1–13.

[4] See Martha C. Nussbaum, *Love's Knowledge: Essays on Philosophy and Literature* (Oxford: Oxford University Press, 1990), Richard Eldridge, *On Moral Personhood: Philosophy, Literature, Criticism and Self-Understanding* (Chicago and London: Chicago University Press, 1989) and Daniel Brudney, 'Knowledge and Silence: *The Golden Bowl* and Moral Philosophy', *Critical Inquiry* 16 (1990): 397–437, and idem, 'Marlow's Morality', *Philosophy and Literature* 27 (2003): 318–40.

[5] Jill Robbins, *Altered Reading: Levinas and Literature* (Chicago: University of Chicago Press, 1999). In *Postmodernity, Ethics and the Novel from Leavis to Levinas* (London: Routledge, 1999), Andrew Gibson's aim is to achieve a 'post-Levinasian ethics of

My aim in this work is to return to and revise arguments concerning the ethics of a sequence of remarkable novels of the long nineteenth century, taking into account new research on key moments in the debates of modernity. The thesis I shall be sustaining here proposes that within the ethics of modernity we can discern an influential line of thought which privileges personal flourishing, that this is interpreted as an active and expansive form of well-being for both men *and* women, and that the novelists who contributed brought to this debate a shrewd understanding of the manifold difficulties that might complicate the realization of such an ideal. I shall be analysing central aspects of novels by Austen, Gaskell, Dickens, Eliot, Hardy and Forster in ways that should yield new insights into narrative ethics, the connections among these novels, and their relationship to modern ethical thought. When it comes to the sphere of ethics these writers look 'modern'; in crucial respects they are 'our contemporaries'.[6] They share modern moral outlooks and notions; they are concerned with typically modern demands and the moral sources which can satisfy them; they are drawn to the problem of what makes lives essentially fragmentary, empty, or incoherent.[7]

Informing my approach to these works of fiction is the premise that in every case the narrative's project envisions or comprehends an ideal of well-being that

---

fiction, both 'an ethics of the event' and 'an ethics of affect'. But see also C. Fred Alford, 'Emmanuel Levinas and Iris Murdoch: Ethics as Exit?', *Philosophy and Literature* 26 (2002): 24–42. Doris Sommer in 'Attitude, Its Rhetoric' discusses the problems of following Levinas and becoming 'the hostage object of the Other subject' in *The Turn to Ethics*, pp. 201–20. In the same volume, Judith Butler conceives of a role for ethics after poststructuralism while considering both Nietzsche's suspicion of ethics and Levinas's ethical demands; 'Ethical Ambivalence', pp. 15–28.

[6] Charles Taylor argues that 'Our Victorian Contemporaries' participate in the modern moral predicament that is due in great measure to the legacy of ideas left by those many-sided cultural transformations that are the Enlightenment and Romanticism. These movements 'made us what we are', which means that 'our cultural life, our self-conceptions, our moral outlooks still operate in the wake of these great events …We still instinctively reach for the old vocabularies, the ones we owe to Enlightenment and Romanticism. That is why the Victorians are so close to us': *Sources of the Self: The Making of the Modern Identity* (Cambridge: Cambridge University Press, 1989), p. 393.

[7] Taylor, *Sources of the Self*, p. 413. Hina Nazar asks 'is Jane Austen a novelist of modernity?' According to Nazar, Austen's modernity consists in the fact that her interest in propriety (a traditional concern) does not preempt her interest in independent judgment. Following Habermas, Nazar takes 'a critical and reflective relation to convention' as the hallmark of modernity. See 'The Imagination Goes Visiting: Jane Austen, Judgment and the Social', *Nineteenth-Century Literature* 59 (2004): 145–78.

In a major study which rejects Marilyn Butler's highly influential view of Austen as asserting a 'preconceived and inflexible morality' that is central to her reactionary tendencies, Peter Knox-Shaw argues compellingly that Austen is to be rated amongst the 'least proselytizing of Christian moralists', she is in fact typical of the sceptical Enlightenment: *Jane Austen and the Enlightenment* (Cambridge: Cambridge University Press, 2004).

implies affirmation through activities that are both personally gratifying and morally acceptable – or better still morally admirable. One of the most attractive features of Enlightenment thought relates to the validation of happiness. For some writers the *summum bonum* consisted in the kind of self-fulfilment that entwined happiness with commitment to the interests of others. In words taken from Archbishop Tillotson's sermons (published in 1820): 'to do good is the most pleasant enjoyment in the world, it is natural, and whatever is so, is delightful'.[8] The novels at the centre of this study covet a life which can be deemed – plausibly deemed – fulfilling: this is a way of life whose happiness is underpinned by a conviction that its activities and achievements are not simply satisfying but truly worthwhile.

Flourishing as a factor must be taken seriously, and to this end harmful forms of self-distortion are to be avoided or overcome. Thriving, most writers seem to recognize, involves the difficult task of achieving the kind of reasonable self-love and healthy self-development that finds expression in undistorted modes of conduct, so that characters neither exaggerate the extent of their duties to the world beyond self, nor pitch their own concerns safely above the needs of others.[9] Virtue is anchored to conceptions of rewarding lives. For these authors if writing about ethics means tackling the question of what makes for a rich and meaningful life, so too does it entail thinking about why things can go wrong. Among the most intricate of problems that the characters of these novels must confront are obstacles to states of 'being well and doing well in being well'.[10] This felicitous expression originates with Alasdair MacIntyre, as does the claim that moderns (by which he means above all modern moral philosophers writing in the period before 1980) have seriously underestimated the importance of debating the implications of eudaimonism. Here I shall be suggesting that it makes sense to think of narratives by Austen, Gaskell, Dickens, Eliot, Hardy and E.M. Forster as engaged in working out responses to the question of what constitutes a fulfilling life: this eudaimonistic prospect is the narrative's desideratum, its secret ambition; it is not its systematic theory. That is only to be expected. The literary text is likely to entertain and promote a diversity of viewpoints, and even modern narratives may well feature disjunction and omission; they can eschew overall coherence and accommodate degrees of indeterminacy and ambiguity. With the prospect of disunity the question arises as to whether the reader can nonetheless form an *all-things-considered* point of view – a perspective that we might identify with that of an 'implied author'. I shall be suggesting that we can attribute to these texts an all-things-considered perspective, that

---

[8] *The Works of the Most Reverend Dr John Tillotson*, ed. T. Birch (10 vols, London: Dove, 1820), vol. 2, p. 205.

[9] Inspired by Nietzsche, Christine Swanton provides an account of virtue ethics which comprises a defence of the self-love that expresses strength and vitality in undistorted ways: *Virtue Ethics: A Pluralistic View* (Oxford: Oxford University Press, 2003), see especially pp. 128–60, 183–91.

[10] Alasdair MacIntyre, *After Virtue: A Study in Moral Theory* (London: Duckworth, 1981), p. 139.

we can reasonably privilege a particular ethical discourse. A rigorous and resourceful ethical reading will clearly be attentive both to patterns of salience and to the problems that attend interpretation, and this means analyzing the disparate and even contradictory elements out of which the text is made.

In certain narratives complications arise through the articulation of moral discourses concerning different types of value. Such discourses may be complementary or antagonistic, for values sometimes pertain to incommensurable perspectives. I shall be drawing attention to the patterns and problems (and especially those connected to the narrative voice) which emerge once we start to focus closely on narrative discourses which favour a eudaimonistic ethical stance. What these narratives share, I suggest, is of the nature of a generic objective; though Hardy's novel, it could be argued, is in some respects an exception: the eudaimonistic prospect in *The Return of the Native* constituting an illusion – perhaps – rather than a working hypothesis.

So what sort of goods will contribute to the goodness of a person's life? What makes for flourishing or a full life? These works were written in a period in which notions of obligation and righteousness were seemingly ubiquitous. Indeed, it seems that such moral rigourism emerged as the defining, the dominant, outlook of the period. In the view of some scholars even Jane Austen shares with Dickens and George Eliot, 'Victorian anxieties' about the saving power of the principled.[11] Victorian morality must often have appeared in the guise of an 'unrelenting and hurtful idealism'.[12] In his *Ethical Studies* of 1876 F.H. Bradley repudiated certain 'fixed habits of thought', comprising the perverse notion that 'morality is a life harassed and persecuted everwhere by "imperatives" and disagreeable duties, and that without these you have not got morality'.[13] What this study should show is that in the narratives analyzed here a variety of moral considerations mixed with other sorts, as novelists reflected about what would have to happen if individuals were to achieve an active and expansive mode of life. Because the accent falls on the quality of lives, because these writers kept their sights fixed on an ethics of well-being, in these narratives moral motives are one set of considerations to be placed alongside others. In the novels of Dickens, for example, characters strive and struggle; they struggle with guilt and they strive to get on. But when in *Great Expectations* Biddy doubts the wisdom of Pip's ambition to become a gentleman, countering with 'I only want you to do well,

---

[11] See, for example, Julia Prewitt Brown, 'The Victorian Anxieties of *Mansfield Park*', in *Jane Austen's Novels: Social Change and Literary Form* (Cambridge, MA: Harvard University Press, 1979), pp. 80–100. But see note 7 above, for the articulation of contrasting views of Austen in recent studies by Hina Nazar and Peter Knox-Shaw.

[12] Jil Larson, *Ethics and Narrative in the English Novel, 1880–1914* (Cambridge: Cambridge University Press, 2001), p. 146. Larson remarks of certain post Victorian writers 'that all recognized the value of traditional morality when purged of its unrelenting and hurtful idealism'. The problem here is what exactly is this 'traditional morality' to which she refers?

[13] *Ethical Studies* (2nd edn, Oxford: Clarendon Press, 1927), p. 215.

and to be *comfortable*', hers is, we realize, the voice of reason (emphasis added).[14] Comfort's contraries, disquiet, distress, pain, are the recurring symptoms and effects of the obsessions that dominate that novel.

For Dickens and others comfort is then a prime consideration, but still one amongst others. Good lives, it would appear, require integrity and authenticity for which considerable self-understanding as well as self-direction would seem to be essential. For most people deep personal relations plus the sense of purpose that goes with beneficent activities are fundamental goods. Good lives are those imbued with a sense that certain interests matter a great deal. It is engagement with meaningful interests that gives a satisfying overall character to one's life. Hence moderns continue to struggle for meaning, and that is what makes them so interesting. On the one side, the social domain does indeed become a site of substantive demands. Attitudes of concern and especially respect for others are seen as somewhere near the centre in anything that can be called an ethical life. Crucially inflecting views of social relationships in this period is the notion of altruism: a notion which arguably distinguishes the ethical stance of modernity.[15]

Altruism is the concern which acknowledges that others, including non-intimate others, can make demands to which we would do well to respond. This sense of rightful concern is exemplified in Austen's last novel *Persuasion* (1818), when Anne Elliot calls on her old school friend in Bath, a friend who 'had the two strong claims on her attention, of past kindness and present suffering'.[16] For moderns, others can make *claims* on us: their need can constitute a valid reason, and will indeed often constitute a decisive reason, for us to act so as to promote their good. The altruist is ready or prepared to put the interests of others first. When considering what to do, Anne Elliot cannot but focus on her old friend's plight, 'her present suffering'. Mrs Smith's need constitutes one claim that features prominently, if not singly, on the horizon of Anne Elliot's moral outlook. It is invested with significance; it must be taken into account.

On the other side, especially in the novels of Victorians, like Dickens, Gaskell, Eliot and Hardy, projects, plans and schemes of various kinds figure largely; they provide individuals with a sense of purpose and endow life with meaning. Some of these plans focus on the welfare, the happiness or potential of others. But what happens when personal interests and projects conflict with what might seem to be moral imperatives? Moderns are going to face predicaments; certain questions will become urgent. Should the individual forgo her own dearest concerns in the service of others? Does morality have to be conceived as a set of negative constraints? Or is morality essential to the

---

[14] *Great Expectations*, ed. Angus Calder (Harmondsworth: Penguin, 1965). Concluding her reading of *David Copperfield*, Annette R. Federico remarks that 'it seems that happiness for Dickens involves both moral exertion and emotional commitment': '*David Copperfield* and the Pursuit of Happiness', *Victorian Studies* 46 (2003): 69–95.

[15] See Richard Norman, *The Moral Philosophers: An Introduction to Ethics* (2nd edn, Oxford: Oxford University Press, 1998), p. 151.

[16] *Persuasion*, ed. D.W. Harding (Harmondsworth: Penguin, 1965), p. 165.

good life? For the authors at the centre of this study narrative ethics means debating some or all of these issues. In short, it means thinking about the fundamentals of a good life and what to do when concerns and strong convictions clash.

It is worth emphasizing, moreover, that in the novels of Gaskell, Dickens and Forster the potent reforming impulse of the times can be discerned in the choice and treatment of topics that link ethics to ideology. These writers investigate the impact of modes of belief that seemed to many to offer – in the words of J.S. Mill – 'the most inspiring prospects of practical improvement in human affairs'.[17] *Hard Times* and *North and South* examine issues of well-being, but they do so in ways that bring into play those ideas regarding personal and social development that pertain to the social formulas or doctrines which were central to the highly influential belief systems of liberalism and paternalism. These novelists assess the implications of practices to which ideologies are committed, but they are convinced that 'though ideologies rise to possess us, we can elect to take selective possession of them'.[18] David Medalie has argued that *Howards End* 'sets up and evaluates many of the ingredients of the New Liberal Programme ...' that it considers 'the trajectory of achievement ...' and suggests that liberal-humanism will be 'overwhelmed by the conditions of modernity'.[19] There can be little doubt that Forster wants to provoke his contemporaries, to get his readers to think about the horrors and the delights of living in a modern, capitalist, liberal, society. But it is the combined ideological *and* ethical question of what is conducive to the 'best use of faculty, opportunity, energy, life' – to borrow a pertinent expression from liberal politician Herbert Henry Asquith, of 1902[20] – the question of what tends to a life well lived, and hence self-fulfilment, that is central to this novel's thematics.[21] In

---

[17] *Autobiography*, ed. John M. Robson (Harmondsworth: Penguin, 1989), p. 68.

[18] Vincent Newey notes that 'to recognize ideology is to be granted the capacity to assess its nature, the advantages it brings, the shortcomings it imposes, its worth as a way of being and living': *The Scriptures of Charles Dickens: Novels of Ideology, Novels of the Self* (Aldershot: Ashgate, 2004), pp. 10–12.

[19] David Medalie, *E.M. Forster's Modernism* (London: Palgrave Macmillan, 2002). According to Medalie *Howards End* is 'a complex late-Edwardian response to what has been termed the New Liberalism', pp. 4, 7. I shall be suggesting that it is the thought of J.S. Mill as expressed in *On Liberty* that provides Forster with one of the most important *ethical*, rather than specifically political or ideological, points of reference. Mill, arguably one of the founder-thinkers of New Liberalism, is not discussed in Medalie's study.

[20] Asquith's comment continues by stressing the importance of 'education, temperance, better dwellings, improved social and industrial environment, everything, in short, that tends to national, communal, and personal *efficiency*' (emphasis added); from Asquith's introduction to *Liberalism, An Attempt to State the Principles and Proposals of Contemporary Liberalism in England*, by Herbert Louis Samuel (London: Grant Richards, 1902), p. x. Asquith's concern for personal 'efficiency' could be interpreted as concern with self-fulfilment in so far as this notion relates to the complete exercise or development of one's capacities, to making the best of one's self.

[21] The aim or ideal of an individual is to achieve a worthy existence or a life well lived, one of whose consequences will be self-fulfilment.

Howards End this concern coincides with that of the Schlegel sisters and is established early on: they 'desired that public life should mirror whatever is good in the life within'.[22] Thinking productively about social relations entails thinking realistically about human beings: about capacities and the conditions necessary for their fulfilment. What can society do to help others make the best of themselves? What is a fulfilled person? Margaret Schlegel is scathing about those professionals who fail to do the necessary work, who jump to conclusions, who ask the inappropriate questions: 'It is always those who know nothing about human nature, who are bored by psychology and shocked by physiology who ask [them]'.[23] The inner life of aspirations, resistance and receptivity, of responsiveness as a capacity for care and commitment: all these features of the self are salient. Like Dickens and Gaskell, what Forster invites his reader to do is to probe the relations between social ideals and practices, and the moral identity of actual or fully realized individuals; issues of social responsibility and rights, and of character or virtue, morality and meaning, turn out once more to be inextricably intertwined.

For authors with eudaimonistic ambitions meditating on the nature of good lives means grappling with ideas regarding what it is right to do, what it is good to be, and what it is possible to become.[24] And this means considering the interrelated phenomena of a moral life over time. According to William James, a moral life consists of normal stretches ruptured by crises. During the normal phases an individual's conduct is shaped by her virtues and vices and directed by her ideals. But during critical moments we choose new ideals or reaffirm and modify old ones guided by nothing but ourselves: 'our character limits our choices and will be modified by the choice we make'.[25] Concurring with James, these narratives investigate the routine and the quandaries and the devastating dilemmas, and in so doing they illuminate specific aspects of moral agency. Readers of Austen's *Mansfield Park* and Hardy's *The Return of the Native* can reflect on the sources and consequences of a lack of self-understanding which at critical moments blocks the moral mode that manifests fair-mindedness. Elizabeth Gaskell (in *North and South*) and George Eliot (in *Middlemarch*) explore the implications of generosity, focussing on well-intentioned actions that culminate in a crushing sense of loss of self-coherence. Of especial interest to all authors is the subject of self-direction. However determined or concerned, however responsible or committed the aspiring moral agent may be, he or she is invariably caught up in a web of relationships, embedded within a social nexus, and thus continually subject to the pressure of other minds. Few women of Austen's time would want to risk the charge

---

[22] *Howards End*, ed. Oliver Stallybrass (Harmondsworth: Penguin, 1973), p. 41.
[23] *Howards End*, ed. Stallybass, p. 282.
[24] Newey expresses the underlying conviction of writers such as Dickens (but this also applies to Gaskell, Eliot and Forster) in the following terms: 'we all suffer limits, are bounded, but are not bound down'. Hence individuals in these novels are 'in pursuit of the best options for living': *The Scriptures of Charles Dickens*, p. 12.
[25] See Ruth Anna Putnam, 'The Moral Life of a Pragmatist', in Flanagan and Rorty (eds), *Identity, Character and Morality*, p. 87.

of showing ' an abominable sort of conceited independence'; the accusation Bingley's sister levels at Elizabeth Bennet (82). But in *Great Expectations* it is the astute Biddy who suggests that acting independently is much to be desired: Pip's goal to improve himself socially 'might be better and more *independently* done by caring nothing for [Estella's] words' (156, emphasis added). Recognizing that multiple forms of influence are exercised over time, realist and quasi realist novels, like *Great Expectations*, trace the implications of such 'battles' for the mind, suggesting why opportunities are exploited or missed, how the initiative may be gained, lost or sustained; they investigate benefits and costs – the costs to individual welfare.

If modern thinkers are fascinated by intricate subjects that transgress the boundaries of social or political or ethical theory, one of the most intriguing of such problems consists then of identifying practices that can promote 'self-government' or 'individual independence' given, in the words of John Stuart Mill, 'the magical influence of custom'.[26] The objective is to discover how and why some individuals are able to challenge and transcend the limitations of both their environments and their traditions (making themselves in significant ways strangers to them) in order to achieve distinctive ways of thinking and acting that have important personal and social implications and consequences. Here the *first* question is not whether an individual's character is excellent, but whether it is her own. The ideal consists of an moral agent who is self-directed and clear-sighted, self-reliant and responsible. However, given the categories and norms according to which we are brought to think of ourselves, the criteria, the imagery, we habitually use to judge ourselves, our practices and customs, those by means of which we regulate ourselves and others – those various aspects of the templates that Nikolas Rose calls 'the historical a priori of our existence'[27] – given all of these factors, how can responsible self-direction be achieved?[28] From a moral perspective, autonomy is highly desirable because individuals need to be alive to their own culture's failures, its blindness to or acceptance of what leads to wrong and even evil. One of the most important purposes of this kind of socio-ethical study is then to identify the strategies and the self-images that are most fruitful to or consonant with forms of ethical self-creation. This is self-creation that is envisaged in terms of self-assertion and expansion, experimentation and acquisition, where prime amongst acquisitions are precisely the critical and self critical modes or outlooks so highly prized by modernity.

---

[26] *On Liberty*, ed. Gertrude Himmelfarb (Harmondsworth: Penguin, 1974), p. 64.

[27] Nikolas Rose, *Inventing Ourselves: Psychology, Power and Personhood* (Cambridge: Cambridge University Press, 1996), p. 167.

[28] Thus see philosopher Gary Gutting's critique of poststructuralism: in so far as its practitioners have contributed 'little to our philosophical understanding of freedom … they remain content with a naive, pre-reflective commitment to the unquestionable status of transgression, novelty, plurality, and difference as absolute ethical ideals. There is, accordingly, no inclination to ask difficult questions about the roots and limits of human freedom; the consuming task is to expose and overcome all obstacles to unrestricted expansion': *French Philosophy in the Twentieth Century* (Cambridge: Cambridge University Press, 2001), pp. 388–90.

The question of what constitutes freedom is of fundamental concern to philosophers of the modern period.[29] But what seems to have most interested the authors I discuss are the implications arising from the difficulties of preserving one's own (informed) point of view – given the various and insidious forces and pressures that facilitate the move towards uniformity and conformity. Mill described the captivating power of an ethos or ideology in his *Autobiography*: 'Some particular body of doctrine in time rallies the majority around it, organizes social institutions and modes of action conformably to itself ... and by degrees it acquires the very same power of compression, so long exercised by the creeds of which it has taken the place' (190). What matters to writers of fiction is not simply that an individual is able to defy such 'compressing' convictions so as to preserve intact his or her own viewpoint (one grounded in considerations of the good and/or the just), but that this moral outlook be motivating, vital, effective. Thus whether we take a novel by Austen or Eliot, Dickens or Forster, a character becomes exemplary because such an individual is – when it matters – essentially self-directing. And this means that desires, beliefs, and values have been endorsed, substantially integrated, *and* are made manifest in action. Anne Elliot sets off to visit the déclassé Mrs Smith in Westgate-Buildings (in *Persuasion*), Dorothea Brooke arranges to meet the disgraced Dr Lydgate (in *Middlemarch*), and John Thornton organizes a canteen in his factory for his combative workers (in *North and South*). For all three acting means moving *controcorrente* – encountering the disapproval or misgivings of their families or social circles. These are the kind of constructive non-conformists that communities clearly need. They demonstrate great determination while also possessing that 'elasticity of mind' or keen intelligence that Austen rates so highly.[30] Their conduct will surprise the conventional though it probably will not shock. But with Helen Schlegel Forster introduces a moral radical who belongs in another dimension; for this is a character whose conduct is at times utterly unpredictable, erratic, reckless, shocking; who exhibits a total lack of concern for those unwritten social codes that provide guidelines as to what is inappropriate and unacceptable behaviour.[31]

Yet however flexible and firm or eccentric some characters may be, all are continually subject to social influence. So when is 'influence management' possible, so that the ideas of others, of authority figures or friends and family, function as a repository of possibilities or a stimulus to creativity rather than just providing a constraint? Contending with such phenomena, 'Realism supposes that, in our

---

[29] For a major recent work on the subject see J.B. Schneewind, *The Invention of Autonomy* (New York: Cambridge University Press, 1998).

[30] This quality is attributed by Anne Elliot to Mrs Smith: 'here was that elasticity of mind, that disposition to be comforted, that power of turning readily from evil to good, and of finding employment which carried her out of herself, which was from Nature alone'; *Persuasion*, ed. D.W. Harding (Harmondsworth: Penguin, 1965), p. 167.

[31] For example, Helen turns up at wedding reception in order to make a scene so that wrongs be righted.

encounter with reality we can produce new and more adequate knowledge'.[32] That it is necessary to make sense of our circumstances if we are to negotiate our social world with some success, or even hope to change it, is an underlying premise of any eudaimonistic project. The experiences of certain characters – even well-intentioned characters like Fanny Price (of *Mansfield Park*) and Clym Yeobright (of the *Return of the Native*) only go to show how very difficult 'making sense' of one's circumstances may turn out to be.

As it explores diverse aspects of the wide-ranging subject of modern narrative ethics, my study has a further objective. Here I shall be retrieving from obscurity non-fictional works that enable us to get a better picture of particular features of this lively debate. I shall be presenting the results of new research relating especially to the intellectual context within which these narratives appeared. An historical perspective which is at once broader and more focussed will help us to gain a better idea of the significance of a point of view, to understand how a certain concept is interpreted, or how an ethical position is extended or reformulated.[33] In this study I aim to identify the strands of ethical thinking to which authors respond; different writers investigate different facets of their ethical tradition. I begin with Jane Austen's response to the Enlightenment preoccupation with the state of mind that is amenable to reason. Locke had suggested in his analysis of Reason that 'it is the Nature of the Understanding constantly to close with the more probable side, but yet', he continued, 'a Man hath a Power to suspend and restrain its Enquires'. There are ways of evading 'the most apparent Probabilities'. In *Mansfield Park*, Austen discloses the 'refuge[s] against *Conviction*', to which Locke refers, investigating 'the secret motives' that hinder both knowledge and assent, and that are characteristic of an attitude of unreasonableness.[34]

---

[32] Harry E. Shaw's is a fine attempt to defend realism from its influential critics. In so doing he stresses the importance of the work of Lukàcs. Yet he adds that his picture of how realism achieves its ends seems incomplete: 'Lukàcs's account leaves out the way narrative fiction sets the mind in motion, instead of freezing knowledge into static, concentrated images ... In fact, there is for realist fiction no question of the achievement of a crystalline embodiment of the essential structure of an age ...' (35). Rather 'nineteenth-century realist fiction makes most sense when it is viewed as an attempt to deal with situations which involve partial knowledge and continual approximation, and in which history, existing on a continuum with our other forms of experience and being, can be known and respresented with various degrees of accuracy' (29): *Narrating Reality: Austen, Scott, Eliot* (Ithaca and London: Cornell University Press, 1999).

[33] Important recent studies by Charles Taylor, J.B. Schneewind and Stefan Collini have all contributed to our understanding of the diffuse movements or frameworks of thought that distinguish the modern period. See Charles Taylor, *Sources of the Self*, J.B. Schneewind, *The Invention of Autonomy* and Stefan Collini, *Public Moralists: Political Thought and Intellectual Life in Britain, 1850–1930* (Oxford: Oxford University Press, 1991).

[34] '*We can hinder both Knowledge and Assent, by stopping our Enquiry*, and not imploying our Faculties in search of any Truth': *An Essay Concerning Human Understanding*, ed. Peter H. Nidditch (Oxford: Clarendon Press, 1975), pp. 715–17. Locke is not an important figure in Peter Knox-Shaw's recent discussion of Austen's Enlightenment interests.

Introduction 11

In Austen's novels attitudes acquire importance. As early as *Sense and Sensibility* (published in 1811) she creates a heroine whose virtue is linked to her disposition to respond to others with 'the candid allowances and generous qualifications'[35] they may well deserve. Social and moral codes fuse when Elinor Dashwood exhibits the 'forbearance of civility' that on occasions also characterizes the conduct of Elizabeth Bennet. But the novel questions how far in the name of either civility or propriety a sensible person might adopt an accommodating attitude towards unwelcome intrusions and even the downright embarrassing or hurtful interventions of others. When should a woman speak out?

In *Mansfield Park* Austen suggests that certain basic attitudes offer us our best bet of establishing viable or mutually enriching relations with those with whom we come into potentially meaningful contact.[36] Reasonableness should make our own lives go better, functioning as a crucial aid in the struggle against emotional or morbid dependency on the one hand, and resentment or prejudice on the other. The chances are principled attitudes will contribute to the pleasures and benefits of lasting attachments. For Austen, the modern moral mode of reasonableness entails a willingness to recognize and make the most of the opportunities to do and be well. Or – to put it another way – it means circumventing the (comfort-giving) mental state of denial and closure; it means finding the mental strength to resist the often unwarranted hostility or antipathy to others that frustrates a process of mutual growth and expansion. Reasonableness is the attitude of receptivity of one who is prepared to entertain the ideas of others because living well means ascertaining what is just and sensible and right to do. Whether in times of stress and discomfort her heroine is capable of such a positive attitude the reader will discover. The reading I shall be offering questions a construal of Austen that has long been prominent in critical studies of her work, and that pictures her as: 'a figure out of key with her time'.[37] This is hardly an appealing

---

[35] *Sense and Sensibility*, ed. Tony Tanner (Harmondsworth: Penguin, 1969), p. 126.

[36] John Finnis defines reasonableness both as a guide (an instrument) and as an attitude – a willingness to remain open to the opportunities which intelligence makes available to us, and thus open to the possibility of integral human fulfilment; unreasonable habits include exaggerating, discounting and distorting: *Fundamentals of Ethics* (Oxford: Clarendon Press, 1983), pp. 56, 75–6.

[37] This expression belongs to Peter Knox-Shaw, whose study *Jane Austen and the Enlightenment*, has sought to dispel the myth of the 'time-warped' 'party-pooper'. According to Knox-Shaw 'what can be said is that the whole thrust of the novel's commentary is profoundly secular, that its concern with religion centres in conduct, and that human happiness is integral to its morality': p. 173. Mary Waldron attempts to understand Austen's religious bearings in 'The Frailties of Fanny: *Mansfield Park* and the Evangelical Movement', *Eighteenth-Century Fiction* 6 (1994): 259–81. On this view *Mansfield Park* does not 'accomodate itself to early nineteenth-century moral and political reaction, but can be seen as a serious challenge to its increasing reliance on a system – Anglican Evangelicalism – which made moral and social responsibility a simple matter of duty, quietism, and example, taking far too little account of the complexity of human affairs': p. 281.

image of Austen, yet over the years Marilyn Butler's much-discussed study has continued to make converts of a kind; her analysis of *Mansfield Park* suggests that Austen's own attitudes are to be read as moralistic, the unfortunate legacy of her early acquaintance with old-fashioned sermons and conduct books.[38] Nowadays we are not likely to want to celebrate such an outlook on life, but we should still try to understand, it has been argued, 'the science, genesis and aetiology' of her heroine's 'moral fastidiousness'.[39]

Here I shall be proposing that it is reasonableness that Austen admires. And reasonableness can be discerned when characters, like Elizabeth Bennet (of *Pride and Prejudice)*, manifest an attitude of respect for truth and the mental agility that enables them to achieve a sundry-things-considered mode of responsiveness. The beginning of her change of attitude to Darcy is marked by a Lockian process of 'reconsidering events' and 'determining probablities'.[40] Though initially anything but willing to do Darcy justice – to accept that he might have reason on his side – as she reconsiders his letter, Elizabeth gradually becomes more reasonable and more knowledgeable. Reason, the ever influential Locke had ascertained, 'must be our last Judge and Guide in everything'.[41] In this context reason works out connections between ideas.[42] Applying herself to discover 'agreements' and 'disagreements', Elizabeth follows Locke's precepts and re-orders her ideas. As she reflects, remembers and compares, the connections become clearer: she recognizes the correspondances between Darcy's account of past events and her own experiences and observations. The mortifications pile up as a miserable Elizabeth realizes she 'had driven reason away' (237). The confessions of Darcy himself that 'it was sometime … before I was reasonable enough to allow [the justice of Elizabeth's expressions of reproof]' reveal that his proper pride is grounded in a view of himself as a person capable of acting in a way that is reasonable and just. His words are welcome testimony to the underlying moral affinities of the happy couple (376). For the most worthy and delightful of her characters Austen devises 'the happiest, wisest, most reasonable end' (357).

Decades later what Forster finds very attractive in Margaret Schlegel is the reasonable attitude that eschews both cool disengagement and the exuberant intensity

---

[38] Marilyn Butler, *Romantics, Rebels and Reactionaries* (Oxford: Oxford University Press, 1981), p. 102.

[39] In Roger Gard's reading we are meant to see 'how her negatives are functions of her real suffering': *Jane Austen's Novel's: The Art of Clarity* (New Haven and London: Yale University Press, 1992), p. 136.

[40] *Pride and Prejudice*, ed. Tony Tanner (Harmondsworth: Penguin, 1972), p. 237; first published 1813.

[41] *An Essay Concerning Human Understanding*, ed. Nidditch, p. 704. For Leslie Stephen Locke was 'the intellectual ruler of the eighteenth century'; see Hans Aarsleff, 'Locke's Influence', *The Cambridge Companion to Locke*, ed. Vere Chappell (Cambridge University Press, 1994), pp. 252–89.

[42] *An Essay Concerning Human Understanding*, ed. Nidditch, pp. 525–30. Hence Elizabeth finds that Darcy's account of Wickham's dealings with the Pemberley family '*agreed* equally well with his own words': 234, emphasis added.

of pity that propels overreaction. While the propensity to appreciate other people's good or good-enough *qualities*, is as important for personal flourishing as appreciating the good *things* life may offer.

A would-be self-directing subject is, it would appear, a striving subject, one who exercises her faculties, attending closely to and interpreting reality, endeavouring to overcome distortion and see through error.[43] Something like 'an enlargement of the capacity for experience' can ensue from the practices of heeding and reasoning.[44] The kind of critical or discriminating outlook, the distinctive attitudes, the often powerful propensities that such an individual develops will clearly affect the dynamics of social interaction. Our conception of this subject and her attributes could become ever more intricate. But the point is that the ethical perspective now emerging allows for a socio-psychological theory of character and agency which recognizes that individuals form (more or less stable or integrated) identities; that an identity is constituted – through time and by means of significant experiences – by a configuration of traits; and that such traits will have practical implications. Some traits 'typically make a systematic difference to the course of a person's life, to the habit-forming and action-guiding social categories in which she is placed, to the way she acts, reacts, and interacts'.[45] On this view, what will count for a great deal in an ethical life are thus not only the

---

[43] Recently the theory of 'situationism' has sought to cast doubt on the validity of ethical preoccupations with character, it questions the centrality of the questions What is the best kind of person to be? and How can people become more virtuous? Its adherents are greatly impressed by experiments by psychologists that apparently show that non-moral 'forces' can overcome moral dispositions; put to the test, people, it appears, do not possess character in the sense required by virtue ethics. Situationists believe that people are typically unaware of what is influencing their behaviour in morally significant ways; they are moved by trivial or non-moral motives to act inappropriately in moral dilemmas. Nevertheless although John M. Doris questions the validity of a characterological approach to moral philosophy, he does affirm that generally speaking 'people manifest considerable reliability with regard to variables like beliefs, goals, values and attitudes; at any rate, more so than they do with overt behaviors ... attitudes, or at least attitudes strongly held, can be quite resistant to change': *Lack of Character: Personality and Moral Behavior* (Cambridge: Cambridge University Press, 2002), p. 87. For a robust rebuttal of situationism see John Sabini and Maury Silver, 'Lack of Character? Situationism Critiqued', *Ethics* 115 (2005): 535–62. They conclude, inter alia, 'We think that the import of the social influence studies is that the exercise of practical intelligence, is, in specific circumstances, harder than the commonsense view expects': p. 562, n .59.

[44] Herbert McCabe contrasts the moral practice of those 'law-abiding' agents, who have internalized a sense of what authority would want, with those who are capable of analyzing their activities by exercising themselves in the question, given the facts, what is it reasonable to do? It is the latter who stand most chance of discovering the goods inherent in ways of being active that involve the practice of the virtues: *The Good Life: Ethics and the Pursuit of Happiness* (London and New York: Continuum, 2005), pp. 47–51.

[45] Amélie Oksenberg Rorty and David Wong, 'Aspects of Identity and Agency', in Flanagan and Rorty (eds), *Identity, Character and Morality*, p. 19, emphasis added.

active processes of deliberation and resolution, but also (as we have noted) attitudes – dominant or deep-seated outlooks on life: those unreflective patterns of expression or responsiveness that are grounded in underlying evaluative notions, suppositions, and judgments.[46] For these realist authors what is worth investigating closely is not just the issue of how people deliberate, but how they tend to face up to types of situation: on certain occasions fear and trembling may be combined with suspicion and scepticism, supreme self-confidence may be characteristically informed by deference.

Not everyone in realist fiction, as in life, gets to form dominant (moral) attitudes. As John Kekes explains, some remain deprived: 'their attachment to individual ideals and projects is loose, their commitments are weakly held, and their concerns and interests are frequently changing. Yet others may be prevented from having a dominant attitude by doubt, despair, cynicism, superficiality, or fear of failure, and they live day to day without a coherent evaluative perspective'.[47] Furthermore, dominant attitudes can and at times do mutate abruptly – for better and for worse. As situations become tricky, pathetic or dramatic, Forster's reader is invited to appraise the reasonableness of the often admirable attitude of tolerance. How far, the question arises (in *Howards End*), can/should you stretch tolerance for the 'male' way of doing things? As this novel enters the stage of climax and closure, Forster identifies the combination of factors that ensure an appropriate degree of female assertiveness; that account for a radical change of attitude.

The novels at the centre of this study are clearly engaged in the elaboration of multifaceted ethical issues. And in this work one of my main aims is to draw attention to those non-fictional texts that can now be seen to have contributed to the generation of pivotal themes.[48] Some of these texts have hitherto been neglected by literary scholars. Hence while I shall be discussing the ways in which ideas of major thinkers are taken up and revised – tracing, for example, the importance of the ideas of Kant to George Eliot, of F.H. Bradley to Hardy, and John Stuart Mill and John Ruskin to Forster – I shall also be bringing clearly into focus little known works by authors such as Edward Tagart, a priest and friend of Dickens, William Maccall, a preacher and leading light within Elizabeth Gaskell's Unitarian community, and philanthropist Helen Dendy Bosanquet, wife of the more famous scholar, the philosopher Bernard Bosanquet. The ideas of these now obscure writers, I shall argue, were of considerable interest to the authors discussed here. By connecting non-fictional texts and realist

---

[46] On the relations between moral responsibility and attitudes see Angela M. Smith 'Responsibility for Attitudes: Activity and Passivity in Mental Life', *Ethics* 115 (2005): 236–71.

[47] *The Art of Life* (Ithaca and London: Cornell University Press, 2002), p. 189.

[48] Thus Mary Gordon notes of *Howards End*, the tone is 'one of conviviality, well-bred judiciousness, a quiet urge to pleasure. It belies the book's tremendous scope, its willingness to take on some of the large questions that we live by ... novel of the sexes, novel of the classes, pastoral novel, allegorical novel, novel of the cultured few: the richness of *Howards End* is that it can be read in all these ways, and more': '"Things That Can't Be Phrased": Forster and *Howards End*', *Salmagundi* 143 (2004): 89–103.

narratives, this work should serve to colour anew our perspectives on much discussed novels. These connections should enable us to see why a certain ethical concern receives the attention it does.[49]

Furthermore, I shall take advantage of the richness of material currently to be found in the sphere of moral philosophy to point out significant points of contact and divergence between old texts and new with regard to key topics or concerns. As Martha Nussbaum has written 'one cannot find for generations – since the time of John Stuart Mill, if not earlier – an era in which there has been so much excellent, adventurous and varied work on the central ethical and political questions of human life'.[50] Thus, for example, in the case of *Hard Times*, if we are now able to trace the impact of Edward Tagart's studies on the Cambridge Platonists, and note how Platonic visions of the good will influenced Dickens's conception of the moral personality, so too can we find in the recent work of philosopher Harry Frankfurt analyses of the good will that suggest that both writers are thinking along very similar lines.[51] When elements of both these texts are brought into the picture, fundamental features of Dickens's ethical viewpoint become more distinct *and* distinctive. In short, if one of my aims is to begin to re-contextualize major novels by returning to salient moments in contemporary debates, so too at times do I adopt a comparative methodology which is meant to aid in the business of clarification. These voices from our own times should further our understanding of the implications of the emphasizes that are given in these literary texts to certain sets of concepts and questions.[52]

My approach to the ethics of a fictional text thus makes use of a variety of critical techniques, bringing into play, when appropriate, elements of intellectual history, moral psychology and the history of philosophy. Such an eclectic method should highlight the ways in which realist narratives elaborate ideas on a wide variety of issues, issues which continue to interest moderns. Just like Charles Taylor, in discussing the ideals and expectations of 'our Victorian contemporaries' and their near relations, one of

---

[49] Jil Larson writes 'despite all the emphasis on particularity, context and narrative in recent studies of ethics and literature, scholars working in this field have directed surprisingly little attention to the question of why an ethical problem or set of ethical concerns dominates in narratives written during a given historical period': *Ethics and Narrative in the English Novel*, p. 20.

[50] *Love's Knowledge*, pp. 169–71.

[51] Harry Frankfurt, *The Importance of What We Care About* (New York: Cambridge University Press, 1988).

[52] In *The Presence of Persons: Essays on Literature, Science and Philosophy in the Nineteenth-Century* (Aldershot: Ashgate, 1998), William Myers brings a variety of thinkers into view from the nineteenth century as well as from our own times (Newman, Dennett and Wittgenstein; Herbert Spencer and Monod against Hardy, Mill and William Hamilton), showing how their arguments throw light on the question as to whether the self is entirely constructed. For Myers Victorian writers such as John Henry Newman had sound arguments to back up their views of 'the real presence of the self', which is the *sine qua non* of all thought. Out of such disputes Myers finds that the stronger arguments belong to those who hold that the self always has a moral and substantively free dimension.

my goals is to suggest why the arguments of these writers are still salient, why they continue to resonate. And one way of achieving this end is to bring prominently into the discussion of single texts eloquent voices (including those of Charles Taylor, Harry Frankfurt and Susan Wolf) from other times and places.

Debates in modern moral philosophy may well seem interminable, apparently holding out no chance of resolving questions of the good or the right once and for all, and attitudes of disdain for modern writings on traditional ethical issues are still conspicuous in some quarters. And yet, as Paul Kelly has remarked, 'unless one is actually predisposed to the idea of the *Good* as sanctioned by divine law, then the closure of debates on certain moral issues can seem either repugnant or foolish'.[53] Why this should be so, why it makes sense to sustain an intellectual community in which a variety of ethical viewpoints continue to be expressed, are questions to which Amélie Oksenberg Rorty provides clear and compelling answers:

> Under the best of circumstances, individuals with various moral mentalities acknowledge the advantages of moral pluralism; they recognize that they benefit from their differences ... a sound political system is well served when its citizens represent the mentality and psychology of a wide and apparently competing range of distinctive moral systems ... Indeed, unless an emphasis is pressed by some opposition, it runs the danger of going amok, transforming virtue into a classically tragic flaw, sometimes a vice. Whether or not we acknowledge it, we depend on moral pluralism, on a variety of well-developed distinctive yet complementary moral mentalities.[54]

It is during the long nineteenth century that such well-developed and distinctive moral mentalities and discourses come to be discernible in major works of fiction.

Examining such discourses entails attending closely, I suggest, to the question of how narrative texts can scrutinize or anatomize a variety of interrelated ethical issues. But it also means recognizing that the reader is often expected to work to uncover meaning, and hence must unpack the implications of the connections set up by a crucial word, expression or sentence. Thus the question of how, given the nature of their medium and its conventions – which cannot allow for the rigorous analyses of concepts or the fine-tuned arguments of the philosopher – novelists go about participating in on-going ethical debates, how, in other words, they *organize and develop* intricate and nuanced discourses on the subject of what makes for admirable or successful lives, is central to my approach. For D.H. Lawrence this is completely the wrong way of viewing things. For Lawrence it is literature, rather than the logical analysis offered by philosophical texts, that can 'make the subtle distinctions life demands':

---

[53] 'MacIntyre's Critique of Utilitarianism', in John Horton and Susan Mendus (eds), *After MacIntyre: Critical Perspectives on the Work of Alasdair MacIntyre* (Oxford: Polity Press, 1994), p. 143.

[54] 'To be sure', Rorty continues, 'we might well fear that practical polyphony can turn into chaotic cacophony. Which among the various types should be stressed varies with time and circumstance. It cannot be determined by rules or principles; it is under constant negotiation': 'What It Takes To Be Good', pp. 43–5.

quite simply 'the novel is the highest example of subtle inter-relatedness that man has discovered'.[55] It is the novel that can trace the finest implications and repercussions of actions, attitudes and intentions, of memory and moments of moral crisis.

Part 1 of this work illustrates topics and distinguishes central features of the problematics of narrative ethics. In Chapter 1 I present a panorama or overview of a rich and distinctive ethical terrain. As I survey some of the most thought-provoking contributions to an ethics of eudaimonia to emerge during the long nineteenth century, I trace patterns and make connections, but equally, I identify the crucial divergences in thought that require signposting. Chapter 2 engages with aspects of narrative technique. In particular it examines a number of problems that attend interpretation of these texts, the configuration of narrative voice being one of the most significant. In Part 2 my intent is to analyze in depth the salient features of each ethical design and disclose the ways in which they contribute to a novel's 'substantive argumentation'. This kind of argumentation can aim at establishing the soundness of a viewpoint, as opposed to making claims for its universal validity.[56] In an afterword focussing on Bruce Chatwin's novella *Utz*, I tackle a theme debated in *Howards End* which centres on the question: When can the requirements of personal meaning reasonably take precedence over those of morality? Self-indulgence can be a fairly harmless activity. But when one starts evading or trampling over the claims of others (to respect, privacy or even justice) in pursuit of the desirable, then, as Elinor Dashwood points out to her sister Marianne, the question of justifying one's actions crops up (*Sense and Sensibility*, 98). I shall be comparing Chatwin's narrative with a philosophical approach to the issues that are linked to the predicament of the Polish collector, Utz. My account of the ways in which novelist and philosopher articulate their versions of the collector's desires and beliefs, actions and reactions, is an attempt to discover why one rather than the other offers the most satisfying exposition of, and justification for, certain modes of being and sensibilities. Chatwin's quirky novella provides an example of opportunistic drivenness, but also an argument for authenticity and integrity, for a life of 'subtle inter-relatedness'. If formally Chatwin's text embraces the postmodern, evincing a penchant for radical or dislocating devices, thematically its focus is modern as it debates the goods that a good life necessitates.

---

[55] See Allan Ingram, *The Language of D.H. Lawrence* (Basingstoke: Macmillan, 1990), p. 52.

[56] See Stephen Toulmin's distinction between texts (such as those of Montaigne) which provide 'substantive argumentation' and works of philosophy. The first are historically situated and rely on the evidence of experience; the best they can do is to aim at soundness, putting a conclusion 'beyond a reasonable doubt' and establishing 'the strongest possible presumption on its behalf'. While the rigour of philosophy aims at establishing the 'validity' of formal arguments, 'whose conclusions are determined by the starting points from which they are deduced': *Return to Reason* (Cambridge, MA: Harvard University Press, 2001), pp. 15–26. It is worth noting also that in his *Autobiography* Mill's standard for assessing the contribution of certain works lies first not in whether they make good on claims to truth, but whether they show an overbalance of sound arguments.

PART 1
WHAT MATTERS (MOST)

Chapter 1

Modes and Sensibilities: Varieties of Ethical Thought

From 1800 onwards one major English author after another took up the topic of eudaimonia. These moderns had plenty of ideas about what makes for lives that are satisfying, worthwhile, meaningful. Flourishing was the novel's aim and ideal – if not a character's motivating thought. But failure to achieve fulfilment often seems likely to be the fate of a heroine or hero. Fanny Price comes pretty close to disaster, while Margaret Hale and Dorothea Brooke face anguish and self-doubt. All their striving, all their idealism,[1] cannot prevent them from experiencing the horror of breakdown. Ravaged at the time of his wife's death by self-conflict, unknowing as to what he is and what made him that way, Clym Yeobright admits that he is 'getting used to the horror of [his] existence' (444). At these times the 'imperial self', abhorred by the postmodernist, gives way to a rather more fragile creature, one who is faced with an unbearable sense of incoherence.

To get to be one's own person, to be clear-headed, responsible *and* self-controlled, was a feat the difficulty of which John Stuart Mill, the heir to the Enlightenment, and one of the 'great self-dissatisfied' (to borrow a term from Nietzsche) did not underestimate. In looking at Mill's *Autobiography*, at the breakdown experienced by this thinker, we are invited also to consider conditions that must be met if an individual is even to embark on an ethical project. The type of account Mill gives us at a certain point in his *Autobiography* – a sort of personal case-history or narrative-cum-commentary of the effects of certain states of mind and being – seeks to further our understanding of the psychological prerequisites of meaningful endeavour – which may in turn contribute to a sense of self-fulfilment.[2]

The *Autobiography* is the story of Mill's life-long pursuit of activities that might count as truly worthwhile: these are the 'inspiring prospects' that give 'colour to one's existence', and are thus worth the effort of achieving. However, as he endeavours to make sense of his life, his aims and relationships, so does Mill come up against the brute fact of moral disempowerment, a condition which is strictly connected to what

---

[1] Their idealism does not consist in self-fulfilment; such idealism involves the fulfilment of their interests or projects, rather than themselves. In other words, self-fulfilment may surface as a preoccupation but it is not a goal.
[2] The *Autobiography* was published in 1873. John Stuart Mill, *Autobiography*, ed. John M. Robson (Harmondsworth: Penguin, 1989).

he diagnoses as a fundamental psychological lack – the cause of which Mill attributes to the profound impact of analytical ways of thought. Where postmoderns want us to confront the potential violence of the self, Mill's account invites us to reconsider the ethical implications of 'ego-loss', of a self bereft of certainty, of self-esteem, of all sources of comfort. It invites us to take a look at a state of moral paralysis. For Mill meaningful endeavour cannot get going in the absense of self-affirming moral attitudes. Crucially, he finds, as if awakening from a dream, that he is not on 'good terms with himself'.[3] He is left hopeless by a dire self-conception that he seems unable to do anything about. Stranded in this state of wretchness, he cannot summon up the 'pleasure of sympathy,' the feelings of empathy or benevolence that might propel his reforming ambitions. His development, such as it has been is, he senses, anything but harmonious.

Mill's self-found therapy draws upon two crucial resources; another story of the self is instrumental in setting to work the power of the imagination: Mill is able to (re)create a 'conception' or visualization of a significant scene (that in Marmontel's *Memoirs*, where the author tells of his father's death), and it is this scene that serves, in turn, to trigger the emotions that are essential to a satisfactory self-image: 'I had still it seemed, some of the material out of which all worth of character, and all capacity for happiness, are made' (117). In Mill's *Autobiography* moral attitudes and meaning are tightly intertwined, but the possibility of pursuing what gives life meaning, and thus happiness, depends in the first instance on acquiring a (minimal) sense of psychological coherence. In exercising his creative faculties, Mill revives and refashions the psychically healthier self he desperately needs. He learns from his experience 'that the passive susceptibilities needed to be cultivated as well as the active capacities, and required to be nourished and enriched as well as guided' (118). Nurturing and protecting certain capacities in order to create a viable self: Mill discovered that certain modes and sensibilities were required to sustain his arduous ethical enterprise.

J.S. Mill is a substantial presence in this study. In more than one chapter Mill's thought constitutes a crucial point of reference. Gaskell shares with Mill a common source of inspiration; Dickens shares grave doubts about the value of his Benthamite legacy; Forster respects but also queries facets of his 'developmental' model. Significant connections can be made between Mill's thought and that of his contemporaries and followers. But of the three terms that seem most applicable to the works of these and the other realist authors at the centre of this study – complexity, subtlety and diversity – it is the fact of diversity that I shall be highlighting here. A survey of the ethical interests of all these authors should point up the striking variety within their ethical

---

[3] See Nicholas Rescher on the importance of being 'on good terms with oneself': *A System of Pragmatic Idealism* (3 vols, Princeton: Princeton University Press, 1993), vol. 2, p. 128.

thought.[4] These novelists certainly share fundamental concerns about the possibility of achieving eudaimonia, but they present the reader with contrasting conceptions of virtue or morality; they add something distinctive to discourses on the subject of what is conducive to well-being.[5] These eudaimonistic designs are informed by specific conceptions of moral psychology, by a variety of ideas about capacities that should be energized and others that are best modified or suppressed. So how might we conceptualize the ethics of each author? What aspects of moral phenomenology will matter most? What is the proper place of morality in a good life? What kind of intuitions serve as a background 'theory' of healthy self-functioning? What does a fine or fertile responsiveness to the challenges of life entail?

*

Writing at the time Jane Austen was approaching adulthood, the philosopher Thomas Reid remarked that the good life was the virtuous life so that any man who believed that 'virtue was contrary to his happiness, on the whole' 'was reduced to the miserable dilemma whether it is better to be a fool or a knave'.[6] Another way of putting this thought is to claim that for a rational being virtue is inseparable from his/her overall best interests: we cannot live well prudentially independently of living well morally. For Reid 'moral perplexity may arise because of the plurality of basic [moral] principles', but on the whole 'the path to duty is a plain path'.[7] For readers well versed in recent criticism of Austen's novel *Mansfield Park*, it would be easy to conclude that Austen is in full agreement with Reid. The good life is above all the moral life, where the moral life is interpreted in terms of moral steadfastness and righteousness, acute sense of duty and obedience to principle. And this virtuous mode of proceeding will show an individual where her best interests lie. I would suggest, however, that Austen would have found much to agree with in the writings of Forster's contemporary, William James.

---

[4] In *Trollope and Victorian Moral Philosophy* (Ohio: Ohio University Press, 1996), Jane Nardin notes that 'different writers emphasize different aspects of their moral heritage ... Because no morality is unambiguous or static, consensus on moral issues can never be complete. Understanding this, many British novelists of the eighteenth and nineteenth centuries problematize their own moral tradition even as they use it to define the dilemmas their characters face. And they find the tension within that tradition a fruitful source of fictional conflict': pp. 1–2.

[5] As John Kekes points out a 'eudaimonistic conception of a good life is not to be understood as the endorsement of a particular form of life. It is rather a regulative ideal that specifies some general conditions to which all good lives conform': *Moral Wisdom and Good Lives* (Ithaca and London: Cornell University Press, 1995), p. 24.

[6] See Henry Sidgwick's discussion of Reid's *Essays on the Active powers of Man*, 1788, in *Outlines of the History of Ethics* (London: Macmillan and Co, 1906), pp. 228–9. On Reid see also J.B. Schneewind's *The Invention of Autonomy* (New York: Cambridge University Press, 1998), pp. 395–403.

[7] Schneewind, *The Invention of Autonomy*, p. 402

For James ethics must attempt to settle the issue of what is good or valuable, or really important, what makes life worth living, what gives it meaning or point and substance. And part of this enquiry into what matters (most) must ascertain 'the relation of the good we call virtue, the qualities of conduct and character that we commend and admire, to other good things'.[8] Ethics is thus practical when it seeks to integrate the different claims constituted by the interests and welfare of others to whom we are more or less attached, and to reconcile these claims with other aims, and in particular with the aim of personal well-being, which may take the form of self-realization or self-perfection.[9] It is the view of James that serious thinkers who possess sensibility, cannot but engage in attempts to find 'the measure of the various goods and ills that men recognize, so that the philosopher may settle the true order of human obligations'. This is a pressing need. For 'every end of desire that presents itself appears exclusive of some other end of desire ... Some part of the ideal must be butchered, and [the ethical philosopher] needs to know which part'. From the perspective of the individual life, although this may seem simply to entail choosing goals, and the means to achieving them, such an aim is, at critical moments, linked to the question of who one chooses to be:

> [When] we reach the plane of Ethics ... choice reigns notoriously supreme. An act has no ethical quality whatsoever unless it be chosen out of several all equally possible. To sustain the arguments for the good course and keep them ever before us, to stifle our longing for more flowery ways, to keep the foot unflinchingly on the arduous path, these are the characteristic ethical energies. But more than these; for these but deal with the means of compassing interests already felt by the man to be supreme. The ethical energy par excellence has to go farther and choose which interest out of severally, equally coercive, shall become supreme ... When he debates ... his choice really lies between one of several equally possible future Characters.[10]

In Austen's ethical vision the sort of morality that envisages and encourages attractive self-refashioning counts for a great deal, but so does personal well-being or comfort (a term which flourishes in this text). And well-being is achieved through the enjoyment of great goods: in fact a wide variety of goods makes for the best kind of life. The intelligent Henry Crawford's list of the goods he can offer Fanny Price is pretty comprehensive: 'happiness, comfort, honour, and dignity in the world' (130). (Consider that of Mrs Norris, who values 'the comforts of hurry, bustle, and importance', 154.) Certainly high up on Austen's wish-list are honour or consequence (as improved social status and recognition), influence and intelligent conversation, as well as the affection that is grounded in shared tastes and esteem. All these goods contribute to

---

[8] *The Principles of Psychology* (2 vols, New York: Dover Publications, 1950), vol. 1, pp. 287–8.

[9] As John Kekes notes, 'If good lives were identified with virtuous lives, then such lives may lack satisfaction' so that 'while it may be true that a good life is virtuous, there is more to it than living virtuously': *Moral Wisdom and Good Lives*, pp. 36–46.

[10] *The Principles of Psychology*, vol. 1, pp. 287–8.

personal well-being as well as to one's capacity to promote the happiness of others less fortunate. Morality matters, but the morality that works best is a morality of reasonableness and fairness. Such moral skills and qualities make for the best kind of interpersonal relations and provide for the kind of moral stance that is essential for thinking through dilemmas, and hence for making the right choice. While this activity, in turn, may constitute a significant step in the business of self-improvement. Attitudes of reasonableness combined with resolute attempts at fairness supply the conditions for promoting mutual recreation, so that the steady and unadventurous (Fanny and Edmund) may become more animated, and the animated (Mary and Henry) a little more steady. In *Mansfield Park* these virtuous modes of being offer the means of bringing about the most inclusive ideal.

Yet Austen's novel reveals that even the most staunchly principled, those who intend to do what is right, to do their duty, may be insufficiently alert at times to their own unreasonableness. And this is often because specific but inadmissable intentions prevail. These can become of paramount influence in the process of reasoning whereby states of doubt and anxiety are overcome. As in her other novels, a rhetoric of virtue permeates the text, but in *Mansfield Park* she is intrigued by patterns of behaviour that frustrate the creative process of virtuous self-refashioning.[11] For Austen normative ethics is checked by psychology. This does not mean that the distinction between the actual and the ideal simply disappears from sight. It means that articulating moral ideals and principles is 'appropriately constrained by knowledge of the basic architecture of the mind, core emotions, patterns of development, social psychology, and the limits of our capacities for rational deliberation'.[12] The question which faces Austen's reader is whether an individual can ever achieve the necessary state of self-awareness that reasonableness requires. Locke could see the difficulty and held it to be a 'Disease' or sort of 'Madness', though one common to 'very sober and rational Minds':

> There is scarce any one that does not observe something that seems odd to him, and is in it self really Extravagant in the Opinions, Reasonings, and Actions of other Men. The least flaw of this kind, if at all different from his own, everyone is quick-sighted enough to espie in another, and will by the Authority of Reason forwardly condemn, though he be guilty of much greater Unreasonableness in his own Tenets and Conduct, which he never perceives, and will very hardly, if at all, be convinced of.[13]

---

[11] Jenny Davidson discusses Austen's equivocal conclusions about virtue and concealment in *Hypocrisy and the Politics of Politeness: Manners and Morals from Locke to Austen* (Cambridge: Cambridge University Press, 2004), pp. 146–69. For Davidson, Fanny's hypocrisy is seen as a 'legitimate manifestation of female dependance'. Hypocrisy's respectable 'alias' comprises manners, civility, decorum, self-control and politeness.

[12] See Owen Flanagan and Amélie Oksenberg Rorty, Introduction to *Identity, Character and Morality: Essays in Moral Psychology* (Cambridge, MA and London: MIT Press, 1993), pp. 1–3.

[13] *Essay Concerning Human Understanding*, ed. Nidditch, pp. 394–5.

'Custom', Locke observed, 'settles habits of Thinking in the Understanding' (396). And Fanny Price, her cousin noted was one 'over whom habit had most power, and novelty least' (349). Like Gaskell and Eliot, Hardy and Forster, Austen is only too well-aware of what can make good lives elusive: the lasting antipathies of early impressions, the unruliness of desire, the impact of pseudorationality and multiple forms of evasion, compulsive self-doubts and delusions. She never underestimates the difficulty of disentangling motives so as to gain mental clarity.[14]

Of all the novelists discussed here it is the ironists Austen and Hardy who reveal the greatest degree of scepticism about the possibility of successful, in the sense of *reliable*, self-interpretation. In *Mansfield Park* Austen wonders whether failure is largely a matter of up-bringing, temperament, or the consequence on occasions of the power over the mind of a particular rationale. If her heroine, Fanny Price, had perused Franklin's *Autobiography* she might – but probably would not – have recognized the appropriateness of a certain, ironic, passage: 'so convenient a thing it is to be a *reasonable creature*, since it enables one to find or make a reason for everything one has a mind to do'.[15]

The idea that reasonableness must prevail if challenging, but also stimulating and mutually supportive, personal connections are to be forged, is central to Austen's vision of possibilities. Here reasonableness must be perpetually striven for. The capacity of the mind to engage in this kind of struggle is revealed in the endeavour to overcome the propensity to both self-serving modes of thought and the slide into censoriousness, the self-righteous or severely judgemental attitude. Like Edmund Bertram (her hero), Austen cannot admire a mind that 'does not struggle against itself' (116); that fails to break a habit of going for the easier, the most congenial, option.

Fanny Price is certainly remarkable in sustaining an unusual degree of mental autonomy, sticking earnestly to her own ideas of what is right and wrong. She may be truly anxious to please – a state of mind, which, it has been suggested, is far from conducive to winning the inner struggle to keep one's own thoughts intact.[16] But

---

[14] In *Love's Knowledge: Essays on Philosophy and Literature* (Oxford: Oxford University Press, 1990), Martha Nussbaum argues that because of its techniques literature is in many respects better able to convey significant features of our moral lives than academic moral philosophy, which suffers from the 'plainness' that is characteristic of its prose. She seems to have doubts, however, whether works of literature can develop more or less structured arguments, as opposed to the salient insight. On the subject of the relations between literature and moral philosophy see also Cora Diamond, 'Having a Rough Story about What Moral Philosophy is', *New Literary History* 15 (1983): 155–69. Diamond claims that 'we cannot see the moral interest of literature unless we recognize gestures, manners, habits, turns of speech, turns of thought, styles of face as morally expressive – of an individual or of a people. The intelligent description of such things is part of the intelligent, the sharp-eyed, description of life, of what matters': p. 163.

[15] Benjamin Franklin, *Autobiography and Other Writings*, ed. Russel B. Nye (Boston: Houghton Mifflin, 1958), p. 32. First published in French in 1791, emphasis added.

[16] Hilary Mantel, 'Giving up the Ghost', *Learning to Talk* (London: Fourth Estate, 2003), pp. 143–4.

anxious or not, she remains true to her own moral vision. This does not mean, I have suggested, that she realizes or obtains what she might have done. On this reading Austen is interested in investigating why Fanny Price fails to exploit certain opportunities, and hence fails to achieve the truly enlightened, or enhanced and enhancing, life that the novel projects for her. In fact if this study leaves the reputations of certain characters enhanced – Dorothea Brooke and Margaret Schlegel belong in this group – those of both Fanny Price and Clym Yeobright lose some of their lustre.

*

When depicting the highs and lows of sexual dynamics (and there are many lows), Gaskell may have learnt a lot from Austen: *Pride and Prejudice* certainly had an impact on the plot of *North and South*. But, like Dickens, Elizabeth Gaskell takes up ethical issues that are very much of her time. In *North and South* she reveals a way of thinking about the newly influential ideology of classical liberalism that places her very much to the fore of radical thought. Gaskell's novel can be read as a timely response to the contemporary debate regarding the conflict between liberal and paternalist modes of conceiving of human welfare, of the tension between the core ideals of rights and responsibilities. At the same time she seeks to problematize the practice of gendered discourse on social and political problems. But what also connects Gaskell to major thinkers of her period, and to J.S. Mill in particular, is her central concern with the question of what it means to be the author or orchestrator of one's own life. If a self-directed person is one who is herself, then the novel asks, What does it mean for a person to be herself? How can a greater degree of individuality be achieved? On Gaskell's view with the spread of individuality 'new things become thinkable', which means that the quality of lives can be enhanced.[17]

What matters to Gaskell is that an individual should be not only self-reliant, but intellectually vigorous and argumentative, open-minded or sensitive to other points of view. Such qualities serve to counteract the distorting perspectives of hegemonic social groups and promote the introduction of practical reforms. Gaskell may have agreed with Mill that 'the moral influences, which are so much more important than all others, are also the most complicated, and the most difficult to specify with any approach to completeness'.[18] But like him, she wants to identify the possible sources of self-direction. So within a carefully delineated context characterized by striking shifts of thought and practice, Gaskell traces positive influences that leave their mark, those factors that make for greater individuality. She looks at education, expectations and ideals, investigating the dynamics of family life, examining the role and status of

---

[17] For a fine discussion of the ways in which 'new things become thinkable' see Nikolas Rose, *Inventing Our Selves: Psychology, Power and Personhood* (Cambridge: Cambridge University Press, 1996), in particular 'Assembling Ourselves', pp. 169–97.
[18] Mill, *Autobiography*, p. 49.

fathers and mothers, and especially daughters. She explores the trajectory of passion and the implications of admiration. She considers the opportunities afforded by community, but also the significance of solitude, of temperament, of the desire to talk as well as the ability to listen. In noting the relations of self to self, she distinguishes the rigorous from the protective mode. Working into her narrative all these interacting elements, Gaskell traces salient sources of authority *and* independence, while she draws out the ethical implications of personal initiative. Given the right mix of qualities and conditions, self-improvement and self-fulfilment are possible. Good lives in this narrative are those characterized by both autonomy *and* authenticity. These are points on which Forster seems to be in complete agreement with Gaskell. For both writers authenticity rightly sets limits to the scope and stringency of morality.

In critical studies of *North and South* one issue that resurfaces from time to time relates to the implications of Margaret Hale's authority. John Thornton's eventual transformation appears to owe much to the urgings of this mostly strong-minded heroine. His classical liberalism is found to be seriously deficient in many respects and by the time he gets to marry the heroine he has set out on a more experimental approach to social relations. His ethical outlook is indeed transformed to a significant degree, and this would seem to be in response to Margaret Hale's endeavours. Yet it is clear that he does not take on board key features of her paternalist vision. Here the reader may find difficulties not only in understanding what this change signifies in itself – what kind of transformation has taken place – but the problem also arises as to how this particular reformation fits into the novel's overall ethical vision or ideology. What is worth noting, then, is that while in the process of conversion the major role is assigned to the converter and she sets the goals, the objectives and modality of change, for Gaskell, as for Mill, although the individualist may require 'helps' towards 'the cultivation of his higher nature',[19] the objectives he (energetically) cultivates are his own. Margaret Hale will set a challenge, but John Thornton will determine the new programme. 'Insofar as men and women have attained genuine individuality,' notes Harry Frankfurt, 'they know their own minds. Furthermore, they have formed their minds not merely by imitating others but through a more personalized and creative process in which each has discovered and determined independently what he himself is'.[20] In *North and South*, the heroine's influence is at once crucial and yet curtailed.

It may be suggested that one reason why Gaskell – and Forster – apparently resist the idea of a convergence or conformity of individual viewpoints has to do with what is fundamental to their system of beliefs. Thus although reformation may be auspicated at a personal and social level, to be avoided at all costs within a narrative is any impression that negates the significance of diversity, of individuality, and of a plurality of values and viewpoints. Both novels fulfill Lionel Trilling's demand

---

[19] These expressions are borrowed from *On Liberty*, p. 135.
[20] See Harry Frankfurt, 'On the Necessity of Ideals', in G. Noam and Thomas E. Wren (eds), *The Moral Self: Building a Better Paradigm* (Cambridge, MA: MIT Press, 1993), p. 17.

for works that 'recall liberalism to its first essential imagination of variousness and possibility, which implies the awareness of complexity and difficulty'.[21] But both novels are also consonant with Seyla Benhabib's refashioned liberal ideal of achieving an 'enlarged way of thinking', by showing that their leading characters are able to reach, if not consensus with significant others, then 'some reasonable agreement in an open-ended moral conversation'.[22]

*

Like Gaskell, Dickens's ethical concerns are in large part the response to profound social and ideological anxieties. Both question the kind of assumptions that the perspicacious Beatrice Webb discerned in her mother's characteristic mode of proceeding, assumptions that seemed to be an engrained part of the Victorian liberal mindset: 'only by [the] persistent pursuit of each individual of his own and his family's interest would the highest general level of civilization be attained'.[23] Neither Gaskell nor Dickens could prize the liberal culture that continued to link private enterprise tightly to individualism or to the fulfilment of self-interest.

Where Austen favours an ideal of reason conceived in terms of reasonableness, in *Hard Times* Dickens challenges the current utilitarian focus on reason, which is interpreted narrowly as instrumental rationality: a form of rationality which promotes self-interest.[24] But what matters most to Dickens is neither reasonableness, nor individuality. And he offers a very different conception both of what it takes to be good and what makes for good lives. Dickens was clearly responding to what he discerned as the increasing and insidious influence of Benthamite Utilitarianism on social practices as well as on notions of personal well-being. While he was registering his disapproval and disgust, so was J.S. Mill engaged in the attempt to revise those features of utilitarian doctrine that he found unacceptable. This philosophy, Mill wrote in his essay on Bentham:

> will enable a society which has attained a certain state of spirtual development, and the maintenance of which in that state is otherwise provided for, to prescribe rules by which it may protect its material interests. It will do nothing (except sometimes as an instrument in the hands of a higher doctrine) for the spiritual interests of society ... It can teach the

---

[21] *The Liberal Imagination: Essays on Literature and Society* (New York: Viking, 1950), pp. xii–xiii.

[22] *Situating the Self, Gender, Community and Postmodernism in Contemporary Ethics* (Oxford: Polity Press, 1992), pp. 8–9.

[23] Beatrice Webb, *My Apprenticeship* (London: Longmans, 1926), p. 15.

[24] As Charles Taylor has observed, with the modern scientific world-view has emerged a new ideal of rationality, so that 'Reason is no longer defined in terms of a vision of order in the cosmos, but rather is defined procedurally, in terms of instrumental efficacy, or maximization of the value sought, or self-consistency': *Sources of the Self: The Making of the Modern Identity* (Cambridge: Cambridge University Press, 1998), p. 21.

means of organising and regulating the merely *business* part of the social arrangements. Whatever can be understood or whatever done without reference to moral influences, his philosophy is equal to; where those influences require to be taken into account, it is at fault.[25]

But for all Mill's revisions, Dickens, it seems, still had a point: utilitarianism may well be incompatible with the pursuit of personal meaning.

For utilitarians morality was/is to be conceived in terms of what is good from the perspective of the moral community. As Mill put it in his essay, 'Utilitarianism', the 'utilitarian standard is not the agent's own greatest happiness, but the greatest amount of happiness altogether'. And this standard is for the moral agent to constitute 'an habitual motive of action'. This is a morality in which the austere ideal of impartiality becomes of paramount importance. Mill specified that his ethics did not require 'that people shall always act from the inducement of promoting the general interests of society': 'Utilitarians are quite aware that there are other desirable possessions and qualities besides virtue, and are perfectly willing to allow to all of them their full worth'.[26] Nonetheless, it has been argued by Charles Taylor and others, that the classical utilitarian outlook is insufficiently accomodating to the moral and non-moral interests that are a shaping force in the identity of individuals. These relate to their personal commitments, their ideals and ambitions, in short, to what gives their lives meaning; and hence, it would seem, to all that contributes to making them effective moral agents. For utilitarians, in certain circumstances, personal ideals and affections are just one set of considerations to be put alongside the needs of others. The maximization of social utility is after all the basic criterion of this kind of morality. The upshot is, in Taylor's words, 'a reduction and homogenisation' of ethical life.[27]

Dickens was clearly precisely of the same opinion. And this unreservedly antagonistic view informs the bleak stories of the lives of the children and workers who populate the world of *Hard Times*. There is a telling moment in the novel when Louisa Gradgrind is asked by her father whether she wants to marry the blustering and bullying banker, Bounderby. For an answer she talks about the shortness of her life: 'While it lasts, I would wish to do the little I can, and that little I am fit for. What does it matter!' Her father – the 'unbending, utilitarian', Thomas Gradgrind – the narrative continues, 'seemed rather at a loss to understand the last four words; replying, "How, matter? What matter, my dear?"' He asks her when she would like to be married. 'What does it matter!'[28] she repeats. And Gradgrind is still perplexed,

---

[25] 'Bentham', in John M. Robson (ed.), *Essays on Ethics, Religion and Society*, in *Collected Works*, vol. 10, pp. 99–100

[26] 'Utilitarianism' (1861), in John M. Robson (ed.), *Essays on Ethics, Religion and Society*, in *Collected Words of John Stuart Mill*, vol. 10, pp. 213, 218, 221.

[27] 'The Diversity of Goods', in Amartya Sen and Bernard Williams (eds), *Utilitarianism and Beyond* (Cambridge: Cambridge: University Press, 1982), p. 132.

[28] David Craig (ed.), *Hard Times for These Times* (Harmondsworth: Penguin, 1969), p. 136.

but makes no further attempt to deal with her evident apathy, or lack of purpose; a condition whose genesis, we are to understand, is to be sought in the effects of an education permeated by one all-powerful and yet spiritually impoverishing theory. Dickens, it is clear, thought the thoughts that later critics have articulated: 'It is difficult for utilitarianism to answer the question of why anything should matter, for the ideal that utilitarianism sets up is a purely impersonal one, a concern for consequences which stand in no significant relation to oneself'.[29]

Forthright in his rejection of the utilitarian vision, Dickens was attracted by the ideals of the Cambridge Platonists, whose work was at that very time being republished by his friend Edward Tagart. For the Platonists John Smith and Ralph Cudworth, the ability to act rightly is given to us through a good will, rather than through our powers of reason: 'We want not so much *Means* of knowing what we ought to do, as Wills to doe that which we may know'.[30] As *Hard Times* reveals, for Dickens the will functions best when it is connected to and guided by the power of sight: a power which is to be discerned in a mix of acute perception and sympathetic attention. But the will also works well when it is bolstered by the loyalty that grows out of the love or affection that is an integral part of an individual's life. In *Hard Times* and *Middlemarch* such loyalty contributes to a heroine's sense of identity and gives her life meaning. The willingness of Sissy, Rachel and Dorothea Brooke to act steadfastly, to remain loyal, is the natural expression and consequence of a strongly felt sense of the abiding meaningfulness of certain connections.

*

If Dickens's vision of the good will can be traced to a revival of interest in the Cambridge Platonists, in *Middlemarch* George Eliot's conception of the way the will works within the moral personality owes much to her extensive reading of Kant.[31] For Eliot moral skills may involve a form or version of Kantian practical reasoning: to avoid moral stasis or escape from a paralysis of confusion and doubt, the will is obedient to the dictates of self-legislating reason. Kantian universalism provides Dorothea Brooke with a way, a necessary way, of avoiding the appeal to self-image. Kant's principle also avoids the 'disturbing aspect of the encounter with exteriority':[32]

---

[29] Richard Norman, *The Moral Philosophers: An Introduction to Ethics* (Oxford: Oxford University Press, 1998), p. 196.

[30] John Smith quoted in C.A. Patrides, *The Cambridge Platonists* (London: Edward Arnold, 1969), p. 139.

[31] *Middlemarch*, ed. W.J. Harvey (Harmondsworth: Penguin, 1981). All references in the text are taken from this edition. For the books that George Eliot and her partner G.H. Lewes acquired on, and by, Kant, see T*he George Eliot-George Henry Lewes Library: An Annotated Catalogue of their books at Dr Williams's Library London*, ed. William Baker (New York: Garland, 1977).

[32] See Catherine Chalier's discussion of Kant in *What Ought I to Do?: Morality in Kant and Levinas*, trans. Jane Marie Todd (Ithaca and London: Cornell University Press, 2002), p. 26.

an appeal which issues from a vision of the other, the fragile, needy other. This is an appeal which for the 'saintly' may turn out to be simply disastrous.

In Hume's view, when judging whether a life is good or not, self-endorsement will play a significant role. For Hume as we act and interact with others we must at all times be able to bear our own survey.[33] Central to the notion of sustaining the kind of viable identity which is crucial to a good life, is the idea of fostering the self-esteem that belongs to an admirable self-image. However, both George Eliot and E.M. Forster can see that the appeal of morality to one's self-image can be highly problematic. Even when the action that an individual contemplates undertaking is consonant with or necessary to the demands of her valued self-conception, it is by no means certain that this act would be one that an ideal or impartial observer would also endorse.

Thus during the long night of inner conflict when Dorothea is asked by her dying husband to continue with his abstruse researches even after his death, the images of herself as assailant and her husband as victim are terribly potent: she must give in to his desires, however unreasonable. To do otherwise would do violence both to him and to her own conception of herself: 'She saw clearly enough the whole situation yet she was fettered: she could not smite the striken soul that entreated hers'. Compelled to give in by the prospect of a totally unacceptable self-image (of herself as aggressor 'smit[ing]' her husband's 'striken soul'), Dorothea is freed from submitting to her 'doom' only by his providential death (521–3). Her mind in vehement conflict, Dorothea views her strength in terms of aggression, and opts, finally, for docility. But this is virtue 'beyond her strength'.[34] By agreeing to excessive demands on herself, Dorothea connives in her own collapse: though eventually freed from the demand for self-abnegation, she is left in a state of severe ill-health, of profound psychic distress. This psychic incoherence is the natural consequence, Eliot implies, of her decision to embrace moral incoherence: to act in a way which collides with her own conception of the good.

Earlier in the same chapter Eliot's narrator had already recognized 'the need of freedom asserting itself within her' (510). For Kant what we value most is our freedom or autonomy. And this is a decisive factor in ensuring that we will choose to be moral in a Kantian manner. On this view an individual is free or self-determining in so far as her will is good. But her will is good when as a rational agent a person chooses to act according to a conception of duty that she has formulated or endorsed; this duty being an axiom she can consistently will as a law. Such a law will constitute a reason for anyone to perform in similar circumstances. From this perspective

---

[33] 'This constant habit of surveying ourselves, as it were, in reflection, keeps alive all the sentiments of right and wrong, and begets, in noble natures, a certain reverence for themselves as well as others, which is the guardian of every virtue': *Enquiries Concerning Human Understanding and Concerning the Principles of Morals*, ed. L.A. Selby-Bigge, rev. P.H. Nidditch (Oxford: Oxford University Press, 1975), p. 276.

[34] See Christine Swanton's discussion of being 'virtuous beyond our strength' in *Virtue Ethics: A Pluralistic View* (Oxford: Oxford University Press, 2003), pp. 64–5, 204–5.

freedom, rationality and morality go together as the individual recognizes what it is Right to do.

This is the moral perspective from which Dorothea's last moral crisis can be understood. Having fled the house in which she finds Will Ladislaw embracing Rosamund Vincy, Dorothea endures another night of anguish. But the tumult of emotion, of anger and despair, is overcome only when she comes to realize that 'The objects of her rescue were not to be sought out by her fancy, they were chosen for her. *She yearned towards the perfect Right, that it should make a throne within her, and rule her errant will*' (846, emphasis added). Dorothea comes to desire that her will be obedient to an ideal of Right action – or Justice: it is a 'maxim' which could be consistently willed as a moral law. This 'recognition within reflection' provides a stopping point in the chaos of her thoughts and emotions. As Catherine Chalier puts it, such recognition is 'a point of certainty within reflection'.[35] Dorothea realizes where her duty lies and achieves the necessary state of (Kantian) calm resolve. Thus she makes her second attempt to 'see and save Rosamund'. And as a result most appropriately finds happiness for herself.

Yet Eliot's ethics are by no means exclusively Kantian, and *Middlemarch* examines modes of thought and belief that ensure both moral competency and moral excellence. As she takes stock of the prevailing attitude to women, an attitude that is generally undermining of constructive endeavour beyond the bounds of domesticity, George Eliot offers an interpretation of what belongs to the supreme virtue that is 'moral saintliness'. This is virtue that recognizes no constraint in the form of domestic boundaries or conventional notions of what it is fitting and not fitting (for a woman) to do. In *Middlemarch* the greatest and yet the most hazardous of the virtues is (over) trust. This wholehearted belief in another's goodness is what prompts Dorothea to rescue the disgraced Dr Lydgate, to make his life 'whole' again. Dorothea is George Eliot's life (restoring) force. Her loyalty to her friend is of a very special kind: it is infused with a super-abundance of trust.

In the Finale Dorothea's own life becomes fulfilling when she is able to participate in the 'beneficent activity' that characterizes her companionate marriage. In a quiet way, at the end of *Howards End* Forster's heroine acts beneficently too, distributing a large part of her unearned income to the needy. The lifestyles that Dorothea Brooke and Margaret Schlegel are able to achieve are hardly raptuously protagonistic. If they are not disappointed neither it seems should we be, and that is because by and large these modes of living satisfy their own intellectual and affective needs.

*

'Yeobright loved his kind': perhaps Hardy's narrator wants to attribute to his hero the Humean quality of sympathy that entails taking pleasure in general happiness,

---

[35] Chalier, *What Ought I to Do?*, p. 19.

in the well-being of humanity. This sense of wide-reaching sympathy, experienced forcefully during his time in Paris, underpins Yeobright's aspiration to do something useful for mankind. In *The Return of the Native*, of 1878, Clym Yeobright's self-conversion is the point of departure for the main plot. Doubt brings him back to Egdon, the place of his past, whose relevance is central first to his reflections on the kind of unsatisfactory materialistic life he has been living, and subsequently to his considered goal of teaching.[36] These reflections and evaluations would appear to be the first steps in a learning process promising to bring still greater understanding and knowledge. Yet it is precisely as he strives to gain a more expressive and valuable kind of life, that Hardy's hero will slide into a moral void. Hardy's narrative shows Yeobright trying to make sense of his life, trying to live according to his own idealistic goals. However, not only does he fail to convince even the least experienced of his listeners, the country folk, that he has a good reason to carry out his new plan. But perhaps more significantly, at the most critical moment in his life the reasons for his own words and actions elude him.

On his return to the Heath, Clym Yeobright puts the 'burning question' to his Mother: 'what is doing well?'.[37] In Yeobright's version of a good life it is fulfilling a sense of purpose or the achievement of meaning that takes precedence over gratifying emotions, or happiness as comfort: 'I want to do some worthy thing before I die' (233). Yeobright finds, to adopt F.H. Bradley's words, 'that the end is for me as active, is a practical end. It is not something merely to be felt, it is something to be done'.[38] Rejecting his mother's vision of a good life as one constituted by affluence and the respect that derives from enhanced status, Yeobright seems to be endorsing Bradley's view: 'the breadth of my life is not measured by the multitude of my pursuits, nor the space I take up amongst other men; but by the fullness of the whole life which I know as mine' (189). If all goes well the feeling of 'self-realizedness' will ensue though the end is a state of self-realization (125). And this enviable condition of fulfilment will occur through acceptance of one's duties to and in a community. Yeobright acknowledges that his life will be hard, that he will have 'to do without what other people require' (234). All lives are subject to adversities, but the eudaimonist will find

---

[36] Thus following Susan Wolf, we may want to maintain a distinction between the pursuit of happiness and the search for meaning – which may or may not promote happiness. For some individuals a good life entails a commitment to finding meaning, which implies that at times considerations of happiness cannot be paramount. First and foremost these people care about the meaningfulness of their lives. 'As Camus pointed out, if a thing is worth living for, it may also be worth dying for, and *a fortiori* it may be worth living with much pain and sorrow for. Having a reason to live, then, and a reason to care about the world in which one lives, is linked fundamentally not with happiness but with meaning': 'Meaning and Morality', *Proceedings of the Aristotelian Society* 47 (1997): 303.

[37] *The Return of the Native*, ed. George Woodcock (Harmondsworth: Penguin, 1978), p. 234. All references in the text are to this edition.

[38] *Ethical Studies* (2nd edn, Oxford: Clarendon Press, 1927), p. 143; first published in 1876.

a way of coping with such difficulties so as to minimize any ill effects.[39] In Bradley's words, 'He sees evils which can not discourage him, since they point to the strength of the life which can endure such parasites and flourish in spite of them' (184). In Hardy's world adversities come in many forms: near blindness, emnity between close relations, and a figure from his wife's past, all intrude. How he deals with these problems will make a great difference to the 'goodness' of Yeobright's life and the lives of those with whom he is most intimate.

At first glance, personal well-being would hardly seem to count for much on Egdon Heath. But 'seems' is probably a most appropriate term, given the importance Hardy's hero later attaches to the happiness he derives from being a furze-cutter. The outdoor exercise not only 'does him good', but provides him with that close contact with nature that becomes a source of bliss. Such are the complications of Hardy's novel. In any case, Clym Yeobright's face seems at first to express 'a view of life as a thing to be put up with, replacing that zest for existence which was so intense in early civilizations'. For this 'modern' type of man the good life is certainly not to be equated with the notion of personal flourishing which was fundamental to the 'Hellenic idea of life' (225). This is the kind of flourishing which was connected to a teleological belief that an individual possessed the potential necessary for the harmonious development of his faculties, that he might legitimately endeavour to achieve the personal excellence that is expressed in a virtuous life, and that this would constitute the fulfilment of his essential nature. This endeavour, remarks the narrator, simply 'grows less and less possible as we uncover the defects of natural laws and see the quandary that man is in by their operation' (225). As Hardy charts his hero's attempt to live a better life, which means eschewing the temptations of a materialistic world in order 'to follow some rational occupation among the people I knew best, and to whom I could be of most use' (229), so does he trace the fatal influence of these 'laws' on the moral life.

For Hardy, it is his hero's 'darkened' self-understanding that undermines the possibility of the moral stance that is manifest in self-responsibility for actions. This is the sense of responsibility which belongs to or informs personal initiative. Failing to take the initiative at crucial times, Yeobright fails those closest to him: his mother and his wife. In assessing what is good in and about Yeobright's life, we shall, Hardy insists, have to examine also the nature of his relationships with those with whom he is most intimate. In the case of both his mother and his wife, what sympathy he possesses does not seem to be highly effective. It is not enough to constitute a decisive influence over his actions: to prompt him into taking action once he is aware of their unhappiness, their suffering.

If Clym Yeobright lacks the capacity to act in the right way at the right time for the right reasons, so too at a dramatic moment is he unaware of the implications of his speech acts. In general agreement with F.H. Bradley's views on the impact of language,

---

[39] See Kekes, 'Permanent Adversities', in *Moral Wisdom and Good Lives*, pp. 51–72.

which both 'penetrates' and 'infects',[40] Hardy finds that at times the self may be left simply defenceless before their power of contagion. Anticipating the theories of French sociologist Gaston Bouthoul, Hardy highlights the fundamental implications of language inheritance, and points up the ways in which certain expressions are connected to an individual's thought patterns, or his *mentalité*.[41] The imprint of his cultural heritage is a significant factor in any attempt to understand why the hero of this tale acts in such a 'barbarous' manner. Thus the fundamentally ironic stance of this novel: although the narrator insists on the 'forwardness' of his hero's views, of his 'relatively advanced position', the narrative discloses the deadly traps that culture may lay for the most idealistic of its members. In what amounts to a case study of the nature and implications of *mentalité*, Yeobright can be seen to assimilate and articulate the expressions of his (primitive) world without ever realising that such a thing has happened. He remains unaware that he has succumbed to their influence. In certain circumstances, Hardy suggests, the inner life becomes inseparable from the outer, the self inseparable from its culture, so that Yeobright's conversion to a new ideal of life seems inevitably, and ironically, to restore him in crucial ways to an earlier mode of existence, and eventually to a more primitive way of thinking. Trying to reinvent himself as a scholar, he is soon transformed into an invalid, before assuming the ways and even the words of the uncultivated men and women of the Heath.

*

Forster's novel *Howards End* presents the reader with two sisters for whom culture is of the utmost importance. Both Margaret and Helen Schlegel seek out and appreciate the goods that belong to 'high' culture: the beauty of architecture and music, the cut and thrust of intellectual conversation. Written only a few years before *Howards End*, G.E. Moore's highly influential work, *Principia Ethica*, of 1903, seems to have provided Forster with a conception of the good life that his heroine – Margaret Schlegel – could wholeheartedly endorse. Attempting to show that the good life is a life in which a great deal of certain intrinsically valuable goods contribute to the experiencing of desirable states of mind, Moore's list of values accords pride of place to the pleasurable consciousness that derives from the ultimate goods of human relationships and beauty.

> By far the most valuable things, which we can know or can imagine, are certain states of consciousness, which may be roughly described as the pleasures of human intercourse and the enjoyment of beautiful objects. No one, probably, who has asked himself the question, has ever doubted that personal affection and the appreciation of what is beautiful in Art or Nature, are good in themselves; nor if we consider strictly what things are worth having

---

[40] 'When he can separate himself from that world, and know himself apart from it, then by that time his self, the object of his self-consciousness, is penetrated, infected, characterized by the existence of others': *Ethical Studies*, p. 172.

[41] Gaston Bouthoul, *Les Mentalités* (Paris: Presses Universitaires de France, 1952).

purely for their own sakes, does it appear probable that any one will think that anything else has *nearly* so great a value as the things that are included under these two heads.[42]

Moore's thesis impressed contemporaries within the Bloomsbury circle, at least for a time. Among them, Forster, it would seem, had his doubts, however. It is with equanimity that on her marriage to Mr Wilcox, Margaret Schlegel relinquishes precisely such highly valued goods – literature, art, the stimulating conversation of her friends – on the grounds that they are no longer the most desirable of 'things'. They are in fact abandoned surprisingly easily: 'It was doubtless a pity not to keep up with Wedekind or John, but some closing of the gates is inevitable after thirty, if the mind itself is to become a *creative* power' (emphasis added).[43] Given her revision of the good life, it is more appropriate, apparently, that her own energies are employed in *constructing* the more exclusive companionate partnership she now desires. Margaret Schlegel intends to do some transforming, and reckons that she can reassemble out of the promising fragments of her future husband's personality a new man, so that their happiness may be ensured as another kind of beauty is gained – the beauty of an harmonious relationship: 'By quiet indications the bridge would be built and span their lives with beauty'; 'she might yet be able to help him to the building of the rainbow bridge that should connect the prose in us with the passion', 188, 187). It is the creation of this new relationship with its particular goals and mutual commitments that takes precedence; the important sources of satisfaction are those that can be shared with the person with whom she will be most intimate.

Commitments, it has rightly been observed, change attitudes, narrow attention and influence action by limiting freedom of manoeuvre.[44] Margaret Schlegel may be able to redirect her energies and focus, demoting the great goods of art and friendship, and so achieve happiness. But what Forster will not dismiss from Margaret's life are the claims of Morality as rendered substantial in the form of the young clerk Leonard Bast, and even more problematically in the shape of Jacky, 'Mrs Lanoline', whose presence is accompanied by 'the odours of the abyss'. Once Leonard Bast has lost his umbrella, for Margaret Schlegel a moral issue starts to impinge, to make a new impression: in Margaret's upper-middle class world Leonard Bast stands for, stands before her as, a telling example of deprivation. He is someone who is physically and mentally malnourished; someone in need. But what exactly are his greatest needs, and who is to provide? For Margaret there is serious thinking to be done about their relationship and her 'role'. And here a comparison with Margaret Hale's assurance in similar circumstances is telling; for Margaret Hale has no doubts about what her responsibilities to the deprived entail. Fifty years later, Forster's narrative raises questions about the kind of claims the deprived can legitimately make on us (and

---

[42] *Principia Ethica* (Cambridge: Cambridge University Press, 1922), pp. 188–9.
[43] *Howards End*, ed. Oliver Stallybrass (Harmondsworth: Penguin Books, 1989), p. 258. All references in the text are to this edition.
[44] James Griffin, *Well-Being: Its Meaning, Measurement and Moral Importance* (Oxford: Clarendon Press, 1986), p. 198.

'us' means both middle-class women and middle-class professional or businessmen), how one might respond, what it makes sense to do. In other words Forster tackles the questions: When should caring transmute into commitment? and When can Meaning reasonably take precedence over Morality?

It is important, Forster suggests, to be concerned with finding answers to the questions What do I most care about? or What matters most at this moment in time? This propensity to engage in moral appraisal, and thus determine the worthiness of goals and commitments, will entail appreciation of the morally salient aspects of different situations. If it is right to characterize a valuable life as one that has both a sense of direction and yet remains open to value of any kind, then it is a life the direction of which is largely shaped by what an attentive individual by means of practical reasoning comes to appreciate as really being of consequence. The wise are good at grasping and reflecting on the central features of situations; they possess soundness of judgement.[45] Moreover, since consistency is not always a virtue, Forster's heroine realizes there will also be critical times when emotions (alone) rightly dictate responses; and this is because 'affection, when reciprocated, gives rights' (285). These are special rights to unconditional attention. But what is not a good idea is to allow the deference that accompanies conjugal love to become a habit. Such continued 'spoiling' of husbands – is not at all wise. In *Howards End* Forster takes a look at the factors that will impact more or less profoundly on the business of situational appreciation and the exercise of virtue.

The Schlegel sisters start out lucky, for a time they have each other to try out ideas upon. Together they can reflect upon and discuss what matters to them and why. But what Forster is able to suggest is how their views of what they should do, and indeed how they should behave, are in ways of which they are not always fully aware, subject to the influence of others. So that their searching intelligence notwithstanding, the flux of their thought is keenly responsive to the pressure of sociality. Margaret Schlegel's is certainly a 'fertile' or resourceful and undogmatic mind. But how open is it good for a mind to be? On one occasion constrained somehow by the presence of their brother, Tibby, they are 'stirred to enthusiasm more easily' once he leaves the room, and only then become appreciative of Leonard Bast's tale of imaginative endeavour, of his determination 'to see once in a way what's going on outside, if it's nothing particular after all' (127).

Clearly it is precisely their combined intelligence and tolerance for other points of view that makes them receptive to new ideas. But in responding to the views of others, Margaret's vision of possibilities can shrink – and shrink dramatically. Later the same evening, provoked by the other debaters at their informal discussion club, she becomes convinced that 'independent thoughts are in nine cases out of ten the result of independent means', and suggests that the solution to Leonard Bast's

---

[45] Kekes observes that 'because this human psychological capacity, once developed, is likely to be lasting and important, it can be identified as a character trait': *Moral Wisdom and Good Lives*, p. 6.

predicament would be to give him money. Then attacked by her fellow debaters, she can see that acquiring the sort of culture that enhances life requires more than money or determination: 'she admitted that an overworked clerk may save his soul in the superterrestial sense, where the effort will be taken for the deed, but she denied that he will ever explore the spiritual resources of this world, will ever know the rarer joys of the body, or attain to clear and passionate intercourse with his fellows'. In other words, she agreed that he might never develop those competencies which will enable him to enjoy the goods of Moore's good life. Margaret's initially optimistic attitude begins to mutate, her vision of what she can achieve seems to become clearer, and as it does, so do her aspirations narrow: 'Doing good to humanity was useless: the many-coloured efforts thereto spreading over the vast area like films and resulting in a universal gray. To do good to one, or, as in this case, to a few, was the utmost she dared hope for' (134). Later, alone again with Helen, Margaret doubts whether she or they can embark on a constructive relationship with Leonard Bast: 'It's no good, I think, unless you really mean to know people. The discussion brought that home to me. We got on well enough with him in a spirit of excitement, but think of rational intercourse. We mustn't play at friendship. No, it's no good' (136). At this point, unlike Elizabeth Gaskell's heroine, Margaret Hale, Margaret Schlegel has become convinced that when the object of altruistic attention is someone whose mental make-up is so different from one's own, Morality and Friendship will not mix. There are certain goods, such as intelligent conversation, that they seem unable to share, and that prospect stands in the way of any meaningful sense of identification with Bast and his aspirations. Certain bonds cannot be forged: commitment cannot grow out of concern. And then just as Margaret is concluding that 'I quite expect to end my life caring most for a place' (137), Mr Wilson appears on the scene and things take another course: Margaret finds 'it was pleasant to listen to him now ... ' (138). In fact his influence will prove to be more important for the way they act than either would care to admit, challenging their own capacity for truly 'independent thoughts'. For the present he provides the knowledge, the 'facts', that (apparently) changing the situation provides a potent reason for them to change their views of what they might do: their views of what it is worthwhile to do.

> 'Let us write to Mr Bast as soon as ever we get home, and tell him to clear out of it at once'.
> 'Do; yes, *that's worth doing.* Let us'.
> 'Let's ask him to tea'. (143, emphasis added)

Chapter 15 ends then with the sisters in agreement about what to do, and some kind of social intercourse, friendship of a kind, with the lower-class clerk is now envisaged. Chapter 16 ends, after Leonard's outburst in front of Mr Wilcox, and Mr Wilcox's dismissal of him as a 'type' (a dangerous word in this book) to be avoided, with the sisters ever tolerant and still in apparent agreement that Bast is 'worth pulling through' (153). His worthiness is recognized in his resourcefulness, in his admirable endeavour to grasp at those good things – literature especially – that can make life go better.

However, from this point in the novel, the sisters' views as to what it makes sense to do will begin to diverge radically. 'Prosperous vulgarian' or man of 'Olympian' laugh and charm: Forster shows how the ideas of the two sisters with regard to whether and how they should help Leonard Bast, take shape to a considerable degree in their response to this other person. It is their changing attitudes to Mr Wilcox, the kinds of feelings they develop for him – affectionate and respectful or suspicious and then hostile – the importance that they attach to his views, that at times will infiltrate their assessment of what they might do for Leonard Bast.

At moments of crisis, however, Margaret Schlegel will have to decide for herself the 'true order' of her personal obligations. And that decision, as William James had argued in *The Principles of Psychology,* of 1890, will bear upon the question of the character or person one wants to be. Forster highlights the various factors, the points or *people* of reference, the beliefs and the emotions, that help to determine 'what being [she] shall now resolve to become'.[46] Margaret Schlegel does change, but in the special sense that she *reclaims* a significant conception of herself. Retrieving and reappropriating a self-conception that reinstates her in her role as her idealistic father's daughter and her sister's fellow feminist, she decides to become what she once was.

As the narrative unfolds, Forster pursues his interest in the question of what exactly counts or is decisive in judgements as to what it makes sense to do by considering what may be sufficient for attempting a good action (Margaret's on behalf of Leonard, when she tries to get him a job with Mr Wilcox), and yet may be insufficient for getting fully involved. That you simply cannot manufacture a personal interest or emotion or desire is obvious (as Margaret remarks to Helen at the very end of the novel, 'Don't drag in the personal when it will not come', 328). In accounting for her own attempted good deed she suggests that her response has nothing to do with a sense of obligation, rather it is tied to a strictly limited kind of desire, one which, it may be noted, is stirred into activity by Helen's intervention:

> *Nor am I concerned with duty.* I'm concerned with the characters of various people whom we know, and how things being as they are, things may be made *a little better*. Mr Wilcox hates being asked favours; all business men do. But I am going to ask him, at the risk of a rebuff, *because I want to make things a little better*. (226, emphasis added)

When her endeavour to aid the Basts fails, Margaret allows them to disappear from sight. She will not get involved. What it makes sense to do becomes separated from what is worth doing. As Henry's wife, it makes no sense for her to pursue this particular interest. Her forthright rejection of the often efficacious notion that the privileged have a duty towards the deprived would seem to be the marker of a radically discriminating or independent mind.

But is it? Margaret's marriage to Henry Wilcox provides Forster with the opportunity to trace the many ways in which influence may be exercised. Margaret will adopt his vocabulary, sometimes apparently unknowingly. She will entertain

---

[46] William James, *Principles of Psychology*, vol. 1, pp. 287–8.

his ideas, usually guardedly, and will even be persuaded into changing some beliefs. Then there are the occasions when she may not fall in with his ideas but lets him have his way. But at a time of suspence, drama and conflict, Forster will investigate, also, what makes for a crucial change of attitude; he will examine the different phases of thought and emotion that constitute the dynamics of her rebellion as she works to regain the initiative. Through pity, guilt, indignation, and finally anger, Margaret Schlegel comes to recognize what or rather who at this moment matters to her most. It is a sense of outrage that fuels a change of attitude and that accompanies a radical shift in her sense of moral identity. In attempting to understand why people react and respond the way they do, we should take a look, Forster suggests, at the critical roles of both influence and identification.

This is a moment in the novel in which Forster introduces an ethical issue that we have already seen greatly interested George Eliot. Though the reader's attention in this novel is drawn to the predicament not of the moral saint but of the socially-mobile man of business, both characters have problems dealing with the ethical implications of self-image. 'Human psychologies,' Janet Coleman has suggested, 'can be spoken of in two ways, one of which emphasizes our capacity to be aware and the other our capacity to desire'.[47] And what we are definitely aware of, if not all of the time, is a notion or picture, however blurred, we have of ourselves. In its most rigorous mode the moral appeal to self-image requires not just 'being on good terms with oneself',[48] rather confirmation that all is as it should be occurs when a valued self-image can be fully endorsed, when the standard of endorsement typically relates to stringent notions of decency or integrity. Yet Forster can see the difficulties with this moral mode of proceeding when the moral shades into or even fuses with the social: when notions of the responsibility that belongs to social status inflect the moral mindset.

In *Howards End* at a moment of high drama, a caring, earnest, and eventually highly indignant, Margaret Schlegel can be found endeavouring to prompt her husband into self-reflective mode so that he can reconsider his attitude to others. The occasion is not (as in *Middlemarch*) a solitary moment of introspection. Rather a vehement dispute is taking place between them. The kind of reasoning Margaret seeks to get her husband started upon implies that the self can take a look at itself (preferably 'seeing things steadily'), perceive where it fits into the larger picture involving others ('seeing things whole'), evaluate self, objectives and values, and then endorse or aim to revise both self-conception and attitude to significant others. However, it soon becomes clear to both heroine and reader that the whole process of enlightenment (which is intended to produce a more favourable attitude to the failings of others) is blocked precisely by Wilcox's keen perception of his own worth. In the case of Henry Wilcox we find that his self-worth is closely bound up with his moral/social code: his

---

[47] Janet Coleman, 'MacIntyre and Aquinas', in John Horton and Susan Mendus (eds), *After MacIntyre: Critical Perspectives on the Work of Alasdair MacIntyre* (Oxford: Polity Press, 1994), p. 75.
[48] Nicholas Rescher, *A System of Pragmatic Idealism*, vol. 2, p. 128.

belief in an ideal of strength of character, which has crucial links with the ethos of the gentleman/warrior. Since the strong character will not tolerate any assault on what is fundamental to his strength – his sense of self-assurance – and the gentleman will uphold at all costs the cause of honour which lies at the very core of his identity (and which brings into play notions of respectability and reparation, which serve to justify the desire to categorize and condemn), this moral endeavour looks set to fail. Urged to reflect, Henry Wilcox raises his 'fortifications'. To pretend that he can promptly divest himself of a self-conception that is rooted in a specific ethic, one which suggests what is appropriate for *a person in his position*, is to fail to appreciate just how strongly social norms and social situation affect moral psychology and self-knowledge. It is left to the plot (so that certain nefarious consequences ensue from holding his beliefs) to prove Forster's pragmatic point that some ways of thinking of our (moral) identity are better because healthier.

*

The heroines of both *North and South* and *Howards End* have a hard time getting enterprising, ambitious, and powerful men to face up to or reflect upon the limitations or confusion and contradiction within their ethical views, so that they can undertake the salutary process of revaluation and self-correction. But it is worth noting that principal characters are principal characters in these novels precisely because they themselves do not need to undergo anything as radical as a transformation. Rather Margaret Hale and Margaret Schlegel experience a process of re-orientation to the good. This means that the wider experience and greater knowledge they come to acquire serves in the business of re-appraisal that is essential to the *recovery* of what is most meaningful, most salient to their sense of what they can and should achieve. As with Dorothea Brooke, it is this act of recognition or re-affirmation that appropriately anticipates the last significant narrative act: the act of union or re-union that rewards, as it strengthens through a sustaining partnership, those heroines whose sense of isolation, longing and need for intimacy has for some time been made manifest.

At the closure of *Mansfield Park* the reader discovers a narrator-author delighted that her lonely heroine is finally exquisitely happy. This is a narrator keen to settle and to reward, to quit the 'odious subjects' of misery and guilt, and 'restore every body, not greatly in fault themselves, to tolerable comfort' (446). 'Tolerable comfort' – we note the (sardonic) qualifier – is distributed only to those pronounced to be deserving. Many decades later the protagonist of *Howards End* manifests an equal concern to promote 'what leads to comfort in the end' (328). In Forster's novel, however, even the 'guilty', those who have transgressed, are accorded a degree of ease that signals a respite from the challenges and complications that invariably arise as individuals move towards that enviable state of 'doing well in being well'.

For Margaret Schlegel, as for Fanny Price, a life that is meaningful, that seems worthwhile, that enables a heroine and her intimate family members to flourish, involves at last what looks like seclusion and retreat. Whether the achievements of a leading character will count as admirable, pretty good or good-enough the reader may well ponder. Our thoughts, George Eliot suggests, might focus finally on whether the lives of others have been made better, or 'not so ill', as a result of someone's 'unhistoric acts'.[49] Were they able to leave the world a somewhat better place?

---

[49] *Middlemarch*, p. 896. Amélie Oksenberg Rorty contrasts a morality of righteousness with significant morality: 'By itself, it does not generate or assure the richness of detail of a morally significant life. Significant morality requires a rich and appropriate array of specific intentions and motives as well as a robust array of abilities to execute these effectively. *It leaves the world a better place for our activity*, beyond the contribution that might be made by the sheer existence of yet one more merely righteous will': 'What It Takes To Be Good', p. 32, emphasis added.

Chapter 2

Narrative Perspectives

Among prominent philosophers of our time Charles Taylor is not alone in taking up and pursuing the idea that literature may help us to make sense of axiological issues, and thereby raise our awareness and perhaps strengthen our judgement with respect to what is good or valuable in lives.[1] In *Sources of the Self: The Making of the Modern Identity* – his highly acclaimed work which examines major changes in ethical thought and the impact of theories stretching from Plato to our own day – Taylor displays a most impressive range of reference to poetry and prose from all periods. Yet when he considers the transformations which took place in the moral outlooks of 'our Victorian Contemporaries', literature is not a major source of ideas, and novels, probably the most read of all the genres at this time, and arguably the richest of literary forms for his purpose, do not make significant contributions in his account of evolving 'pictures of the good'. Such an omission is in the circumstances understandable. Clearly what is essential to the enterprise of interpretation is an acknowledgment, ideally disclosed in some kind of discussion, of the complexity that pertains to the literary text's own favoured strategies, configurations, and modes of expression, and of their effects and implications.

In examining novels for key features of their very different kinds of ethical design we may be able to get away from the idea of fictional texts as engaged above all in a prescriptive process of moral improvement through the fashioning of an exemplary character. We may feel that some texts are not best conceived as a means of *proving* points or providing solutions. Rather, they may 'reveal new dimensions and resonances' of a code or concept, and, moreover, they may do so in unexpected, somewhat 'devious' ways, using deviating techniques.[2] In a wide-ranging discussion

---

[1] In addition to the works of Martha Nussbaum and Daniel Brudney, see also Anthony Cunningham, *The Heart of What Matters: The Role for Literature in Moral Philosophy* (Berkeley, Los Angeles, London: University of California Press, 2001) and Colin McGinn, *Ethics, Evil and Fiction* (Oxford: Clarendon Press, 1997).

[2] Daniel Brudney identifies diverse ways in which philosophy and literature can interrelate: the text can function as 'complex example', literature is often seen 'as a kind of moral training'; or there is the related idea 'that a text might show how some philosophical position "cannot be lived"', or 'what literature might do for moral philosophers is to project some of the *concepts* of moral philosophy. The text will show a new context for applying a concept, one that reveals new dimensions and resonances', thus the text 'would prompt the extension or development of the moral concept': 'Knowledge and Silence: *The Golden Bowl* and Moral Philosophy', *Critical Inquiry* 16 (1990): 397–437.

of the ethics of a variety of modern texts, Adam Zackary Newton has pursued this notion by focussing on forms of storytelling within fictional representations. Newton considers those acts and performances which can be taken as paradigms, and which raise 'fundamental ethical questions about what it means to generate and transmit narratives and to implicate, transform or force persons who participate in them'.[3] Thinking along these lines means acknowledging the crucial functions of literary forms and devices in the shaping of an ethical viewpoint. In this context we might assess, for example, the import of the different narrative strategies that shape reader response to Jane Austen's assiduous pleasure-seekers. In *Emma* and *Sense and Sensibility* personal narratives play a significant role in influencing reader response or attitude. But in *Mansfield Park* a missing narrative deprives Henry Crawford of the chance to gain/regain the confidence of both character and reader. While the charming but devious Frank Churchill (of *Emma*) and the charming but cruelly calculating John Willoughby (of *Sense and Sensibility*) are allowed explanatory, if not justificatory, narratives of their past behaviour, the charming but flirtatious Henry Crawford is permitted no such privileged mode of working on anyone's sympathies. By the time Fanny Price leaves for Portsmouth, he may well have seen the error of his ways, but he is given no opportunity to exercise the art of narrative persuasion. Crawford may be eloquent and expansive in 'life', but the novel's tight construction imposes strict limits on his narrative forms of expression. Given the novel's ironic vision, Fanny Price has to be seen to be 'right' – in her suspicious/sceptical view of him, a view which he cannot entirely dispel – but also 'wrong' because to the end she is susceptible to unreason. The plausibility of closure in exclusion requires fastidious adherence to a principle of verbal restraint; it relies on a finely-tuned awareness of what should and what cannot be said.

We may have to give some thought, then, to the wide variety of devices which structure narratives, including juxtaposition, foregrounding, *peripeteia*, suspension and omission. In the case of *Mansfield Park* I shall be taking into consideration not only textual features that solicit the reader's attention, but take note when scenes or episodes terminate abruptly, or when the drama of the moment is deliberately downplayed in a form of literary minimalism which makes for minimalization. In Austen's novel these formal devices pertain to strategies which work unobstrusively to direct or redirect perception and interpretation. With a highly skilled ironist like Austen such devices may be part of a subtle strategy aimed at provoking a potential misreading by encouraging hermeneutic overlooking and underestimating. Our interest is curtailed, our attention deflected, for reasons which we might do well to ponder. In fact drawing out and working out the ethical implications of these critical points or narrative junctures should contribute to a process of revaluation of the ethics of the text.[4]

---

[3] Adam Zackary Newton, *Narrative Ethics* (Cambridge, MA: Harvard University Press, 1995), p. 7.

[4] This means that the kind of assessment we find in even the most recent studies of the novel requires rethinking: Thomas Williams repeats conventional critical wisdom when he claims that 'Fanny Price is the one character whose judgment never leads her astray'.

Of particular importance is the issue of how at any one time we envisage the narrator's function and contribution, for this dimension of the text will count for a great deal in our interpretation of the ethical perspective of the work, that is the novel viewed in its entirety. Such a task will involve, interalia, a perception of the attitude, or perhaps the shifting attitudes, expressed by the narrative voice, and an assessment as to whether these are indicative of a specific agenda, or a stance that is more or less ironic or provocative, or judicious or biased, or knowledgeable or authoritative, or complicit (as when in free-indirect discourse it merges with the thought of characters).[5] For there is a question we can always ask of the narrative voice: To what extent does it approximate to that of an ideal observer or impartial spectator? In novels such as *Hard Times*, *Mansfield Park* and *Middlemarch* we find that the narrative voice represents a source of tension, of dissension and dissonance within the text.[6] So that at times the reader is left with antagonistic tendencies that refuse to co-exist within a single perspective. These texts are composites and the faultlines can be discovered.

A basic hermeneutic problem clearly involves discerning each novel's underlying ethical/ideological perspective(s). And it is usual critical practice to conceive of this 'position' in terms of the point of view of an 'implied author'.[7] Yet the idea of the

---

Discernment is the 'characteristic virtue of the outsider': 'Moral Vice, Cognitive Virtue: Austen on Jealousy and Envy', *Philosophy and Literature* 27 (2003): 223–30. For a very different reading see below, Chapter 3.

[5] Harry E. Shaw asks the question 'What sorts of things do authors want their narrators to do?' in 'The Place of the Narrator', *Narrating Reality: Austen, Scott, Eliot* (Ithaca and London: Cornell University Press, 1999), pp. 236–42.

[6] Patricia Ingham finds a similar kind of disparity of viewpoints in *Little Dorrit*: see 'Nobody's Fault: The Scope of the Negative in *Little Dorrit*', in John Schad (ed.), *Dickens Refigured: Bodies, Desires and Other Histories* (Manchester: Manchester University Press, 1996), pp. 98–116.

[7] For a discussion of this topic see Martha C. Nussbaum, *Love's Knowledge: Essays on Philosophy and Literature* (Oxford: Oxford University Press, 1990), pp. 8–10. Nussbaum distinguishes between the narrator, the authorial presence that 'animates the text taken as a whole', and the real-life author. However, her reference to the narrator as an 'author-character' is problematic in so far as it suggests that this is a privileged and reliable voice which necessarily explicates the author's 'intentions and thoughts'. In *Upheavals of Thought: The Intelligence of the Emotions* (New York: Cambridge University Press, 2001), following Wayne Booth, Nussbaum again runs together aspects that make for a very different conception of the 'implied author' than the one given here. She notes that the 'implied author' is 'a voice or presence or sense of life that animates the work taken as a whole': p. 252. This definition is also problematic in that the comments of the 'voice' can only ever refer to a part of the novel or some idea or ideas that are raised by the work, and not to 'the work taken as a whole'. So that the comments of such a 'voice' – such as the parting words in *Hard Times*, to which Nussbaum refers, are best understood as enunciated by the narrator, or more precisely, a 'narrator-as author' or 'narrator-as-moralist'. In my study, on the other hand, the implied author does refer to a stance that emerges precisely from a consideration of the text 'taken as a whole'.

perspective of an 'author' may mislead if one fails to appreciate that what lies behind any such stance or theory or ideology is the construction of a composite picture consisting typically of a considerable variety of narrative elements (which may or may not entirely cohere). This means that in appraising the content of this view what is called for is the recognition of an implicit 'all-things-considered' rationale, which requires of the reader a similar capacity for a wide-ranging assessment prior to the shaping that belongs to interpretation. Such a conception seemingly contrasts with that of critics such as Dominic Rainsford, for whom in texts by Blake, Dickens and Joyce, the 'implied-author' is perceived to function above all as a kind of 'presence', a version of the author himself, though one deprived of the real author's daily concerns.[8] Instead, in this work I shall be adopting the theory of narration that conceives of the various sources of meaning in terms of different layers of discourse. We can imagine then that behind the '*narrator* as author' or the 'narrator as subscriber', one who does at some point give the reader a sense of his presence by firmly advocating a certain point of view (and who is to be distinguished on this occasion from a narrator *tout court* or a 'narrator as *character*'), we find the 'implied author', which term signifies a more inclusive, indeed, an '*all-things-considered* stance'. Occupying another conceptual dimension, is the controlling presence of author him- or herself.

With respect to *Hard Times* one question to be considered is how Dickens's method of organizing the various stories that have to do with his governing themes on forms of virtue and forms of social/political relations, helps to shape what is to count in any final analysis of the novel. For many readers the conversion of the utilitarian character Thomas Gradgrind is pivotal. In *Hard Times* this moment of enlightenment occurs at the very end of the novel, when the 'man of realities' comes face to face with his degraded and dishonest son, the unmistakeable proof of the failure of his teaching scheme to produce rational bodies. It is a transformation that makes for controversy, for the end-weighting of the moment of revelation would seem to endow it with particular significance. In Gradgrind's conversion to the wonderous ways of the circus, in his new found loyalty to his son and concern for his daughter's emotional well-being, we are – according to influential critical views – not only to discern a final and decisive repudiation of the Benthamite utilitarian outlook, but we are also to endorse the idea that its power can be deviated or defied if the resources of family affection and the creative imagination are drawn upon. The moral model that the closure affirms may not count for much within the context of Coketown, but it is supposed to work its magic on the reader. If Gradgrind repents of his system – which the narrator has suggested is part of a wider phenomenon of reforming ideals which translate into the practice of regulation and even repression – then this is apparently in favour of a paternalist position. This paternalist vision, symbolized in the reformation that brings into being the good (if enfeebled) father, is the novel's 'ostensible', if problematic, 'solution' to

---

[8]   *Authorship, Ethics and the Reader: Blake, Dickens and Joyce* (London: Macmillan, 1997), pp. 4–8.

conflicts and crises both personal and social. In the view of Catherine Gallagher 'the Gradgrind family becomes a model of harmony and security, a paradigm for proper social relations, only by undergoing internal change'.[9] But there are good reasons, I shall suggest in my analysis of this novel, to revise this problematic interpretation and to place Dickens not amongst the shrinking and increasingly powerless numbers of paternalists, but within the influential crowd of liberal critics of liberalism. In the interpretation advanced here, Gradgrind's conversion – which transforms him at a stroke into a disgraced and uninfluential public figure – is not a sign of the novel's ultimately conservative stance: Dickens, remains, like Gaskell, a troubled even angry liberal. To see what makes for such a reading we need to reconsider the function of the various components within the constellation that constitutes the novel's form of argumentation, bringing them into relation with each other so as to identify major patterns of signification.

Dickens's technique, we discover, relies upon the narrative form of contrastive schematism, the logic of which requires different outcomes, each contributing something to the sense of the ending. Gradgrind's conversion is then to be contrasted with the capitalist Bounderby's fervent commitment to *un*conversion. As Gradgrind retreats into the bosom of his family, Bounderby marches resolutely on and into the future. No one is going to change Bounderby, nor, it is clear, Gradgrind's own star pupil, Bitzer, that exemplar of self-reliance and self-mastery, of enterprising and industrious behaviour, the ideal at the heart of classical liberalism. Clearly, if these two are representative of a powerful tendency within the powerful force that is liberalism, then, Dickens suggests, liberals themselves will have to rethink an ideology that can serve as a justification for an excess of self-interest. For this is an ideology which is deficient in ideas for 'carrying forward the members of the community toward perfection, or preserving them from degeneracy' – precisely the problem that J.S.

---

[9] See Catherine Gallagher: 'Gradgrind sacrifices his old principles of reason and self-interest to his new belief in family loyalty ... Thus the Gradgrind family ostensibly comes to embody the virtues of loyalty and compassion, and thereby takes a necessary step toward, becoming an appropriate model for society'. There is a problem however, for Gallagher continues, 'At the very moment Dickens restores the usual optimistic direction of the paternalist metaphor – the ideal family as a model for society – the parallel between the Gradgrind children and the working classes collapses ... For the Gradgrinds, therefore, becoming a model family means cutting themselves off from the larger social considerations and retreating into the morality of clannishness': *The Industrial Reformation of English Fiction: Social Discourse and Narrative Form 1832–1867* (Chicago and London: University of Chicago Press, 1985), pp. 154–5.

In the view of Rosemarie Bodemheimer 'the stories of *Hard Times* offer a social critique so bleak, a vision of society so fractured, that only Marx could have accomodated it to mid-nineteenth-century ways of thinking. Is it any wonder that Dickens falls back on the paternalist appeals, evoking the image of a world in which rulers might touch the lives of the ruled?': *The Politics of Story in Victorian Social Fiction* (Ithaca and London: Cornell University Press, 1988), p. 206.

Mill had identified and was seeking to address at the very time Dickens's novel was being written.[10]

If social change is not to mean alienation, and if a richer and more inspiring moral vision is to take hold, then radical changes will have to be made, Dickens implies, in what is becoming established as the most influential ideology of the time. Here, then, an 'all-things-considered' appraisal would avoid placing the weight of salience on the shoulders of any one (reformed or reforming) character: the usual candidates being Gradgrind and Sissy Jupe. Rather this mode would take into account both of the novel's major concerns as developed through its thematic patterning: concerns relating both to forms of virtue that inform individual lives and to the wider social and political practices that determine the well-being of communities. Thus a consideration of the interrelations of the larger issues the novel explores would leave us with the thought that in this novel Dickens proposes that political belief be permeated by the recognition that ethical codes, however strong and complete, are necessarily insufficient to promote the fulfillment of human interests, though political practice cannot consolidate or extend particular interests without strong ethical foundations.[11]

Complicating the hermeneutic issue in *Hard Times* – as in *Middlemarch* and *Mansfield Park* – is the contribution made to the novel's ethical discourses by that influential element in the text, the narrator. For a close reading of these novels may well cause us to reflect on the function(s) of the narrative voice. Whereas Adam Zachary Newton claims that we will be, or must expect to be, 'schooled' by the narrator in 'the correct evaluation of and response to character and moral situation', I would suggest that we firmly resist the idea of succumbing to these didactic impulses so as to achieve a more appropriate, because more comprehensive, reading of the text.[12] Particular caution needs to be exercised when we come across an advocate or 'a narrator as subscriber', and that is a narrator who is committed to a particular notion or theory to which the reader is also invited most warmly or urgently to subscribe.

In *Hard Times* we may expect to encounter discursive cohesion; we may expect sooner or later to find a harmony or a convergence of interests and a unity of viewpoints

---

[10] John Stuart Mill, 'Remarks on Bentham's Philosophy', in John M. Robson (ed.), *Essays on Ethics, Religion and Society*, in *Collected Works*, vol. 10, p. 9. Mill strongly criticized Bentham's use of the term 'interests', as in the following passage: 'self-regarding interest is predominant over social interest; each person's own individual interest over the interest of all other persons taken together'. 'By the promulgation of such views of human nature', maintains Mill, 'and by a general tone of thought and expression perfectly in harmony with them, I conceive Mr Bentham's writings to have done and to be doing very serious evil ... The effect is still worse on the minds of those who are not shocked and repelled by this tone of thinking, for on them it must be perverting to their whole moral nature': pp. 14–15.

[11] See Vincent P. Pecora, 'Ethics, Politics and the Middle Voice', *Yale French Studies* 79 (1991): 205, whose point I have slightly modified.

[12] *Narrative Ethics*, p. 9.

established between the narrator and the 'implied author'.[13] Thus we may assume that the function of the narrator is precisely to promote the novel's key values. Such assumptions may well be unwarranted, however. In other words we may discover that the narrator is not a truly authoritative voice in that he is not responsible – cannot be responsible – for expressing what is in fact a multifaceted ethical argument. As in *Middlemarch*, the narrator of *Hard Times* is much concerned with the moral function of the emotions, while clearly also very much alive to the crucial role of the creative imagination. Indignant and scornful, this narrator is out to make a lasting impression:

> Utilitarian economists, skeletons of schoolmasters, Commissioners of Fact, genteel and used-up infidels, gabblers of many little dog's-eared creeds, the poor you will have always with you. Cultivate in them, while there is yet time, the utmost graces of the fancies and affections to adorn their lives so much in need of ornament; or, in the day of your triumph, when romance is utterly driven out of their souls, and they and a bare existence stand face to face, Reality will take a wolfish turn, and make an end of you! (192)

Because in *Hard Times* the narrator's rhetoric aims to promote an ethics of affect – which is shown to be most efficacious when conjoined with the keen perception that is characteristic of a good will – the reader may well underestimate the salience of those themes which serve to develop Dickens's views on the need for other key goods. Foremost amongst these goods are mutual respect, freedom of expression and toleration: those life-goods that Dickens finds in short supply in the liberal society which is precisely the broader target of the narrative. There is a risk then, in succumbing to the power of the narrative voice in being disabled when it comes to seeing how the different themes relating to ethics and ideology interrelate or fit into the novel's overall design, its extensive social and moral vision, its meditation on the advantages and disadvantages – mostly the disadvantages – of living in a newly emerging liberal state: a state whose underlying political premises and social and moral doctrines are perceived to be in need of considerable revision.

That the narrator may serve as but an imperfect guide to the ethics of the work in which he/she figures is a conclusion we may come to once more when we consider a passage from *Middlemarch*, or more precisely, if we examine the relation between two juxtaposed discourses, those of narrator and character. The temptation for the reader is to presume that the semi-integrated thought processes we are presented with can be made to integrate fully as one ethical discourse. In this passage both lines of thought are concerned with Dr Lydgate's anguish and with understanding his 'grief' in the context of what has happened to his 'honourable ambition'. (Though the whole is rendered still more complex by the importance the narrator also attaches to the manifestation of certain moral emotions.)

---

[13] As D.A. Miller observes, 'once the ending is enshrined as an all-embracing cause in which the elements of a narrative find their ultimate justification, it is difficult for analysis to assert anything short of total coherence': *Narrative and its Discontents* (Princeton: Princeton University Press, 1981), p. xiii.

> He felt himself becoming violent and unreasonable as if raging under the pain of stings: he was ready to curse the day on which he had come to Middlemarch. Everything that had happened to him there seemed a mere preparation for this hateful fatality, which had come as a blight on his *honourable ambition*, and must make even people who had only vulgar standards regard *his reputation* as irrevocably damaged. In such moments a man can hardly escape being unloving. Lydgate thought of himself as the sufferer, and of others as the agents who had injured his lot. He had meant everything to turn out differently; and others had thrust themselves into his life and thwarted his purposes. His marriage seemed an unmitigated calamity; and he was afraid of going to Rosamond before he had vented himself in this solitary rage, lest the mere sight of her should exasperate him and make him behave unwarrantably. There are episodes in most men's lives in which their highest qualities can only cast a deterring shadow over the objects that fill their inward vision: Lydgate's tender-heartedness was present just then only as a dread lest he should offend against it, not as an emotion that swayed him to tenderness. For he was very miserable. Only those who know the *supremacy of the intellectual life – the life which has a seed of ennobling thought and purpose within it* – can understand the grief of one who falls from that serene activity into the absorbing soul-wasting struggle with worldly annoyances.
>
> How was he to live on without vindicating himself among people who suspected him of baseness? How could he go silently away from Middlemarch as if he were retreating before a just condemnation? And yet how was he to set about vindicating himself (793–4, emphasis added).[14]

Here the narrator can acknowledge at the start of her musings that Lydgate's actions (though well-intentioned) have led to evil consequences with regard to both his plans and his reputation. But what to her is of greatest import, it becomes clear, is the threat now posed to that supreme way of life that is the 'intellectual life'. The idea/ideal of pursing an 'honourable ambition' fits into a wider vocational theme; a theme which throughout the novel has identified an ethical end in the kind of realization that is noble (or soul enhancing) because aimed at the achievement of a great social good – in this case the goods are beneficial scientific discoveries. The aim is not ennoblement, but both honour and a profound sense of satisfaction are clearly welcome consequences of success. Failure is measured in terms of an inability to measure up to one's (great) potential. Lydgate's predicament is thus viewed as, and can only be fully understood by those able to appreciate the dangers of, 'a soul-wasting struggle with worldly annoyances': the worldly annoyances being debts.

But in Lydgate's thoughts, we discern, notions of honour have become detached from considerations of ambition or sense of purpose, however noble. Honour is now connected with (ordinary) reputation rather than with the glory of noble achievement. At the point we are given his free indirect self-questioning ('How was he to …') Lydgate begins to dwell entirely on the personal implications of loss of dignity. In this case failure is bound up with loss of respect and even self-esteem; it is a loss which is potentially devastating because he will be faced, it seems, with the humiliation (and not simply with 'worldly annoyances') that derives from a condition of imagined 'baseness'.

---

[14] *Middlemarch*, ed. W.J. Harvey (Harmondsworth: Penguin, 1956, reprinted 1981).

What we discover in this text is then a disjunction which may be reconceived as an intersection where ethical interests meet but cannot ever become a merger: distinctive ethical modes are formulated as the voices talk past each other. Lydgate's discourse constitutes one element – but a most significant one – in a complex of devices that work throughout the final chapters towards establishing the premises of an eudaimonistic ethics. This is an ethics of 'doing well *in being well*' – an ethics which in its commitment to personal welfare recognizes the legitimacy of constraints on the ambition that drives perfectionism. Lydgate's dilemma suggests that a viable self-conception – which is essential for well-being – will involve acknowledging the significance of what are simply basic components: his reputation and self-esteem. On this reading, the different elements that pertain to the narrative's argumentation in favour of a eudaimonistic ethics provide an intelligible check on the claim to primacy which the narrator's perfectionist ethos seeks to make.[15]

The question of how narrators contribute to the way we read or perhaps misread the ethics of certain realist novels merits yet further attention. Turning to *Mansfield Park* we find that there are times when Austen's narrator would appear to possess the very qualities that are looked for in characters as well as readers: reasonableness and fairness above all. Hence this narrator can distance herself from her heroine and invoke the standard of impartiality when Fanny Price errs by sliding into censoriousness:

> Experience might have hoped more from any young people, so circumstanced, and *impartiality* would not have denied to Miss Crawford's nature, that participation of the general nature of women, which would lead her to adopt the opinions of the man she loved and respected, as her own. (362, emphasis added)[16]

But at the moment of closure, as if exasperated by the evidence of so much human folly, and as if deliberately defying the reader to object, the 'narrator as author' takes sides; unashamedly, as it were, she *now* declares for the heroine: '*My* Fanny indeed at this very time, *I have the satisfaction of knowing*, must have been happy in spite of everything' (446, emphasis added). However, although such a re-positioning on the part of the narrator might lead us to think that the final arrangements – whereby Fanny Price gets what she has always wanted – are to be judged highly satisfactory, the text works in various ways to undermine our confidence in any such conclusion.

---

[15] This is a teleological vision according to which moral action is construed primarily in terms of the endeavour to achieve a highly desirable goal or intrinsically valuable attainment. The Prelude to the novel expresses such an end as promising 'some illimitable satisfaction ... which would reconcile self-despair with the rapturous consciousness of life beyond self' (25). As Richard Norman puts it, a perfectionist ethos pertains to an impersonal or detached perspective, while values which include specific obligations belong to a personal perspective. Such points of view are concerned with incommensurable values which cannot be ranked or weighed against each other on a single scale: *The Moral Philosophers: An Introduction to Ethics* (Oxford University Press, 1998), pp. 200–201.

[16] *Mansfield Park*, ed. Tony Tanner (Harmondsworth: Penguin, 1966).

Summing up, the narrator looks to the future as she comments on the past. In her assessment we find that the idea of personal responsibility and moral action are bound up – as in *Hard Times* – with the idea of the crucial influence of early education. The evil consequences of the wrong kind of education thus supply an essential element in any explanation of the novel's closure in exclusion – the exclusion from Mansfield Park of so many of the characters.

> Henry Crawford, ruined by early independence and a bad domestic example, indulged in the freaks of a cold-blooded vanity a little too long. Once it had, by an opening undesigned and unmerited, led him into the way of happiness. *Could he have* been satisfied with the conquest of one amiable woman's affections, *could he have* found sufficient exultation in overcoming the reluctance, in working himself into the esteem and tenderness of Fanny Price, there would have been every probability of success and felicity for him. His affection had already done something. Her influence over him had already given him some influence over her. *Would he have* deserved more, there can be no doubt that more would have been obtained; especially when that marriage had taken place, which would have given him the assistance of her conscience in subduing her first inclination, and brought them very often together. *Would he have* persevered, and uprightly, Fanny must have been his reward – and a reward very voluntarily bestowed – within a reasonable period from Edmund's marrying Mary.
>
> Had he done as he intended, and as he knew he ought, by going down to Everingham after his return from Portsmouth, he might have been deciding his own happy destiny. But he was pressed to stay for Mrs Fraser's party; his staying was made of flattering consequence, and he was to meet Mrs Rushworth there. Curiosity and vanity were both engaged, and the temptation of immediate pleasure was too strong for a mind unused to make any sacrifice to right; he resolved to defer his Norfolk journey, resolved that writing should answer the purpose of it, or that its purpose was unimportant – and staid. (451–2, emphasis added)

It is worth noting for a start the refrain set up by the phrase 'could he have' which is synonymous with 'if only he could have'. The passage, we find, becomes a kind of lament for a missed opportunity: 'could he have ... could he have ... would he have ... would he have ...'. But this is an opportunity that – given the apparently decisive effects of nurture on his character – was, it would appear, no real opportunity or 'opening' at all. We are to view Henry Crawford's actions as subject time and again to the promptings of vanity: vanity that has become exacerbated through over-indulgence. But if we insist, nonetheless, that within the passage there lurks the idea that there was such a thing as an opportunity, which could have led to happiness for both Henry and Fanny in marriage ('there would have been every probability of success and felicity'), then such a notion would seem to require a corresponding idea of an agent who is sufficiently free, or unconditioned by his past, to be able to appreciate that this is an opportunity which he might make something of. Thus the phrase 'could he have' might trigger the thought that perhaps he could have acted otherwise – could have avoided involvement with Maria. So that the phrase 'Would he have persevered', might be followed by another thought: 'why did he not persevere?' The narrator provides a short answer to this last question by dwelling again on Crawford's vanity – the result of too much early spoiling – which apparently prevented him from taking advantage of what chance had placed in his way. According to this view, it is as if Crawford simply *found* something valuable, was unable to realize its potential, and then thoughtlessly threw it away. He could not derive an opportunity out of a contingency. Yet all that has gone before in the previous intricate narration of thoughts, intentions, words and actions, all that occurred in the synthetic or composite text, gives us reason to object that this is a partial and partisan answer. For a better one might take into consideration the history of a rejection – Fanny Price's rejection of him – which is also a history of denial, withdrawal, resistance and omission. For the narrator's is an explanation which misses out on a salient factor. What is absent in this, the narrator's gap or evasion, is any mention of the story of another evasion – indeed a series of evasions and deviations – on the part of the other person involved: the heroine of the story, who was offered an opportunity, an opportunity *created* for her by Crawford. For the text as History, rather than Moralizing Summary, is deeply interested in the question of why Fanny Price does not even for a moment consider that an alliance with Henry Crawford might be an opportunity for herself (and/or others), not that is until, ironically, it has become too late. And it gives us abundant reason to ask whether her attitude could be described as reasonable. The narrative itself thus provides us with a very good reason to query the sufficiency of the narrator's explanation.

What we find as we read *Mansfield Park* are suggestions that we view responses and reactions through the lens of a standard of reasonableness. Fidelity to this norm of openness, moderation and fairness, is of the essence if mutual understanding is to be achieved. A multifaceted notion, reasonableness, it is implied time and again, is a most desirable feature of attitudes and outlooks and ways of thinking. According to this viewpoint – this 'rationalist' stance which we are invited to adopt – what is required of both character and reader is a review of both attitudes and reasons so as to gauge their sufficiency, cogency and appropriateness.

In Austen's text it is important to note, then, when we are and when we are not given the opportunity to examine the kind of reason that is involved in her characters' reasoning. But it is also important to distinguish who at crucial moments is able to exert most influence and perceive how this influence is exercised. What counts ultimately in this novel is not the power to command and compel – the prerequisites of the patriarchal system – but rather the power to convince as well as the capacity for self-conviction. We will discover that it is the particular mode of reasoning, the mode of self-persuasion of her heroine, the habitual outsider, which will contribute decisively to a closure which we will be expected to view as unfortunate or even troubling. Troubling for several reasons, not least because it marks an abrupt and decisive break with the text's characteristic mode of proceeding, its own complex mode of comprehension. The upshot of all this is that an unmistakably partisan narrator is able to attribute responsibility for the near-but-not to-be conversion – of both Henry *and* Fanny – to Henry Crawford alone, effectively disallowing Fanny any significant part in the action.

Ostensibly preoccupied with a form of virtue that is conceived as a strict adherence to principle and sense of duty, this novel's ironic focus captures in its anatomy of the mind the intricacies of human 'self-abuse'. It traces in the particular logic of practical reasoning the role played by desire, fear and resentment in the achievement of the self-conviction that is constituted by self-deception, disingenuousness and denial. What emerges from such a reading is Austen's shrewd appreciation of the psychological needs and purposes that such practices can serve. We may well wonder, therefore, whether we are to take seriously the narrator's satisfaction with her heroine, and whether the 'implied author' is content with the way things turn out. In short, we may query whether the final arrangements and attachments celebrated by the narrator are in fact consonant with the 'author's' ethical ideal. Here the text's many discourses – that of the narrator included – permit through the adoption of irony and hyperbole, ambiguity or dissonance to prevail.[17] This text invites and entertains difference or disagreement, and it does so to the last, where dissent is prompted as a response to what is represented as a fitting end.

---

[17] Hence this reading endorses the views of Pam Perkins that 'Austen stresses the arbitrariness of the resolution that she actually provides and forces readers out of any uncritical contentment with her allotment of conventional rewards and punishments ... Dour and moralistic Fanny might be, but *Mansfield Park* itself is no humorless sermon': 'A Subdued Gaiety: The Comedy of *Mansfield Park*', *Nineteenth-Century Literature* 47 (1993): 22–5.

PART 2
ETHICAL DESIGNS

Chapter 3

On Being Un/reasonable: *Mansfield Park* and the Limits of Persuasion

At a crucial moment in the novel *Mansfield Park*, Fanny Price receives a letter from Mary Crawford urging her to avail herself of the opportunity to return 'home'. 'Tell us to come,' Mary writes, 'It will do us all good'.[1] Fanny thinks for a short while whether she should accept the offer, but then refuses. For many of Austen's critics what Mary wants would not be good for Fanny Price at all. Rather what is of value is some special quality or characteristic of the heroine herself, who, seemingly rewarded for her good behaviour, finally returns to the great house in the company of Edmund Bertram in a state of exquisite happiness. No longer 'the lowest and last', a poor relation occupying an ambiguous position within the Mansfield household, the timorous Fanny is now hailed as the daughter Sir Thomas Bertram always desired, and she will shortly be the wife of Edmund, his son, which is what we know she has desired all along. Clearly if the reader has been brought to desire Fanny's good or well-being, there will be pleasure when in the final summary settling of circumstances – when comfort and consequence are conferred – the happiness of this unlikely heroine is secured. In this chapter I attend to the much debated question of this novel's conception/s of the good, or of what we are required to appreciate and praise – or condemn.

So what does this most impressive of novels require from its reader? Are we supposed to find its heroine's point of view essentially correct, and hence admire what might (or might not) be called her nobility of purpose? Given Austen's habitual delight in both the lively and the absurd are we really to read Fanny Price – as so many critics have done – as a model of exemplary feminine behaviour, an ideal of submissiveness and obedience, and so imagine a solemn-faced Austen in a perpetual Sunday-morning mood devotedly devising an apologia for the pietistic?[2] Is 'the picture of good' that brings the narrative to a close the one we are expected to endorse,

---

[1] *Mansfield Park*, ed. Tony Tanner (Harmondsworth: Penguin, 1966), p. 424, emphasis added. Henceforth all further references in the text are to this edition.
[2] In Marilyn Butler's highly influential reading Fanny Price is the character who is able 'to discern the true nature of evil, to choose the future course of her life, and, through a period of total loneliness, like a true Christian to endure': *Jane Austen and the War of Ideas* (Oxford: Oxford University Press, 1975), p. 236.

when our considerations as to what is good might extend to ideas of what is just, fair, reasonable and/ or – as Mary Crawford intends it – beneficial or advantageous?

My reading concurs with the view expressed by Claudia Johnson that Austen's novels are increasingly concerned, not simply with the realization of an existence that is 'sweet and dear', but with achieving a more active, expansive and personally fulfilling happiness. *Mansfield Park*, is not an exception. Just like *Persuasion*, this narrative implies that a life of 'doing well in being well' is well worth the striving.[3] Indeed, from an ethical perspective, precisely because it envisions a more active and expansive conception of well-being, Austen's fiction constitutes an important moment in the story of modern literature. But *Mansfield Park* differs from her other fiction, crucially, in so far as the reader is left, even encouraged, to doubt whether the more active and expansive conception of well-being is the one with which the novel closes.

The ethical question this novel pursues relates to the problem of what Fanny Price can achieve given all her disadvantages. Or rather, to be more precise, what is of interest here are two interlinked questions: What is it possible to accomplish? and What is it possible to become? In this reading I propose to show why in *Mansfield Park* 'doing well in being well' is so very difficult. My analysis should reveal how Austen's vision of ethical possibilities is constrained by her appreciation of the nature of distinctive elements of psychological phenomenology. This means that she recognizes and – unlike, say, Richardson, Dickens or George Eliot – insists on preserving the tension between ideals and expectations. What is of considerable interest in this novel is Austen's grasp of the role and implications of vital psychological defence mechanisms. And I shall be noting how in her remarkably perceptive – and subtly ironic – study of her heroine's attitudes, the characteristic coping strategies of subliminal self-defence complicate those responses which for Austen are constitutive of a desirable ethical outlook.[4] Fanny Price, we discover, is especially adept when it comes to operating a transference or displacement of interest and mental energy from one subject to another, so achieving a specific and necessary objective. (These are precisely the self-protective mechanisms that Freud was to investigate and theorize several decades later.) However, before we examine more closely Fanny Price's function in the History that is *Mansfield Park*, as a way of understanding the wider

---

[3] *Jane Austen: Women, Politics and the Novel* (Chicago: Chicago University Press, 1988), pp. 164–6.

[4] Other critics have observed that Fanny's behaviour exhibits self-protective mechanisms, but seen these as contributing to a 'strategy of goodness' so that Fanny is both a 'suffering' and an 'exemplary' heroine. This is the view of Bernard J. Paris: 'Here is the goodness of a terrified child who dreads total rejection if she does not conform in every way to the will of those in power. It is rigid, desperate, compulsive. Fanny is not actively loving or benevolent; she is obedient, submissive, driven by her fears and her shoulds. Her goodness provides, moreover, the only outlet for her repressed aggressive impulses': *Character and Conflict in Jane Austen's Novels: A Pyschological Approach* (Detroit: Wayne State University Press, 1978), p. 49.

issues involved it will serve, I think, to take a critical look at some influential earlier accounts of Austen's ethics.

In his classic work on ethics, *After Virtue*, Alasdair MacIntyre advances what would seem to be a very good reason to admire Austen's shy and shrinking heroine. Arguing for a view of the ethical life that affords a central place to an Aristotelian conception of disposition, MacIntyre claims that certain character traits or virtues are the *sine qua non* for the pursuit and attainment of the good. And in *Mansfield Park*, it is constancy, Fanny's constancy, that is the most highly rated of the virtues, and which justly earns its reward. That Fanny is 'constant' and that it is due in great part to this virtue that she finally achieves 'a certain kind of happiness', might seem indisputable.[5] And yet to assume that her 'constancy' actually connotes excellency of character may be to assume too much. Thus we might prefer to think of her rather as consistent or immutable or even intransigent. In fact another way of appreciating Fanny's behaviour would be to adopt the norms favoured by the enlightened minds of Austen's time, and inquire how 'reasonable' she may be judged to be, thus recalling Mary Wollstonecraft's desire: 'I wish to see women neither heroines, nor brutes, but reasonable creatures'.[6] We might then ask: How reasonable is such constancy? We might suspect, furthermore, that at the time she was composing *Mansfield Park* Austen was rereading Richardson's *Pamela*, where an equally modest and principled heroine successfully exerts her influence over the socially superior rake Mr B. By the second half of the novel now his most complaisant wife, Pamela must listen to an account of his requirements for their future relations. Mr B. insists that he will expect nothing from his wife that is not '*reasonable, or just*'. But Pamela wonders who will decide what reasonable behaviour might be.[7] *Mansfield Park* shows Austen thinking the subject over, her ideas on reasonable and especially unreasonable behaviour shaping the logic that drives the plot. In her earlier novel, *Pride and Prejudice*, Austen had insisted that closure coincide with the manifest reasonableness of her protagonists' sentiments and behaviour. Her heroine's change of attitude towards the hero is to her own mind 'as *reasonable and just*' as her sister's feelings for Bingley'.[8] While Darcy's account of his tormented reactions to Elizabeth's reproof terminates with the admission that 'it was some time, I confess, before I was reasonable enough to allow their justice' (376).

The notion of reasonableness was certainly central to certain strands of Enlightenment morality. But Austen was the author – I shall be suggesting – who not only ran with the idea but who endowed it with the kind of ironical slant that we find articulated in

---

5   Alasdair MacIntyre, *After Virtue: A Study in Moral Theory* (London: Duckworth,1981), pp. 225–6.
6   *A Vindication of the Rights of Woman*, 1792, ed. Miriam Kramnick (Harmondsworth: Penguin Classics, 1975,) p. 172.
7   Samuel Richardson, *Pamela*, ed. Margaret A. Doody (Harmondsworth: Penguin Classics, 1980), pp. 465, 469, emphasis added.
8   *Pride and Prejudice*, ed. Tony Tanner (Harmondsworth: Penguin, 1972), p. 345, emphasis added.

Franklin's *Autobiography*: 'So convenient a thing is it to be a *reasonable creature*, since it enables one to find or make a reason for everything one has a mind to do'.[9] In *Mansfield Park* Austen teases out the implications of un/reasonableness for an ethics of eudaimonia.

Earlier readings of the novel have typically made much of Austen's heroine's stirling qualities. In Tony Tanner's account these qualities are not really virtues in the traditional sense, rather she is seen as sustaining in her behaviour key social values.[10] Hence a special notion of the good is of relevance to society as a whole. Fanny's firmness, her 'extraordinary immobility' is emblematic of the praiseworthy endeavour to uphold the social values of order and stability, and fine discrimination is called for on Tanner's part in differentiating between Fanny's 'stillness' and Lady Bertram's 'inertia'. The hero of *Northanger Abbey* was of the opinion that 'To be always firm must be to be often obstinate. When properly to relax is the trial of judgment'.[11] But for Tanner Fanny is beyond criticism, the image of 'thoughtful rest', she alone 'resolutely holds on to standards and values' (173). In a novel whose characters can be quite unsparing in their judgements of each other, Fanny Price is the only one, it would seem, who possesses the capacity for 'true judgement' (147).

Many critics have concurred with Tanner. And Margaret Kirkham's reading expresses a similiar high regard: it is Fanny's rationality, or rather 'her rational reflection upon experience' that we are asked to admire.[12] Certainly it is true that the narrative voice claims that she has good sense often enough. Yet we might do well to take a closer look at what happens to Fanny's judgement at significant junctures and examine those crucial moments when even as she attempts to reason herself out of her distress, her reasoning becomes deeply informed and directed by her feelings of like and dislike, her resentment and jealousy, her habitual mistrust of herself and others. Hence such an assessment of her reasoning powers, I shall suggest, may be reasonably re-assessed and even revised. In Austen's carefully constructed text it is worth noting when we are, and when we are not, given the opportunity to examine the kind of reason that is involved in her characters' reasoning.

Clearly then there would seem to be problems in discerning an unambiguous source of the good.[13] And Brian Wilkie has come up with strong reasons for doubting that in this novel Austen is engaged in concerns of an exclusively moral nature,

---

[9] Benjamin Franklin, *Autobiography and Other Writings*, ed. Russel B. Nye (Boston: Houghton Mifflin, 1958), p. 32.

[10] 'The Quiet Thing: *Mansfield Park*', in *Jane Austen* (London: Macmillan, 1986), pp. 142–75.

[11] *Northanger Abbey*, ed. Anne E. Ehrenpreis (Harmondsworth: Penguin, 1972), p. 143.

[12] 'Feminist Irony and the Priceless Heroine of *Mansfield Park*', in Janet Todd (ed.), *Jane Austen: New Perspectives* (New York: Holmes and Meier, 1983), pp. 231–47.

[13] In *Jane Austen's Novels: The Art of Clarity* (New Haven and London: Yale University Press, 1992), Roger Gard confidently claims that 'there is no ambiguity in Jane Austen: the reader is never long unsure about what has happened, and never finally unsure as to how to take it': p. 12.

arguing that she refuses 'to let morality wield pre-emptive force'.[14] Wilkie claims instead that what the novel registers is a prime concern for her heroine's capacity for happiness. It is 'the growing amplitude of personality' that matters most to Austen in *Mansfield Park*. (Nina Auerbach makes the telling point, however, that there would seem to be deliberate irony in Jane Austen's conclusion with 'its pitiless repetition of "happy" [in a paragraph otherwise concerned with] this household of collapsed hopes'. And she adds that 'never in the canon is the happy ending so reliant upon the wounds and disappointments of others ...'.)[15] Wilkie suggests that we focus on Fanny's well-being rather than on the issue of her worthiness and role or activities within the community the novel has created. Here I will attempt to show that it is not only Fanny's well-being that is of concern. For the 'author' can perceive a way of achieving the greatest happiness or well-being of the greatest number of characters through the making of an inclusive, rather than an exclusive, set of connections. The well-being of the members of this group, and in particular Edmund and Mary, Fanny and Crawford, is to be measured not simply in terms of the happiness that derives from reciprocal affection, for reciprocal encouragement may help all concerned to modify certain propensities so as to achieve a more harmonious or well-integrated or well-rounded kind of character, as well as a more rewarding kind of existence. In short, by the forging of these connections, we have good reason to believe that the animated might become more steady and the steady a little more animated. On this view, Austen is still of the idea that good lives – or rather the best lives – are those which find a place for talent and wit alongside propriety and decorum. These are the lives which – as during the evening of the successful mixing of Bertrams, Prices, Crawfords and Grants – manage to make the most and the best of 'steady sobriety' and 'lively turns, quick resources and playful impudence' (249, 254).

But Austen's nuanced conception of personal flourishing takes further elements into account: the state of 'being well and doing well in being well' is conceived also in terms of the potential benefits that the dominant social and economic system of patronage can offer. From this perspective, an optimal state of affairs can be understood to have been reached when comfort, consequence and influence – the influence to promote the good of others – are there to be enjoyed. Thus those who disregard the possibilities of influence that can be gained from creating firm attachments within the best of connections will, like Fanny Price's mother, learn sooner or later of their value.

Indeed, the matter of influence – what forms it takes, who has it, gains it, loses it, how it works and to what end – will turn out to be pivotal in this subtle history of causes and their 'natural results'. Negligible, transient, immediate, profound and substantial, the effects of the attempts to exert influence are everywhere registered. Reviewing this intricate account of group dynamics we find time and again that what counts for a great deal is not the power to command and coerce, but the power to

---

[14] Brian Wilkie, 'Structural Layering in Jane Austen's Problem Novels', *Nineteenth-Century Literature* 46 (1992): 517–44.

[15] 'Jane Austen's Dangerous Charm: Feeling as One Ought about Fanny Price', in Todd (ed.), *Jane Austen: New Perspectives*, pp. 208–23.

convince as well as the capacity for self-conviction. In particular, appreciating the vital role self-persuasion plays at times of opportunity, times for improving attachments or undermining potential connections, should help in understanding why things turn out the way they do in a novel whose analysis of the tactics of the serious and the self-deceived manages to be at once entertaining and profound.

*

To the novel's heroine the implications of influence start to matter very much once the Crawfords have made their dashing appearance at Mansfield Park. Austen has invested both Mary and Henry Crawford with extraordinary powers to animate, whose reach extends well beyond the text, challenging the equanimity of characters and readers alike – as critical reactions typically reveal.[16] Fanny worries for Edmund, becoming deeply, extravagantly, pessimistic: 'God grant that her influence do not make him cease to be respectable' (414). Yet though some may lose their heads, the narrator achieves detachment and even imparts a measured optimism: 'Experience might have hoped more for any young people, so circumstanced, and *impartiality* would not have denied to Miss Crawford's nature, that participation of the general nature of women, which would lead her to adopt the opinions of the man she loved and respected, as her own' (362, emphasis added). Experience and impartiality serve to project a vision of the future which is far more sanguine. While we cannot but note how unfair all with the exception of Edmund often are to Fanny, undervaluing her good qualities, so it becomes increasingly obvious that Fanny finds it difficult – very difficult – to be fair to Mary Crawford. This is a tendency shared by some readers.[17] In the view of Marilyn Butler, Mary is nothing less than a 'really dangerous' figure.[18] But the move to persuade us that Mary is not only flawed but wicked means having to play down the narrator's testimony to the fact that – *just like most people* – she possesses 'the really good feelings by which [she] was almost purely governed' (170). Rather than 'vicious'

---

[16] As Michael Williams has astutely remarked, 'the novel appears to do, pre-eminently, what all art does in some measure: to turn the reader back on himself, to baffle him, to leave him revealing more about himself than the thing he would explain': *Jane Austen: Six Novels and their Methods* (London: Macmillan, 1986), p. 83.

[17] Mary Crawford possesses 'Talents and Shrewdness and Wit', qualities Jane Austen singled out in her description of a young woman, from whom the 'faultless heroine' – 'perfectly good, with much tenderness & sentiment, & not the least wit' – shrinks. This burlesque 'Plan of a Novel' is mentioned by Pam Perkins in 'A Subdued Gaiety: The Comedy of *Mansfield Park*', *Nineteenth-Century Literature* 47 (1993): 18. Perkins's assessment of Mary Crawford can be taken to corroborate the view of her given here: 'Her principles do not stand up to Fanny's careful scrutiny, but her cheerful wit makes her an attractive character despite her inability to live up to the standards affirmed by the concluding vision of Mansfield', p. 5.

[18] Butler, *Jane Austen and the War of Ideas*, p. 233.

or 'evil', the frank, clever, well-informed, and talented, Mary Crawford shares with Mr Bennet (of *Pride and Prejudice)* both a mischievous wit and an almost complete disregard for the finer points of morality; she is lacking in scrupulosity. When viewed from the strict perspective of the moralist this is certainly a noteworthy imperfection or deficiency. Yet it hardly constitutes a major or disfiguring vice.

Mary Crawford certainly has her good points – most notably exemplified in her kindness towards Fanny when she is verbally abused by Aunt Norris – but to expect Fanny Price to feel charitable towards the one person who is a serious rival for Edmund's affections may be to expect too much. Fanny is invulnerable to a special quality that Austen persuades (some of) us that Mary possesses. It is described by Hume as 'something mysterious and inexplicable, which conveys an immediate satisfaction to the spectator, but how, or why, or for what reason, he cannot pretend to determine. There is a manner, a grace, an ease, a genteelness, an I-know-not-what, which some [wo]men possess above others, which is very different from external beauty and comeliness, and which, however, catches our affection almost as suddenly and powerfully. And though this *manner* be chiefly talked of in the passion between the sexes, where the concealed magic is easily explained, yet surely much of it prevails in all our estimation of characters, and forms no inconsiderable part of personal merit'.[19] Hume's description gives us a notion of the moral personality that is intuitively appealing, an idea of merit as comprising also the social virtue of amiability, a mode of being that is attractive and winning, that has sway or seductive power over others. Austen clearly attributes this manner to both Crawfords and to no one else, but the problem is, of course, whether or not the narrative is meant to convince us that they possess the potential to mix such 'magic' with greater moral seriousness. On more than one occasion Mary's conversation is enlivened by the risqué humour of the self-confident and sophisticated entertainer, and though the upright Edmund is often ready to condemn, so too is he ready to blame himself 'for a too harsh construction of a playful manner' (412). Mary amuses as she confounds and intrigues until, compelled by the plot to blunder, she most unwisely exhibits in her letter to Fanny a new line of vulgar innuendo. As D.A. Miller has argued 'the closure that Mary is subjected to involves a necessary simplification of her discourse and the implications it has sustained'. Her liveliness and wit are now transmuted into 'a thoroughly corrupted cynicism'; and this we are to attribute to the influence of London.[20]

In charting Henry Crawford's intent to seduce via 'the power of the word' – the power to impress, move and persuade – Austen's narrative strategy of sexual dynamics is certainly less risky than Richardson's employment in *Pamela* of the aggressive tactics of Mr B. But she still courts the reader's dislike and distrust, for Crawford's

---

[19] David Hume, *An Enquiry Concerning the Principles of Morals*, ed. L.A. Selby-Bigge, rev. P.H. Nidditch (Oxford: Oxford University Press, 1975), p. 267.

[20] On the 'mystery' that is Mary Crawford and the text's changing attitude to her see D.A. Miller, 'Good Riddance: Closure in *Mansfield Park*', in *Narrative and its Discontents: Problems of Closure in the Traditional Novel* (Princeton: Princeton University Press, 1981), pp. 79–89.

initial motive for claiming Fanny's attention consists of nothing less than the desire to exert complete influence over her; to induce her '*to think as I think*, be interested in all my possessions and pleasures' (241, emphasis added). In this novel time and again scenes are designed so as to expose the conditions of persuasion, but we must wait to see which of the characters possesses most influence or whose influence will prove most efficacious, shaping the novel's plot and providing for narrative closure. The final chapters will disclose which characters – and they are both women – are able to exert that remarkable and gratifying power (to be distinguished from the power of those who like Sir Thomas Bertram have inherited the right to command and coerce) which may challenge and combat reason (as in the case of Maria), or even desire (as with Fanny), causing others (Henry and Edmund) at critical moments to change their minds about what to think and/or what to do.[21] But it is worth noting that important though such acts are in ensuring which connections will be created and which attachments dissolved, the text is remarkably compressed: Austen will not divulge the details, providing us with a tantalizingly brief explanation of how her characters went about exerting their influence. There are, in other words, no revelations concerning the precise means by which on those crucial occasions of male vulnerability such female power is exercised.

In the chapters that lead up to the momentous change in the life of Fanny Price – her departure for Portsmouth – her growing power over Henry Crawford is, we find, minutely accounted for. At the same time, the reader is given more opportunity to assess those aspects of his character that suggest he does in fact possess the capacity to change a mode of life which has hitherto been devoted entirely to the pursuit of self-gratification. Yet Fanny is steadfast in her determination not to influence or help to reclaim him (as Edmund desires), nor to be influenced in the slightest by him. In this ironic rewriting of *Pamela* – whose eponymous heroine is made by Richardson to undergo psychological acrobatics in order to accomodate the far more dangerous and far less attractive libertine Mr B. – we are given a Fanny Price who remains consistently mistrustful. Although many critics find Fanny unlikeable, her behaviour nonetheless apparently demonstrates a 'toughmindedness' that is highly commendable. She is a 'true Christian' 'born to endure"claims Marilyn Butler;[22] she 'requires no enlightenment' Yeazell declares;[23] her's are 'the standards by which we are asked to judge', according to Mary Poovey.[24] For Julia Prewitt Brown, Fanny is a sort of 'moral

---

[21] Maria's ascendency is such that she is able to divert Henry Crawford's attention from the 'woman he had rationally, as well as passionately loved', p. 453.
[22] Butler, *Jane Austen and the War of Ideas,* pp. 236–7.
[23] Ruth Bernard Yeazell, 'The Boundaries of *Mansfield Park*', in Judy Simons (ed.) *Mansfield Park and Persuasion* (Basingstoke: Macmillan,1984), p.77.
[24] 'The True English Style' in *The Proper Lady and the Woman Writer: Ideology as Style in the Works of Mary Wollstonecraft, Mary Shelley and Jane Austen* (Chicago: Chicago University Press, 1984), p. 104.

yardstick',[25] for John Wiltshire, 'a high-principled, undeviatingly righteous soul';[26] in Nina Auerbach's critical extravaganza Fanny is 'monstrous' precisely because she is so staunchly virtuous.[27] In Avrom Fleishman's account of the novel as *bildungsroman* 'Fanny is the first young person ... who learns enough of the world to win through to success by moral effort'.[28] In Lionel Trilling's highly influential reading it is 'by reason of her virtue [that] the terrified little stranger in Mansfield Park grows up to be virtually its mistress'.[29] Paul Pickrel agrees that 'Fanny Price is always right' and adds moreover that although she is subject to irony 'it never suggests, as the irony that surrounds Emma does, that she may be headed in the wrong direction. When we see a story from the point of view of a character whose appraisal of what is going on is essentially correct, obviously we do not have to wait to get the true view'.[30] With what almost amounts to critical consensus on the subject, it might seem fanciful to raise the question of how we are to consider Fanny's behaviour.[31] There is, after all, no denying that she possesses modesty and sensibility, and that she believes in the upholding of principles and the dictates of conscience. When Roger Gard remarks that she is 'tender and vulnerable'; 'a beautifully seen case of timidity in adversity', we must agree. Whether we believe his claims for her 'superlative moral rectitude' will depend, however, on our notion of 'moral rectitude', or more precisely, on our idea of what constitutes admirable manners of reasoning.[32] Arguably, unlike her characters, Austen is most concerned – for most of the novel – in looking at character not in terms of 'who is best?', but rather with a view to discerning what they are about, how they deliberate and evaluate. It is no accident that at crucial moments the novel invites us, by presenting us with quite substantial accounts of Fanny's thought processes, to judge for ourselves the extent to which her reasoning is influenced by her principles.[33] So that developing a point made by Martin Price

---

[25] *Jane Austen's Novels: Social Change and Literary Form* (Cambridge, MA: Harvard University Press, 1979), p. 5.

[26] John Wiltshire argues that the value 'set upon conscientiousness is compromised because Fanny's is excessive and unprofitable and in some ways incapacitating': *Jane Austen and the Body* (Cambridge: Cambridge University Press, 1992), p. 96. But more problematically, he also claims that Fanny's 'meditations exemplify her as that self-reflexive moral being, with that ability to "discuss" her feelings and conduct with herself which it is repeatedly suggested is the crucial failure of the other characters to be without': p. 67.

[27] Auerbach, 'Jane Austen's Dangerous Charm', p. 50.

[28] *A Reading of Mansfield Park: An Essay in Critical Synthesis* (Minneapolis: University of Minnesota Press, 1967), pp. 71–2.

[29] Lionel Trilling, *The Opposing Self* (New York: Viking Press, 1955), pp. 207–30.

[30] 'Lionel Trilling and *Mansfield Park*', *Studies in English Literature* 27 (1987): 619.

[31] According to Pam Perkins, 'Austen is very subtly undermining the convention that modesty and moral virtue are sufficient to gain respect and happiness': 'A Subdued Gaiety', pp. 17–18.

[32] Gard, *Jane Austen's Novels*, pp. 130–31.

[33] Jane Spencer is amongst those critics who hold that Fanny possesses 'greater moral sensibility' than Edmund, which is apparently proved later when Edmund learns 'what Fanny already

– who notes the importance Austen attached to 'an unconstricted consciousness'; one that has 'range and stretch' – I shall argue that the novel's paradigmatic moral concept can be taken to be a 'reasonable mind'.[34] This is a mind aware of the need for self-imposed limits on emotions or constraints on partiality, but one that is capable, too, of openness to experience and argument; it is a mind receptive to reasons, in the sense of being willing to engage in reflection on them. Reasonableness, philosopher John Finnis has argued, is an essential requisite for participating in all human goods well. On this view 'doing well in being well' depends primarily on the capacity for reasoning well; and that involves 'attention both to one's own inclinations and to the whole range of possibilities open to one'.[35] Reasonableness thus requires the kind of engagement that calls for a (temporary) estrangement from the self's concerns. It is that virtue which 'provides the indispensable direction needed for all the other moral virtues' (69).

According to philosopher Nicholas Rescher it is only in heeding reason's call – in being *willing* to listen to reasons – that we exercise our freedom and at the same time realize our most positive human potential; while the realization of one's potential is a process that contributes to a condition of flourishing. For Rescher those who are reasonable are not only capable of the understanding and impartiality of which Finnis speaks, they are also well-informed and well-intentioned.[36] Significantly, Austen, also, requires that her reader consider the importance of forms of intention as she discloses their impact on the modes of thought that can make for or hinder flourishing. She discerns the ways in which certain intentions block the possibility of exploring certain sources of information; such intentions make it difficult to listen to the reasons of others. The danger is that becoming well-informed or clear-sighted may in fact impede the achievement of one's long-term, long-cherished, if unexpressed, hopes and desires.

*

In this reading of the novel if Crawford's weakness, his vanity, is a crucial element affecting the outcome of the action, so too is the nature of the reasoning and the attitude – the reasonableness or unreasonableness – of Fanny Price. Her responses and reactions are factors which cannot be left out of any attempt to understand why

---

knows – that only conscience can effect true reform. Any attempt at influence which goes beyond awakening the other's conscience is doomed to failure ... Without that inner moral life, which neither Mary nor Henry possesses, no-one can be reformed by a lover-mentor': *The Rise of the Woman Novelist: From Aphra Benn to Jane Austen* (Oxford: Basil Blackwell, 1986), pp. 174–5. This view suggests that Mary and Henry fail to possess any good qualities, upon the basis of which it might be possible to bring about their 'salvation'.

[34] 'Austen: Manners and Morals', in *Forms of Life: Character and Moral Imagination in the Novel* (New Haven and London: Yale University Press, 1983), p. 70.
[35] *Fundamentals of Ethics* (Oxford: Clarendon Press, 1983), p. 51.
[36] Nicholas Rescher, *A System of Pragmatic Idealism* (3 vols, Princeton: Princeton University Press, 1993), vol. 2, pp. 25–6, 54.

things turn out the way they do. Fanny does not, then, as Mary Poovey maintains, emerge 'victorious simply because the others falter' (105). In fact, just as we can evaluate and *re-evaluate* Crawford's character, given his desire and endeavour to change (so that in Julia Prewitt Brown's words 'we are made to feel that his love ... contains his salvation', 93), so can we assess the evidence – right from the start of their acquaintance – as to reasonableness of Fanny Price's attitude towards him and figure out its implications.

To be sure the novel works hard at creating the impression that Fanny Price *intends* to be 'agreeable to reason', as Dr Johnson defined the condition of being reasonable. But it demonstrates, too, that Crawford, just like his sister, will constitute a challenge of immense difficulty. Thus right at the very beginning of the Crawfords' stay at Mansfield Park, during the apparently trivial but in fact highly significant episode of the riding lesson, we are given the opportunity to track Fanny's thoughts, and find that, determined to exculpate Edmund for the late arrival of her horse, she picks on Henry Crawford instead: 'what could be more natural than that Edmund should be making himself useful, and proving his good-nature by any one? She could not but think indeed that Mr Crawford might as well have saved him the trouble; that it would have been particularly proper and becoming in a brother to have done it himself; but Mr Crawford, with all his boasted good-nature, and all his coachmanship, probably knew nothing of the matter, and had no active kindness in comparison of Edmund. She began to think it rather hard upon the mare to have such double duty; if she were forgotten the poor mare should be remembered' (98).

The placing of this episode is most important; it occurs before the theatricals, and hence before Fanny can have any reason to suspect Crawford of undue levity or moral carelessness. In fact, the underlying cause of this 'attack' has nothing to do with Henry's 'vices'. Henry Crawford simply serves as a target for Fanny's jumbled up feelings of distress and resentment, pity for the horse and pity for herself. Subsequently the narrator notes ironically that 'her feelings for one and the other were soon a little tranquillized, by seeing the party in the meadow disperse ...'. But the feelings she experiences, we may well surmize, are of many kinds. Thus although there is no explicit mention of Fanny's pain as she perceives, or thinks she perceives, Edmund's hand holding Mary's, 'he was evidently directing the management of the bridle, he had hold of her hand; she saw it, or the imagination supplied what the eye could not reach', there is no doubting that pain is what she feels as she views this moment of 'attachment'. And it is this bitter and potent image of the hands meeting that sets in motion her coping or self-protective strategy: a strategy designed to shift the focus of feeling so that her self-centred pain might be eclipsed by or dissipated in an other-centred scorn. Fanny's is an intuitive kind of displacement therapy. Here as elsewhere, Austen is concerned not with narrow issues of right or wrong, rather it is Fanny's distinctive mode of response that interests and that is even subjected to a fine irony: her sorrow for the horse is a symptom of a sensibility pathetically tilting towards excess. Thus what we might do well to examine – I suggest – is the intricate nature of the relation between the novel's ethic and its characters' attitudes.

The kind of attitude Fanny Price displays to Crawford is, Austen makes clear, the manifestation of a particular psychological condition.[37] And what engages her attention, and what she shows great understanding of, are the workings of 'the powerful energy system of the self-defensive psyche', to borrow from Iris Murdoch a most appropriate expression.[38] Resorting to tactics or mental manoeuvres that serve to defend both Edmund and herself, Fanny is being unfair to Crawford, when being fair is an important part of what being reasonable is about, and when being reasonable is the virtue that underpins or inflects (all?) others. What is notable about Austen's ethical design is thus the marked disjunction between values and expectations, for her expectations are grounded in an astute reading of what is possible given the developmental history of the psyche. Whether that tension can ever be dispelled is open to doubt. On this view what shadows the narrative is not dogmatism – as Trilling famously claimed – but a spirit of scepticism born of psychological realism.

Reasonableness, Austen implies, calls for a significant degree of self-awareness and effort. And Fanny comes to appreciate this. Indeed, she wonders and worries at the time of the theatricals whether she will ever understand her own motivation: 'Was she *right* in refusing what was so warmly asked, so strongly wished for? ... Was it not ill-nature – selfishness – and a fear of exposing herself? ... It would be so horrible to her to act, that she was inclined to suspect the truth and purity of her own scruples ...' (174). This doubting about her doubts, this questioning of her own motivation, cannot but strike us as admirable. It is a mark of Fanny's earnest endeavour to do right. At this point Austen has alerted us to Fanny's recognition of a moral problem, and because we know that Fanny is aware of the danger of self-deception we may assume that she will be able to achieve self-understanding. It is worth noting, however, that Fanny grows 'bewildered' and does not resolve her dilemma. Henceforth it remains to be seen, then, whether Fanny will be able to achieve clarity with regard to the impact of her own hopes, desires and fears, and in particular her jealousy and resentment, on her modes of thought, and whether she will be able to strive successfully against the possibility, the lure, of self-deception.

As Austen's ironic gaze focuses on the particular logic of practical reasoning, we discover that on one notable occasion Fanny's intent to be 'rational' or reasonable is prompted even as it is undermined by what we cannot but feel to be an unreasonable and unbecoming desire: it is the desire 'to deserve the right of judging of Miss Crawford's character'. Fanny's desire for the right of such judging not only stakes a cool claim to the moral high ground but anticipates the satisfactions to be derived from sitting in judgement on, that is criticizing or censuring, Miss Crawford: 'It was her intention, as

---

[37] Attitude, Gordon Allport has suggested, is the 'cornerstone of social psychology'; it is 'a mental and neural state of readiness, organized through experience, *exerting a dynamic influence upon the individual's response* to all objects and situations with which it is related' (emphasis added): G.W. Allport, 'Attitudes', in C.A. Murchison (ed.), *Handbook of Social Psychology* (Worcester, MA: Clark University Press, 1935), pp. 1–50.

[38] *The Sovereignty of Good* (London: Routledge, 1970), pp. 81–2.

she felt it to be her duty, to try to overcome all that was excessive, all that bordered on selfishness in her affection for Edmund ... She would endeavour to be rational, and to deserve the right of judging of Miss Crawford's character and the privilege of true solicitude for him by a sound intellect and an honest heart'(271). That Fanny never desires to sit in judgement on Tom Bertram – whose wild and selfish ways could equally be classified as 'wrong' – is telling. Could it be because Tom offers no threat whatever to the happiness that for her is so hard to achieve?

It is significant that our assessment of Fanny's achievements will take place within the context of the prospect of an *all-inclusive* resolution, where the greatest good is, from an 'impartial' point of view (a view which, as we have noted, the narrator has suggested we adopt) the general good. This good is envisaged as a network of life-enhancing and mutually supportive, as well as mutually improving, connections, so that the animated (the Crawfords) may become more steady or serious, and the steady (Edmund and Fanny) a little more animated. That this proposition is invested with 'authorial' approval may be deduced from the sound arguments put forward in those discourses which are advanced to sustain it. Thus faced with the *exclusive* closure,[39] we can agree with Paul Pickrel that 'things need not have turned out as they did' (617). And we can affirm, moreover, that Austen does not contrive the actual ending for conventional moral reasons, whereby sinners and saved get their due reward.[40] There is an obvious irony to be gained in a novel which privileges reasonableness, when its principal character achieves her ends by selectively determining when to be bound by its imperatives.[41]

---

[39] Yeazell discusses Fanny's propensity 'to organize experience by drawing sharp lines of exclusion'. She argues, however, that it is 'the novel' that endorses this kind of exclusion: 'The novel as a whole' goes in for 'this categorical sorting of things into the clean and the dirty, the sacred and the profane', thus 'consciousness maintains its own purity by shutting things out': Yeazell, 'The Boundaries of *Mansfield Park*', pp. 70, 81.

[40] We can thus agree with Trilling that the novel terminates by establishing in 'fixity and closure, a refuge from the dangers of openness and chance', but challenge his view that it anxiously asserts the need to find security, that 'it takes full notice of spiritness, vivacity, celerity and lightness, but only to reject them as having nothing to do with virtue and happiness, as being, indeed, deterrents to the good life', Trilling, *The Opposing Self*, pp. 210–11. Thus whether Austen or the 'implied author' endorses the final 'exclusive' arrangement is, I shall argue, another matter. Moreover, the ending manages to appear to be 'arbitrary', ruthless in its disposal of characters, as Perkins has underlined in 'The Comedy of *Mansfield Park*' (pp. 22–5), while all the time it develops according to the logic that hangs upon the behaviour of Fanny in her expedient resort to unreason.

[41] Nicholas Rescher argues in *Rationality: A Philosophical Inquiry into the Nature and the Rationale of Reason* (Oxford: Clarendon Press, 1988), that reason dictates rather than counsels: 'The factors of self-interest and self-realization contrive to thrust the rationality project upon us as one in which we both self-interestedly *should* be and properly *ought* to be involved ... The obligation to be rational is an *ontological* obligation that inheres in our capacity for self-development and self-realization – a commitment to the full development of our human potentialities ... We have here a rationale that grounds obligations in

That things turn out the way they do is almost always attributed largely to the 'wickedness' of the Crawfords, who in the view of many readers deserve their exclusion from the cloistered security of Mansfield Park. Amongst the novel's characters, Mrs Norris points the accusing finger at Fanny: 'Had Fanny accepted Mr Crawford, this [disgrace/disaster] could not have happened' (435). Fanny, however, thinks that her rejection of Crawford will be seen to be 'justified'. As indeed it is. To the other characters at Mansfield, as to the vast majority of critics, what Fanny did was 'right'. However, as has been suggested, to think in terms of whether Fanny's conduct is 'right' or 'wrong' may not be the most helpful way to gain an understanding of what interests Austen. At a certain point in the narrative Fanny is able to regulate her thoughts and comfort her feelings by a 'happy mixture of reason and weakness' (272). And it is the nature of this 'mixture' that, I have argued, we should be paying particular attention to. As she views the 'vicissitudes of the human mind' Austen is impressed by the debility of a certain kind of reason – the epistemic – a weakness that is manifest all too often at those crucial moments that are decisive for future states of well-being.[42] Thus what we are given in *Mansfield Park* is the kind of nuanced and ironic picture of human fraility that we have been accustomed to finding in her fiction. Austen's is a vision that strives for exactness in its portrayal of the precariousness of sense and self-awareness, the fallibility that, as Pope recognized, characterized the human state: 'Born but to die, and reasoning but to err; / Alike in ignorance, his reason such, / Whether he thinks too little or too much: / Chaos of thought and passion, all confused; / still by himself abused or disabused'.[43] Fanny Price, as we shall see, is no less liable than the other characters of *Mansfield Park* to such mental 'confusion', or, as is more often the case, to a kind of distortion or even self-deception and denial ('still by [herself] abused or disabused'), that must undermine our faith in the claims that have been made for her superior moral awareness. Thus even as the narrative voice functions time and again to deflect criticism away from the 'tender' 'sweet-tempered' heroine, who possesses such 'delicacy of taste, of mind, of feeling' (110), and who tries so hard to do right, at crucial moments the text discloses how difficult it is for her to avoid self-deception and gain full awareness of the motives of her actions, allowing as it does for a thorough appraisal of Fanny Price's responses.

In its pervasive irony, which as Lionel Trilling astutely noted is a method of comprehension habitual to Austen (though he denied that it was present in *Mansfield Park*), this novel, in common with her earlier works, 'perceives the world through

---

considerations of nature (that is of a modality of existence) – by its very nature as such, a being that has a capacity for value realization ought to realize it': pp. 205–6.

[42] Epistemic rationality captures important or useful truths in situations, while normative rationality pushes an agent towards desires which it makes sense to have; ie. which have a rightness independent of the wants and values of the person concerned; arguably at times Fanny lacks also the latter type of rationality.

[43] *An Essay on Man* (1733); *Pope, Poems* selected by Douglas Grant, with an introduction by Angus Ross (Harmondsworth: Penguin, 1985), p. 121.

an awareness of [its characters'] contradictions'.[44] If irony resides in a perceived gap or disjunction, in Austen's sharp analysis of character it is often to be found in an exposed incongruity between forms of intention: in the disparity which exists between an indeterminate aim to do what is right, to do one's duty, to abide by principles, and a specific intent or objective that informing reasoning and attitude is unexpressed, unadmitted, that is indeed inadmissable. At crucial moments her characters – including both Sir Thomas Bertram and Fanny Price – succumb to the temptation to construct and secure, by means of selective focussing and the suppression of certain thoughts and the avoidance of others, the grounds or basis for a highly desired conviction. Their intentions are at the very least murky. Clear-sightedness is not their aim. On notable occasions both characters' reasonings show them attempting to fit world to mind rather than exercise their powers of cognitive rationality, which in its search for truth aims to fit mind to world. Rational conviction, as Austen notes elsewhere in the novel (123), may involve determining probabilities by means of calculation and comparison. It requires a willingness to weigh up reasons, assess their relevance, and then maybe ask further questions and hence produce new reasons for acting. This is not the kind of activity that the inhabitants of Mansfield Park find congenial. Austen's analyses of the mind at work on vital matters disclose the various strategies which pertain to self-conviction of a most expedient kind, and reveal just how shrewdly sceptical she was about the possibility of making much progress in the business of self-understanding.[45]

Early on in the novel, and especially during the theatricals, the reader's attention is drawn time and again to an awareness of the characters' states of anxiety and pain. Feelings are often acute. The text suggests, however, that some kind of potential release from certain kinds of mental suffering may be found in the 'endeavour at rational tranquillity': the tranquillity it would make sense to strive for. Thus Julia suffers: 'Henry Crawford had trifled with her feelings; but she had very long allowed and even sought his attentions, *with a jealousy of her sister so reasonable* as ought to have been their cure; and now that the conviction of his preference for Maria had been forced upon her, she submitted to it without any alarm for Maria's situation, or any endeavour at *rational tranquillity* for herself' (181, emphasis added). Even while registering Julia's distress, the narrator mocks her for her emotional incontinence. Meanwhile, Fanny's own distress is lessened as that of the others' increases, indeed their 'vexation' is precisely the cause of such a diminuition: 'Fanny found, before many

---

[44] Thus, while recognizing Trilling's insight with regard to Austen's typical mode of procedure, this reading counters his claim that '*Mansfield Park* ruthlessly rejects the dialectical mode and seeks to impose the categorical constraints the more firmly upon us': *Sincerity and Authenticity* (London: Oxford University Press, 1972), p. 79.

[45] Hence meditating on the likelihood of Edmund and Mary's increasing attachment leading to union, Fanny's thoughts are narrated as follows: 'Her acceptance must be as certain as his offer; and yet, there were bad feelings still remaining which made the prospect of it most sorrowful to her, independently – *she believed independently of self*': (p. 326, emphasis added).

days were past, that it was not all uninterrupted enjoyment to the party themselves, and that she had not to witness the continuance of such unanimity and delight, as had been almost too much for her at first. Every body began to have their vexation' (184). But Fanny's greater ease of mind founded in the others' growing discomfort is to be short lived, as she is pressed into witnessing the 'increasing spirit of Edmund's manner' to Mary Crawford. Now most unwillingly 'with the office of judge and critic', she cannot bear to watch them rehearsing, and turns away from them 'exactly as he wanted help'. By the actors 'it was imputed to very *reasonable* weariness' (189, emphasis added). We know, however, that the cause is not weariness but rather her own pain at the sight of their 'joy and animation of being ... together'. Presumably then, we can assume that both words in the phrase are inappropriate as a description/ judgement of Fanny's state. She is not weary but – just like Julia – she is jealous, and for Austen Fanny's feelings are, like Julia's, hardly '*reasonable*' – or sensible and wise. That her author finds her absurd on certain occasions testifies to Fanny's feeble hold on reason when this might be summoned to establish limits to feelings, curbing the extravagant or excessive.[46]

Moreover, if reasonableness calls for a combination of self-restraint or moderation, as well as openmindedness in order to secure peace of mind or sound judgement, then Fanny's unreasonableness is manifest in her tendency both to exaggerate and to distort; just as she is prone to exaggerate Edmund's goodness or the threats posed to this goodness by the Crawfords, so she is ready to discount or diminish any signs of good in the characters of the Crawfords.

Later on when Edmund can see good reasons for Fanny to accept Henry Crawford's proposal, his approval of the match has often been interpreted as unreasonable in that it is apparently influenced by his own strong desire for a closer connection with the Crawfords. But Edmund only recognizes what the novel emphasizes – by making these the concluding words to Chapter 30 – and that is the fact that Crawford can offer Fanny some of the greatest goods available: 'What can Sir Thomas and Edmund do, what do they *do* for her happiness, comfort, honour, and dignity in the world to what I *shall* do?' (emphasis added, 301). Crawford is talking with his sister and confidant, Mary, so we may be assured as to his sincerity. The play-acting has ceased; Henry Crawford appears truly convinced that he can offer Fanny Price a rich and beautiful life, and Edmund is convinced that he can too. Book Three of the novel continues to investigate the role played by reason in all the major characters' endeavours to judge, it discloses the traces of intention on modes of reasoning, and reveals the reasons they come up with in their attempts to persuade.

Fanny's capacity for expedient self-persuasion is, we find, as vital as that of any Bertram. Given unmistakeable public proof that Crawford's intentions are serious,

---

[46] While waiting to encounter Sir Thomas on his return 'she found a seat, where in *excessive* trembling she was enduring ... *fearful* thoughts', p. 193. Her thanks on receiving a gold necklace from her cousin Edmund are such that he has to oblige her 'to bring down her mind from its *heavenly* flight': p. 269, emphasis added.

her response is to see it 'all as nonsense, as mere trifling and gallantry, which meant only to deceive for the hour ...' (304). Fanny may feel distress as Crawford presses his suit, but we are surely meant to respond to her 'reasoning' with amusement bordering on exasperation, for it is pretty clear who is deceiving whom here. Fanny reasons but her 'reasoning' all tends in the same direction. There is no attempt at evaluation, no weighing up of possibilities or probabilities. She succeeds in convincing herself in compliance with her desire, that Henry Crawford cannot be serious. 'The difficulty', comments the narrator ironically, 'was in maintaining the conviction quite so absolutely after Mr Crawford was in the room ... But she still tried to believe it' (309). However, arguing against her from now onwards is ranged a formidable group: Edmund, Sir Thomas and Mary Crawford can all find very good reasons for Fanny Price to change her mind.[47]

At this point in the novel, Edmund has usually been taken to be acting in bad faith,[48] while Fanny's point: 'how hopeless and how wicked it was to marry without affection' needs clearly to be taken into consideration. But reconsidering, we shall find, I think, that Edmund has several good reasons for sharing his father's point of view. Moreover, since he can enter sympathetically into the question of Fanny's feelings, his attempt to convince her can be seen to develop the novel's argument as to the validity of the projected alliance. Edmund finds that his father has been 'unreasonable' in expecting Fanny suddenly to feel sufficiently attached to Crawford to want to marry him. And he begins his discourse with the highly reasonable premise that 'I consider Crawford's proposals as most advantageous and desirable, *if* you could return his affection' (343, emphasis added) ... 'As far as you have gone, Fanny, I think you perfectly right ... But the matter does not end here'. It takes time to create a strong regard, he goes on to acknowledge, but if Fanny is 'grateful and tender-hearted' such an attachment can be created. Her vigorous response of 'Oh! never, never, never; he never will succeed with me', is, in his view, 'not like yourself, your rational self' (343–4).

In the ensuing exchange it is worth noting that Edmund responds to all Fanny's objections as he tries to get her to reconsider, as he tries to get her to move on. For

---

[47] So too is Marianne Dashwood confronted by a 'confederacy' of friends, but she is persuaded to marry the man they have decided is right for her: 'With such a confederacy against her ... what could she do? ... Colonel Brandon was now as happy, as all those who best loved him, believed he deserved to be ... and that Marianne found her own happiness in forming his, was equally the persuasion and delight of each observing friend. Marianne could never love by halves; and her whole heart became, in time, so much devoted to her husband, as it had once been to Willoughby': *Sense and Sensibility*, ed. Tony Tanner (Harmondsworth: Penguin, 1969), pp. 366–7. What opponents of their marriage can argue, of course, is that Henry Crawford does not 'deserve' Fanny Price.

[48] In common with many critics, Isobel Armstrong finds Edmund's approval of the match 'in bad faith'. 'Edmund, approving of the marriage because it will bring him nearer to Mary and because it will preserve his closeness to Fanny (another act of bad faith), finds her intransigent': *Mansfield Park: Penguin Critical Studies* (Harmondsworth: Penguin, 1988), p. 79.

Edmund, as for Mary Crawford, it no longer makes sense for Fanny to be mistrustful, to live in the past. He is motivated, it has been argued, by a desire to strengthen his own relationship with the Crawfords. In fact Edmund is quite open about his interest in Henry Crawford's future and unmistakeably concerned about Mary. But this does not necessarily mean that he does not also have Fanny interests at heart, nor that his arguments will be lacking in cogency; and the points he makes are good ones.

For Edmund, it is important that Fanny and Crawford have tastes in common – and the novel will bear this out, will show that Henry Crawford possesses good taste, is in fact a model of delicacy or sensibility. Fanny, however, will not forget the past, and what she believes must continue to influence the present: her perception of Crawford's pleasure in trifling with other people's feelings, 'I received an impression which will never be got over'. Edmund will not deny the wrongdoing, and simply admits that all were in the wrong: 'Maria was wrong, Crawford was wrong, we were all wrong together; but none so wrong as myself' (346). The past will have to be reckoned with and accepted, but it does not have to be the sole or prime cause in determining the future. And Fanny herself has seen signs of Crawford's desire to change. Yet as Locke had emphasized, memory may conflict with reason, be too powerful for reason, 'so that all Representations, though never so reasonable, are in vain'.[49] Fanny's own meditations on the 'inequalities of memory', as she wanders through the shrubbery with Mary, focus – ironically – on its 'incomprehensible powers': 'The memory is sometimes so retentive, so serviceable, so obedient – at others, so bewildered and so weak – and at others again, so tyrannic, so beyond controul!' (222). In her discussion of *Pride and Prejudice*, Margaret Anne Doody has recently remarked on the significance of Austen's notion that 'memory apparently is – or can be – a great handicap to human freedom'. Doody comments on Elizabeth Bennet's assertion, when her sister Jane reminds her of her dislike for Darcy, that 'in such cases a good memory is unpardonable', observing that: 'A good memory can make one suspicious, paranoiac, holding the door shut against the new wind that would blow in the clean fresh air. Far from being the irreplaceable rock on which consciousness and law and human dignity rest, memory is a doubtful Janus-faced entity. Austen expresses the matter ironically – to remember too well is a kind of sin, not pardonable in human relationships ... It is not just the beloved but the self that requires a certain freedom from the bondage of memory. Without some intelligent check on memory, neither freedom nor love is possible'.[50]

Furthermore, on the crucial question of Fanny's feelings, Edmund can find no major difficulty, relying on the idea of the '*natural* wish of gratitude'. 'You must have some feeling of that sort' (emphasis added, 345) – as supplying the desire which can trigger off the emotions necessary for a 'pure attachment'. Edmund's reasoning admits

---

[49] John Locke, *An Essay Concerning Human Understanding*, ed. Peter H. Nidditch (Oxford: Clarendon Press, 1975), pp. 398–9.

[50] '"A Good Memory is Unpardonable": Self, Love, and the Irrational Irritation of Memory', *Eighteenth-Century Fiction* 14 (2001): 94.

that feelings can and do change, and will change more readily if reasons for changing them are first acknowledged. The idea that if, as is quite natural, she begins to feel grateful towards Crawford for all he has done for her brother (in using his influence to get him a promotion) then her other feelings will soften, will not work, however, as Fanny is determined to dislike him. Since the whole of Edmund's discourse makes it only too evident that he has no idea of attaching her to himself, that on the contrary 'Miss Crawford's power was all returning', Fanny would seem to have good reason to re-consider. But she does nothing of the kind, shrinking at the very idea that she could influence Crawford for the better, that she could 'make him everything'. Yet again she depends on the argument that Crawford's request for her hand and heart was unreasonable: 'how was I to be prepared to meet him with any feeling answerable to his own? ... How was I to have an attachment at his service, as soon as it was asked for?' (349). It is but a partial explanation of her feelings, for it keeps securely hidden the vital roles that both Crawford and himself have long played in her vision of her world. What she cannot give an account of is how these feelings shape and structure her (moral) outlook. One has always been of great concern, the other, she has decided, can never be. But Edmund is convinced he now has the truth. He is satisfied 'that everything should be left to Crawford's assiduities, and the *natural* workings of her own mind' (352, emphasis added). How 'natural' Fanny's attitude may be judged to be, is then the question that continues to face the reader, though the 'natural workings' that Edmund has in mind are clearly not simply instinctive responses or inclinations. On the contrary, he expects that as a 'sensible' woman, where there is desire, it will be a desire to exercise the capacities of her nature both with regard to the sentiments and reason: 'I am spoilt, Fanny, for common female society. Good-humoured, unaffected girls, will not do for a man who has been used to sensible women. They are two distinct orders of being. You and Miss Crawford have made me too nice' (351). As Johnson noted in his *Dictionary* 'in conversation [the word 'sensible'] has sometimes the sense of reasonable; judicious, wise'.[51] Edmund is optimistic, certain that Fanny will be reasonable. There is in his discourse a kind of underlying logic to the effect that given time, gratitude may contribute to appreciation (of gifts, favours, talent, wit and an easy disposition), while appreciation may lead to affection, and affection may develop into esteem, which is a state of mind conducive to matrimony. Austen's plot will suggest, however, that one of the main problems with this theory has to do with time or timing. When at Portsmouth Fanny starts to soften a little towards Crawford he will already have left for London.

It is at this point in the narrative that Fanny's powers of reasoning will be subjected to their greatest test. In the endeavour to improve 'her powers of comparing and judging', Sir Thomas Bertram exiles Fanny to Portsmouth, where in that abode of noise, squalor and confusion, she does indeed begin to reassess her past experiences. But it is Mansfield that she estimates, *overestimates*, as ignored by her family she

---

51 On this point see Isobel Armstrong, *Sense and Sensibility; Penguin Critical Studies* (Harmondsworth: Penguin, 1994), p. 3.

broods alone. Mansfield, she manages to persuade herself, is perfect: 'she could think of nothing but Mansfield, its beloved inmates, its happy ways' (384). In contrast to the rest of the novel, the Portsmouth chapters focus almost entirely on the concerns of Fanny Price, and yet of the workings of her mind at those crucial moments when she meets the man who is courting her, we are provided with less information than we might have expected. What we are given is a timely reminder of her good sense, which 'will always act when really called upon'. But we find that her feelings are often 'overpowering', and must suspect that the account of the unexpected arrival of Henry Crawford is intended to be ironic. He *'wisely and kindly'* devotes himself to her mother while she 'fancied herself on the point of fainting away', and is even described as 'trying to keep her self alive' (392, emphasis added). Whether we are supposed to sympathize with her or find her rather foolish is unclear. That at this stage the reader has problems is a function of Austen's own dilemma. In Chapters 41–3 she faces some tricky problems, and these include trying to render the confused mix of feelings that constitutes Fanny's ambivalence without fully commiting her either way, while gauging how much of her heroine's feelings for Henry but also for Mary she can divulge to her reader.

At Portsmouth Fanny is portrayed as fastidious and ashamed and desperate: desperate to escape from the squalor yet bound by the narrowness of her views (or the 'purity' of her principles?) to a determined dislike or suspicion of the very people who would like to help her. Thus she continues to find Crawford unsuitable, and yet, since she is tender-hearted and Henry Crawford is indeed kind, if not always wise, such kindness will have an effect. But how much of an effect it should have was clearly for Austen a consideration of some nicety. Crawford and the reader might well expect some kind of development to take place. Throughout his visit Crawford displays exemplary delicacy or fineness of awareness; when 'it was not unreasonable to suppose' that Fanny is ready for his attentions, he then devotes himself to her; he is considerate, amusing and, we are informed, shares the 'same sentiment and taste'. Austen was most satisfied with her brother Henry's admiration for Crawford: an admiration expressed 'properly', she wrote to her sister, Cassandra, because valuing him 'as a clever, pleasant man'.[52] However, the narration of Fanny's reactions to Crawford is so curtailed as to make comprehension of her mind a difficult business. What we do find, however, when finally we are given access to her thoughts, is a distinctive kind of reasoning, for she begins to display signs of 'imaginative rationality'. This is significant but also ironic, because by then Crawford has left Portsmouth, left dissatisfied, and we can imagine, frustrated and perhaps mortified by her lack of interest.

According to Nicholas Rescher, 'rationality in all its forms calls for the comparative assessment of feasible alternatives', and one of the major faculties involved is imaginative rationality. This is the capacity 'to entertain alternative possibilities, project hypotheses, and perform "if-then" thinking' (11). That Fanny is willing to engage in the business of 'if-then' thinking' is revealed as she meditiates on the fate

---

[52] Quoted by David Nokes, *Jane Austen, A Life* (London: Fourth Estate, 1997), p. 436.

of her sister Susan: 'that a girl so capable of being made every thing good, should be left in [the hands of her parents] distressed her more and more' ...

> *Were she likely* to have a home to invite her to, what a blessing *it would be*! – And *had it been possible* for her to return Mr Crawford's regard, *the probability* of his being very far from objecting to such a measure, *would have been* the greatest increase of all her own comforts. *She thought he was really good tempered, and could fancy his entering into a plan of that sort, most pleasantly.* (409–10, emphasis added)

Such thoughts of an alternative scenario stop here, most abruptly.

A plausible continuation, a possible development of ideas, had already appeared in Austen's previous novel. With only a few changes that text might have supplied a fitting ending to this chapter:

> She certainly did not [dislike] him. No ... the respect created by the conviction of his valuable qualities ... had [now] ceased to be repugnant to her feelings ... It was gratitude ... Gratitude not merely for having once loved her, but for loving her still well enough, to forgive all the [coldness] of her manner [towards] him. (284–5)

Elizabeth Bennet's 'revolution of mind' provides a plausible model for Fanny Price. (Clearly, however, Jane Austen would not have wanted two novels to conclude in such a similar fashion.) That Fanny could have changed sufficiently to want to marry Crawford is attested to later on by no less an authority than the narrator (451). But Fanny Price does not think these thoughts, and so is saved from regretting 'what might have been'.

Fanny Price neither fully converts Crawford, nor undergoes her own full conversion. Indeed her own action, or rather refusal to act, is a decisive factor in blocking the 'all-inclusive' plot resolution. It is resolution which could have been brought about, as Mary Crawford indicates, by Fanny's return to Mansfield Park in the company of the Crawfords: her brother, she will suggest, influenced and firmly attached by Fanny Price, would have been impervious to the temptations or passion of Maria Bertram/Rushworth; strengthened by success he would have been capable of resisting the potent mixture of hostility and erotic challenge that Maria incarnates. But when previous to his return to London, Crawford offers to take Fanny back to Mansfield she refuses. About Fanny's state of mind, now, the text evinces remarkable reticence; that the confused nature of her response is left unintelligible points up Austen's difficulties at this juncture: 'Fanny thanked him again, but *was affected and distressed to a degree that made it impossible for her to say much*, or even to be certain of what she ought to say' (403, emphasis added).

The exact nature of Fanny's emotional incontinence is not disclosed, but we may suspect that her thoughts and feelings are not of the admirable sort. This, it would seem, is the silence of what is best left unsaid. (It is only later, when she refuses a second chance to return to Mansfield Park with the Crawfords, that Austen will supply her with an explicit reason that can justify the state of her feelings.) Fanny is at this moment susceptible to two states of mind, neither of which can be fully explicated, nor distinctly rendered. There is the habitual negative train of thought, which involves never giving in to the Crawfords. These negative thoughts are (for the sake of Fanny's reputation) better only hinted at. It is the usual story, however, Fanny cannot bring herself to accept favours from the Crawfords however great a pleasure to herself might ensue, if this would also bring them pleasure, and the only way she can deal with this situation is to transform the proffering into an act of aggression, about which she may then feel aggrieved. However, we may also surmise that on some level she is aware that such feelings are hardly admirable; thus she is distressed because aware of her own feelings of ill will when he is all good will. If the manner of delineating Fanny's consciousness in her confrontations with Crawford is usually perspicacious and precise, here the text registers the strain of refusing to commit Fanny Price to a distinctive point of view.

Yet there are indications of a softening towards Crawford, and soon after this her change in attitude becomes ever more apparent as she begins to dwell on Susan's plight. Then she begins to meditate on the possibilities of Crawford's 'good temper'. And so most reluctantly she comes round to endorsing the view expressed by the narrator that he is after all 'a clever, agreeable man' (394). But she cannot do more than this, she is not ready to. Fanny Price, as Edmund Bertram recognizes, is, 'one over whom habit [has] most power' (349). Throughout his Portsmouth sojourn she gives Crawford not the slightest hope of ever succeeding.

With the advent of spring and Tom's illness, Fanny's longing to return to Mansfield becomes intense. Thus when Mary's offer is made to take Fanny back – 'write directly, and tell us to come. *It will do us all good*' – Fanny is very much tempted (424, emphasis added). But Mary's letter with its most indiscreet, most injudiciously expressed, thoughts as to what might happen if Tom died, only reinforces Fanny's dislike. However could Mary ever imagine seeing 'Fanny smile and look cunning', and then joke about never having bribed a physician in her life!? Mary's gleeful review of Edmund's prospects is so uncharacteristically unseemly as to inspire disbelief: in providing Mary with such flagrantly self-seeking thoughts, Austen provides the reader with a reason to share Fanny's 'disgust'. Such a reason may or may not influence us; in effect, preventing us – perhaps – from examining closely Fanny's own mode of reasoning, encouraging us to overlook the troubling implications of *Fanny*'s way of thinking and subsequent mode of acting.[53]

One thing is immediately apparent: Fanny's mode of thinking registers a major change. The idea occurs to her that she might 'weigh and decide between opposite

---

[53] On Austen's treatment of Mary Crawford see D.A. Miller 'Good Riddance: Closure in *Mansfield Park*', reprinted in Judy Simons (ed.), *Mansfield Park and Persuasion*, pp. 37–48. Miller notes that 'A narrator whose point of view cannot be identified with theirs simply watches on, as it were, not hostile to their activities, but neither wholly committed to them'. However – contrary to the view expressed here – he then goes on to affirm that 'At the moment it takes place, the closure practised on Mary Crawford voids the text of a certain linguistic richness, but the riddance is felt to operate in the interest of the good': pp. 46–7.

inclinations and doubtful notions of right', that she might reason or attempt to judge 'impartially'. But uppermost in her thoughts, we discern, is her 'extreme reluctance to bring the writer of [the letter] and her cousin Edmund together'. And it is convenient then, all too convenient, that she hits upon a 'rule' that will dissolve any problem of 'judging impartially whether the concluding offer might be accepted or not'.

> Happily, however, she was not left to weigh and decide between opposite inclinations and doubtful notions of right; there was no occasion to determine, whether she ought to keep Edmund and Mary asunder or not. She had a rule to apply to, which settled every thing. Her awe of her uncle, and her dread of taking a liberty with him, made it instantly plain to her, what she had to do. (425)

We find then that the thought which she fixes on as decisive (as providing a rule) is a motive dictated by an emotion, her fear. That her fear dictates and cuts short the deliberation that belongs to greater self-determination could be interpreted as a form of renunciation: a giving in to weakness. Yet tactically such a move is self-serving. Her thought (of her uncle) is the kind of expedient thought one thinks and seizes upon in order to keep other more unmanageable thoughts at bay. The narration of Fanny's meditations shows mental energy being redirected to a suitable subject so as to distract attention from a problem too difficult fully to confront.

No further attempt is thus made to evaluate the situation or to find some more impressive notion of what she might do. Desire has found a reason not to do so, or rather one desire – not to be the means of bringing Mary and Edmund together – proves stronger than all others. It is a potent desire, though hiding behind another (the desire not to anger her uncle). At the back of things there lies, it seems clear, not a principle but a passion. All in all, it is difficult to see this episode as a vindication of Fanny's integrity.[54]

In the next chapter Mary's letter arrives with hints of the scandal, concluding with her question: 'But why would not you let us come for you? I wish you may not repent it' (426). On realizing what has happened, Fanny may be amazed, agitated, uncomfortable, shocked; she might pass 'from feelings of sickness to shudderings of horror; and from hot fits of fever to cold' (429); but she certainly never repents of her action. It is Mary who has reason, if anyone, to repent: to repent of sending her letter with its most unwise surmises to Fanny. She will never learn however of the uses to which the letter will shortly be put.

At this point, things swiftly speed up as Edmund, suddenly feeling great need of Fanny's company 'in our present wretchedness', arrives in Portsmouth, takes Fanny

---

[54] See, for example, Roger Gard: 'It is essential that she be subjected to the full force of Henry's peculiarly Austenian charm and to survive it by a finger, for if she were not so exposed the point residing in her integrity would be destroyed ... Having achieved the courage to say it, she must be seen to mean "Never"': *Jane Austen's Novels*, p. 141. As we have seen, however, there is no holding fast to principles here.

'home', and relates to her 'pain' and 'delight', the story of his last meeting with Mary in London. He relates at length of his shock both that Mary could show 'no modest loathings' on the subject of their siblings' 'sin', and that she could moreover hope to mitigate 'the crime' by using her influence to persuade Henry into marrying Maria. Mary, in Edmund's eyes, fails to be angry with the right people for the right reasons in the right way.[55] He concludes, or seems to conclude, his long account of Mary's most unhappy, most inappropriate manner of treating the subject of the elopement, with the words 'This has been the greatest relief, and now we will have done'. It seems to Fanny that 'they *had* done'. 'However', we note, 'it all came on again, *or something very like it*' (445, emphasis added).

The final ironic clause is most significant: in Austen's report of the renewed conversation it becomes clear that Edmund is soon talking himself into another frame of mind, and that 'the something very like it', is in fact something rather different. We discern that Edmund is soon well on the way to convincing himself once more of 'how delightful nature had made [Mary Crawford]' (443–4). But here reason comes in useful. Fanny is able to seize an opportunity to intervene with a thought of her own, feeling as she does, 'more than justified in adding to his knowledge of her real character, by some hint of what share his brother's state of health might be supposed to have in her wish for a complete reconciliation'. This timely intervention, though most reasonable, and coming from 'the heart which knew no guile' (Edmund's own words, 442), is not agreeable and is resisted; 'but his vanity was not of a strength to fight long against *reason*' (445, emphasis added). This unobtrusive scene, overshadowed by seemingly more momentuous events and passions, appears by comparison such a quiet moment, and it is certainly one whose emotional import is so played down, so economically drawn, that we are likely – as many a reader has done – to miss its full narrative implications. Fanny is then, it should be stressed, most efficiently, most decisively persuasive. She deals, as she realizes she must for her own future happiness and security, a final blow to Mary Crawford's authority. (For what would happen if Edmund were reconciled with Mary Crawford?) She administers the masterstroke. It is just as well, however, for her reputation for 'true generosity' that we are not given a verbatim account of exactly how Fanny's influence is exerted, nor an idea of what was going on in her mind. It is difficult to see how Austen could have avoided the charge that Fanny fears, that of showing some 'littleness' of character.

For the time being, Fanny must be content with a partial reward for thoroughly opening his eyes to Mary's 'deceitful' nature (though in what way Mary has deceived anyone is not at all clear, given that her preoccupations with consequence have always been openly expressed) in the form of a spiritual attachment/connection: 'Fanny's friendship was all that he had to cling to' (445). In the final chapter, however, affairs are

---

[55] If one adopts an Aristotelian view of the virtues and vices – Aristotle described virtuous behaviour as having 'the right feelings at the right times on the right grounds towards the right people for the right motive and in the right way', this is 'to feel them to an intermediate, that is to the best, degree; and this is the mark of virtue' – it is difficult to identify Mary's vice. For Edmund she does not show sufficient anger, but she is hardly lacking in spirit;

settled in a more satisfactory manner, with a connection that rewards this heroine for her timely and influential act whereby she was able to 'add to [Edmund's] knowledge of [Mary's] real character'. Fanny's 'comfort' is ensured as Edmund transfers his affections to her. Comfort is indeed distributed most generously to those 'not greatly in fault themselves' to the evident delight of a narrator who is now anything but impartial: '*My* Fanny indeed at this very time, I have the satisfaction of knowing, must have been happy in spite of every thing' (446, emphasis added). This is a narrator, we discover at this point, with a theory to propound. It is a theory to explain the past which, like many others, offers a sharply edited, a simplified and simplifying, version of events; identifying a fatal weakness in Crawford's vanity: a weakness whose origins are to be traced back to the dire influence of his early education.

But neither the selective strategy of blame, nor the compensatory talk of all the comfort gained,[56] can dispel from the reader's mind the idea of something significant lost – and lost because something was wanting not only on Crawford's part. What is missing from the final taut version of events, from the moralizing interpretation we are left with, is the analysis presented in the narrative itself – of what happened when an opportunity unexpectedly arose. This is the story of a failure to make something of an animating, a stimulating and challenging friendship;[57] a failure to derive something good out of attachments now consigned to the past by the favoured few still residing 'within the view and patronage of Mansfield Park'. If at the closure of *Northanger Abbey* the 'author' is prevented from distributing the glory she would like to share, it is doubtful now whether she can truly 'share in the [comfort] she so liberally bestows' (*Northanger Abbey*, 230).

---

nor if modesty is the mean can she be said to be shameless herself; she may not display righteous indignation but neither does she indulge in malicious enjoyment: *The Ethics of Aristotle: The Nicomachean Ethics*, trans. J.A.K. Thomson with an introduction by Jonathan Barnes (Harmondsworth: Penguin, 1976), pp. 101–4.

[56] For a contrasting reading on the link between merit and comfort see Edward Said, *Culture and Imperialism* (London: Chatto and Windus, 1993), pp. 99–116. Said makes claims for Fanny's steadfastness in the 'face of numerous challenges, threats and surprises'. She acts as 'surrogate conscience' at Mansfield Park, so that 'once the principles have been interiorised comforts follow'.

[57] Thus of Edmund's last interview with Mary Sheila Kaye-Smith and G.B. Stern write 'we are bidden contemplate not the triumph of evil, but certainly what is not far removed from it, the failure of goodness': *Speaking of Jane Austen* (New York and London: Harper, 1944), p. 89.

Chapter 4

Discovering Autonomy and Authenticity in *North and South*: Elizabeth Gaskell, John Stuart Mill, and the Liberal Ethic

Working away on her latest novel, Elizabeth Gaskell was somewhat anxious about 'marring' the character of John Thornton, her hero. Yet he seemed to be turning out alright, and she confided to a friend that he was much as she wanted him to be: 'large and strong and tender, and *yet a master*'. The problem was, she realised, to keep his character 'consistent with itself', despite the changes he would undergo.[1] By the end of *North and South* again a master, thanks to the financial assistance of Margaret Hale, and still possessed of 'a sense of inherent dignity and manly strength', Thornton has become a more enlightened manufacturer, a master who is more concerned for the welfare of his 'men'. In bringing about this change, Margaret Hale would appear to have played an influential role. Despite experiencing the attractions of bourgeois London society and the appeals of luxury, leisure, and self-advancement, this strong-minded heroine has conserved intact the idea of personal involvement in the lives of the less fortunate: an ideal which underlay the social practices in the country village she knew as a child. When her family moves to Milton-Northern, the same ideal seems to offer a solution to the conflict between masters like Thornton and labouring men like Nicholas Higgins. Gaskell's novel charts her troubled relationships with both, the disagreements and misunderstandings, the strongly contrasting emotions.

For the historians David Roberts and Patrick Joyce, the novel's ideological intent is nonetheless unequivocal. Thornton's love for Margaret Hale induces him to become an archetypal paternalist employer: secure in his sense of superiority yet more conscious of his social responsibilities.[2] Yet in recent critical studies of this narrative, interpreting Thornton's change of mind and Margaret's influence is seen to be far more problematic. The readings of Rosemarie Bodenheimer, Margaret Ganz, and Catherine

---

[1] In a letter quoted by Jenny Uglow, *Elizabeth Gaskell: A Habit of Stories* (London: Faber and Faber, 1993), p. 366.
[2] David Roberts, *Paternalism in Early-Victorian England* (London: Croom Helm, 1979), pp. 91–98; Patrick Joyce, *Work, Society, and Politics: The Culture of the Factory in Later Victorian England* (New Brunswick, NJ: Rutgers University Press, 1980), pp. 147–48.

Gallagher suggest that there are difficulties in recovering precise or consistent moral convictions or commitments. Bodenheimer finds 'openness' – which is a good sign – but also 'doubleness' and even 'confusion' in the text. Ganz maintains that the novel lacks both dramatic power and 'significant moral implications'. While in Gallagher's view 'the book suggests a kind of anarchy of signification'.[3]

Recent studies have been more favourable to Gaskell, with critics keen to show that the anarchy Gaskell describes is integral to her interests.[4] Yet Gallagher and Bodenheimer are surely right when they claim that certain paternalist assumptions are challenged in the novel. The problem arises, then, with regard to the implications of this challenge for Margaret's moral status, for the heroine's attitudes and activities are assumed by many scholars to confirm paternalist theories. Moreover, how can we square the novel's apparent rejection of crucial aspects of paternalism with Joyce's detailed account of its importance from the mid-1840s, both as practice and consciousness, in the creation of social cohesion and sense of community in the factory towns of the North?[5] For social unity and stability are clearly among the goals that Gaskell would promote. To understand Gaskell's attitude not only to paternalism, but, equally important, to fundamental liberal doctrines, we need to look closely at the debate between paternalists and liberals at the mid- nineteenth century, whose starting point was the social condition of the working classes, but which embraced wider issues regarding the ethical foundations of society and the quality of life in industrialism. On the one side we find John Stuart Mill standing firmly opposed to the politics of protection, and on the other, paternalist ideologues, like Arthur Helps, Jelinger Cookson Symons, Rev. Samuel Green, and the like, who are more or less susceptible to the liberal ideal of a meliorist society but deeply worried about the prospect of working class independence. In this chapter I shall examine Gaskell's response to these different

---

[3] Rosemarie Bodenheimer, *The Politics of Story in Victorian Social Fiction* (Ithaca and London: Cornell University Press, 1988), pp. 55, 57, 67; Margaret Ganz, *Elizabeth Gaskell: The Artist in Conflict* (New York: Twayne, 1969), p. 82; Catherine Gallagher, *The Industrial Reformation of English Fiction: Social Discourse and Narrative Form, 1832–1867* (Chicago and London: University of Chicago Press, 1985), p. 181.

[4] Hilary M. Schor finds that the anarchy in the novel is not incidental but integral to Gaskell's interests; *Scheherezade in the Marketplace* (Oxford: Oxford University Press, 1992); Barbara Leah Harman's study also takes a more favourable line. On this view, Gaskell's work is not a conservative project of accomodation, rather it seeks to affirm and legitimize female public action: *The Feminine Political Novel in Victorian England* (Charlottesville and London: Virginia University Press, 1998), pp. 46–75.

[5] Roberts refers briefly to the paternalist revival of the 1840s, and maintains, unlike Joyce, that it was shortlived (p. 59). He notes that it continued to exalt the notions of an 'authoritarian, hierarchical, and deferential society' (pp. 99–100), a view which runs contrary to the development of the movement outlined here. Joyce examines in detail the theory and practice of the new paternalist employers of the North in the 1830s and 1840s: *Paternalism in Early-Victorian England*, pp. 134–57.

strands of thought. It is a response, we will find, which is complex and discriminating rather than – as Kettle[6] and Ganz have argued – confused or contradictory.

In Gaskell's novel, I will be arguing, hero and heroine are associated respectively with liberal and paternalist discourses, but both their systems of belief are challenged and emerge transformed to a significant degree. What Gaskell achieves in the symbolism of their marriage is neither a subordination of the one, nor some kind of synthesis of the two revised moral and social codes. Rather central to Gaskell's ethics is the notion of a vibrant individuality: through vital and often vehement interaction John Thornton and Margaret Hale eventually achieve what Gaskell perceives is of fundamental importance to the good life: both are capable of the kind of rigorous reflection that contributes to a crucial refashioning of their individuality. This is a refashioning with broad ethical implications. If initially John Thornton and Margaret Hale function as exemplary members of their respective ideologies, ultimately they achieve a new status, a new moral status, by embracing difference, realizing their potential to move beyond orthodox modes of thought. This means that Thornton will deserve the evaluation Margaret's father makes when linking him to the cultivated Oxford man, Mr Bell: 'You are neither of you representative men; you are each of you too individual for that' (323). Thus, if at first the narrative endows both John Thornton and Margaret Hale with representative status, providing them with the recognizable rhetoric of specific traditions and practices, by the time of their marriage they have both become firmly established as representatives of an ethically superior category of individuals; they belong to the select band of those who are courageous enough to eschew conventional positions. It is worth emphasizing that for Gaskell this diversity is valuable in so far as it tends to promote those 'experiments in living' that improve welfare and reduce conflict. For Gaskell, as for Mill, 'the free development of individuality is one of the leading essentials of well-being'.[7] The privileged and cosseted make an occasional appearance in this novel: though not as sombre as *Hard Times*, *North and South* is nonetheless pre-eminently a tale of trials and troubles, of struggling, suffering and loss. Well-being is not easily achieved. For hero and heroine satisfaction is gained with the sense of accomplishment that individualists realise as they embrace and successfully negotiate new and difficult challenges.

*

At the very same time that Gaskell's novel appeared, John Stuart Mill was preparing *On Liberty*, a text that was to leave its immortal mark on the development of liberal thought.[8] In this treatise Mill stressed the importance of individuality in combatting

---

[6] Arnold Kettle, 'The Early Victorian Social-Problem Novel', in Boris Ford (ed.), *From Dickens to Hardy* (Harmondsworth: Penguin, 1958), pp. 182–3.
[7] *On Liberty*, ch. 3, 'Of Individuality, as One of the Elements of Well-Being'.
[8] M. Freeden has pointed out the importance of Mill's concept of individuality to New Liberalism. According to Freeden, 'He clarified and crystallized a tendency which was to become as central to liberalism as liberty itself, namely, the concept of individuality': *The New Liberalism: An Ideology of Social Reform* (Oxford: Clarendon Press, 1978), p. 23.

the dangers he perceived to be threatening society: the tyranny of custom, of prevailing opinion and feeling, the spread of uniformity and mediocrity. As is well-known, Wilhelm von Humboldt was a major source of inspiration, but in his *Autobiography* Mill also mentions the little-known Unitarian preacher William Maccall as a predecessor in promulgating the 'right and duty of self-development'.[9] Maccall, who lived near Gaskell in Lancashire from 1837 until 1840, when he moved to the South, believed in 'unity' and 'divine harmony', and thought that these could only be achieved if men 'bring forth the entire elements of their nature in their fullness, fervor and variety'.[10] In his published pamphlets he claimed that 'by his example, and by the agencies and ideas which he diffuses [the individual] makes another develope his Individuality' and thus 'forms the links of a progression which is interminable' (118). 'I believe,' affirmed Maccall, 'that every individual bests helps all other individuals to develop their individuality, by most perfectly developing his own; and that Morality is thus simply that fidelity to our Nature in action which Religion is in consciousness.' 'I believe,' he continued, 'that every man in proportion as he developes his own Individuality, will be more desirous that other men should develope theirs; and that thus Tolerance will assume its sublimest aspect.' Instead of indifference, there would be 'cordial rejoicing at, and zealous aiding of, the manifestation of his faculties, however different that manifestation may be from the manifestation of our own'(5). Indeed, 'Individuality alone constitutes happiness' (126).

I have suggested that for Gaskell achieving individuality was crucial to social progress. An earlier novel, *Mary Barton* (1848), had already focused on class relations in Manchester and revealed[11] her ambivalence to the dominant liberal culture of the city with its stress on the reason, interests, and rights of the individual; a culture disseminated among the poor by the Unitarians' Domestic Home Mission. Certain notions central to liberal individualism continued to worry Gaskell, herself a Unitarian and sometime helper of the Mission. While not refuting the principles of personal exertion, self-improvement and self-government, as propounded by the industrious Thornton, she rejects his language of rights and interest, and highlights the absurdity of a character ideal grounded in the notion of self-sufficiency. Her own discourse draws upon Maccall's ideal and elaborates in its delineation of a richly cultivated self-development and of the invigorating encounter of contending modes of thought, a more comprehensive vision of man in society, a pluralistic moral view which has significant points of contact with the new liberalism of Mill. Thus, in *North and South*, Gaskell is concerned with a general view of the human condition which extends beyond the immediate search for remedies for social ills, and proposes a radical rethinking of the relations between the self and society. This concern leads, in turn, to questions about the nature of the mature self and about the relation or interplay of psychological growth and adherence to specific moral codes.

---

[9] *Autobiography*, ed. John M. Robson (Harmondsworth: Penguin, 1989), p. 191.
[10] William Maccall, *The Elements of Individualism* (London: John Chapman, 1847), p. 4.
[11] John Seed, 'Unitarianism, Political Economy and the Antinomies of Liberal Culture in Manchester, 1830–50', *Social History* 7 (1982): 19, 21.

When John Stuart Mill wrote his 1845 critique of Arthur Helps's treatise for employers, *The Claims of Labour* (1844), for the *Edinburgh Review* – later elaborating his arguments in his *Principles of Political Economy* (1848) – he was not, perhaps, being entirely fair to paternalists like Helps. That the patriarchal system 'was one to which [the labouring classes] would not again be subject' was his firm and strongly expressed conviction. 'Modern Nations', he asserted, 'will have to learn the lesson, that the well-being of a people must exist by means of justice and self-government of the individual citizens'.[12] As one might expect, Mill's identification of Protection and Obedience as the two central tenets of traditional Paternalism was precise. Yet his assessment of paternalist thought failed to render the new note of revisionism that appeared in the work of Helps, and that became more pronounced in the essays of his successors: the lawyers Jelinger Cookson Symons and David Power, the civil engineer Simmons, and the reverend Samuel G. Green.

Earlier paternalist ideologues had reasoned that the grateful deference of subordinates was a just return for the protection and patronage of their social superiors: an idea in keeping with their vision of society as fundamentally static and strictly hierarchical, a society in which inequalities were seen as sacred, natural or inevitable. But Helps could not accept such assumptions. To expect obedience and deference was to court delusion and perhaps disaster in the unstable social and political contexts of industrialism and Chartism. 'And can you think,' he demanded, 'that it is left for you to drill men suddenly into your notions, or to produce moral ends by merely mechanical means?'[13] That both the overbearing conduct and the rigid expectations of the upper classes were of fundamental importance in shaping their relations with the labouring poor are ideas that Gaskell shared. Significantly, the riot at Thornton's mill is shown to be precipitated by the sound of his 'commanding voice'.[14] To his fellow Captains of Industry he might appear as a man of 'great force of character', by his striking workers he is perceived to be arrogant, 'not so much unjust as unfeeling' (160).

Helps's version of paternalism was sufficiently broad to admit of no difficulty in holding on both to the belief in the desirability of the father-child model for labour relations and to the idea that employers must promote that 'freedom of thought and action which is necessary for spontaneous development' (157). While liberals could only applaud his plea for greater individual freedom as a prerequisite for self-development, Mill held that in a patriarchal system the labouring classes would lack any incentive to achieve self-control or self-reliance. He could not accept the fundamental tenet of this as of all paternalist theories: that the privileged classes must

---

[12] *Principles of Political Economy*, in John M. Robson et al. (eds), *Collected Works* (Toronto: University of Toronto Press, 1963), vol. 3, pp. 762, 764.
[13] Arthur Helps, *The Claims of Labour: An Essay on the Duties of the Employers to the Employed* (London: William Pickering, 1844), p. 47.
[14] *North and South* (London: Dent, 1975), p. 168. All further references are given in the text.

assume personal responsibility for the well-being and well-doing of the poor and vulnerable. On Mill's account, the problems of the disadvantaged should be left to the processes of the law and to the welfare and educational institutions of the state. In classic liberal fashion, Mill interprets the theory of Protection as a justification for unwarranted interference. And so, too, do Gaskell's two male characters, the manufacturer Thornton and the working-man Higgins.

When is interference justified? is a question that evidently concerns Gaskell. And her narrative highlights the importance not only of the demeanour but also of the desires of upper-classes to make contact with those belonging to the lower ranks of the social hierarchy. How this desire to make contact would be interpreted was a crucial factor in class relations. When Margaret Hale, new to the industrial town of Milton voices her intention of visiting Higgins's home, Higgins is annoyed. To him the proposal carries shades of authority's patronizing condescension, implicitly denying his rights to independence and equality. For Margaret, on the other hand, her interest is the outward expression of sympathy and fellow-feeling. It is the attempt to put into practice her own belief in the principle of connection, in the 'equality of friendship' that should unite the classes. Margaret's impulses are vindicated when Higgins comes to appreciate all she does for his child, Bessy. But there are other elements in the novel's narrative strategy which seem designed to counter Mill's fears of the negative consequences of such 'paternalist' practice.

Mill had repudiated the theory of responsibility and protection essentially on two counts: it encouraged on the one side desires to encroach or coerce and, on the other, habits of dependency which enervated or stupified. To such forms of oppression and repression Gaskell's heroine becomes increasingly sensitive, so that far from endangering the worker's vigorous, self-reliant, and sociable character, Margaret Hale attempts to preserve it at all costs. Though well aware of Higgins's predicament, she seeks to dissuade him from going to the South in search of employment precisely because – as she explains– the conditions of farm labourers are stultifying: robbing 'their brain of life'; deadening 'their imagination …You could not stir them up into any companionship …'. Most significantly, they are no longer capable of dialogue, of discussing and debating: 'they don't care to meet to talk over their thoughts and speculations …' (296). Within the novel's revisionist agenda, Margaret's discourse, the process leading up to it, and its effects, may be taken, within the debate over paternalism, to be making three points: first, the common-sense one that there are certainly situations when the benefits to be gained from good advice or guidance outweigh the disadvantages of intrusion; second, that liberals and 'new paternalists' were in basic agreement that the self-reliance of the working classes must be linked to intellectual and moral improvement; and third, that the conditions of the workplace might well offer most opportunities for such improvement.

Given that the attitudes and practice of the employer were of vital importance, Gaskell's heroine cannot but intrude into the realm of Thornton's affairs. Such interference is doubly productive contributing both to their well-being and, most importantly, to the development of *his* autonomy. By contrast, Mrs Thornton's interference in Margaret's affairs – her stern warning that Margaret's behaviour is gaining her a bad reputation – can only be interpreted as ill-judged. Thornton's mother stands condemned for both her motivation and her manner, for her inability to act as a true friend or counsellor.

What Higgins's initial attitude to interference also indicates, however, is the condition of 'likemindedness'. That in this respect he shares the same perspective as Thornton in disliking any kind of intrusion suggests that the perceptions of both classes are fundamentally similar; such a convergence, Mill and Hobhouse were to argue, was an essential component in class harmony.[15] And the same principle obviously applies, as Gaskell intuited, to positive reader-response to the working classes. Higgins's sense of dignity which demands respect for the privacy of his home is recognized from the outset by Thornton. But what Thornton comes to acquire is a different kind of respect for the working man: a respect which involves admiration and is not merely the acceptance of a right. For Higgins has done something he feels he could not have done himself. In adopting Boucher's children, he has become a (metaphorical) brother to his neighbour and former antagonist.

Belief in an equality of friendship to be founded upon sympathy and mutual respect was in fact a common theme in the treatises of the new paternalists of the late 1840s; though it would probably be more appropriate to call them Christian-humanitarian theorists. Rejecting Arthur Helps's child-father model, they yet feared the moral anarchy that would ensue if those 'in the superior ranks of life' withdrew, as Mill had demanded, 'the protection and guidance of superior mind and station'. In the view of Jelinger Cookson Symons the ideas informing Mill's thesis added up to a mischievous and defective code for the arrangement of class relations: 'There is a strange mixture in this of undeniable truth and very dangerous error', he thundered:

> That a spontaneous education is going on in the mind of the multitude is unquestionable; but that it is of a beneficial kind it were as hazardous to admit, as that the instruction obtained from newpapers and political tracts, such as they mostly read, is 'vastly superior to none at all' ... and we may say, without fear of contradiction from anyone who really knows the working classes, that the 'instruction' they now chiefly have perverts their minds, infidelises their faith, and destroys their morals ... [Mill's] very just dislike of a servile dependence on the part of the lower classes to the higher has, moreover, led him into far too sweeping a notion of the desire of the former to repel the protection of the latter ... If Mr. Mill had said that few of the poor would receive into their hearts *dogmas* of religion and morals authoritatively forced on them, he would have had reason and experience in support of his assertion ... He carries his denunciation of the dependence of the poor on the protection of the rich, to an extent which would go far to exempt the latter from those moral obligations of sympathy and care for the poor with which the highest of all codes clothes them: and on the fruition of which the charities of life and the bonds of society depend.[16]

---

[15] See Gerald F. Gaus, *The Modern Liberal Theory of Man* (London: Croom Helm, 1983), pp. 92–3.

[16] Jelinger Cookson Symons, *Tactics for the Times, as Regards the Condition and Treatment of the Dangerous Classes* (London: John Olliver, 1849), pp. 3, 4, 5, 8.

Quoting Mill's question and answer: 'What is there in the present state of society to make it natural that human beings, of ordinary strength and courage, should glow with the warmest gratitude and devotion in return for protection? The laws protect them: where laws do not reach, manners and opinion shield them', Symons could not repress his indignation:

> Whose manners? Whose opinion? Precisely of those whose protection is here deprecated in terms and admitted in effect! But are there no evils but those of personal outrage or loss of property from which the poor suffer? Are they not the victims of their own unconverted hearts, depraved morals, evil counsellors, bad habits, inveterate prejudices, uninformed minds, gross lusts and countless other internal adversities. Are these not 'serious dangers?' Do they need no better protection from them than their own strength and intelligence? Are those more favoured in mind, knowledge, station and power unable to give it: and are we seriously told that to do so is to restore a relation between the higher and humbler orders of society and *sentiments which belong to Arabian hospitality and to 'a rude and imperfect state of the social union!'* ... I am as anxious to increase this relation of moral tendance and protection on the one hand, and a grateful sense of its benefits on the other, as Mr. Mill seems to prevent its growth and deride its use.[17]

Informing projects for social cohesion and class peace of Christian-humanitarians like Symons, was the desire to instill the governing classes with fraternal rather than paternal sentiments. By so doing they sought to avoid a danger indicated by Mill: 'with paternal care is connected paternal authority'.[18] They insisted – as the Hales will do – on the idea that the rich are God's 'stewards' for the poor, the employer 'but the trustee of the interests of his humbler brother man'.[19] And it is surely no coincidence that when Thornton at the close of the novel describes to Mr Bell how his dining room scheme for his workers is run, his own role is explained in terms of his acting as 'something like that of steward to a club' (351).

But what is crucial for Gaskell, as for Symons, is not kindness *tout court*,[20] but civilized forms of dialogue: the question of maintaining or restoring communication between the members of the different classes is crucial: for Symons 'the kindnesses of intercourse' (13) must be attempted; in Mr Hale's words, instead of expecting 'unreasoning obedience', the 'wise [parent or master] humours the desire for independent action, so as to become the friend and adviser when his absolute rule shall cease' (115). Indeed, great importance was attached by 'paternalist' or 'Christian-humanitarian' theorists of the late 1840s to the idea that personal ties creating a network

---

[17] Symons, *Tactics for the Times*, pp. 5–6.
[18] 'The Claims of Labour', in *Collected Works*, vol. 4, p. 374.
[19] Samuel Green, *The Working Classes of Great Britain, their Present Condition and the Means of their Improvement and Elevation* (London: J. Snow, 1850), p. 11.
[20] Mill had observed that this is an age 'the whole spirit of which instigates every one to demand fair play for helping himself, rather than to seek or expect help from another. In such an age, and in the treatment of minds so predisposed, justice is the one needful thing rather than kindness': 'The Claims of Labour', in *Collected Works*, vol. 4, p. 383.

of solidarity within a shared community were to be forged by the employer *and* his family. In the essays of Green and Simmons, the 'female domestic' ideology that would confine the influence of socially and morally superior women from the upper classes to the home and family, is firmly repudiated. Instead, women from the upper classes were exhorted by Green 'to inquire' and offer 'counsel' and 'aid' to the poor (44); to undertake, in the words of Simmons 'a large and friendly visitation'.[21]

Margaret's experiences in Milton-Northern will provide an account of the consequences, both positive and negative, of what may be interpreted as either 'a friendly visitation' or 'interference', revealing the incomprehensions but also the rewards that might be expected. Equally – and this will be of more concern to us here – Gaskell is interested in the personal implications for the woman who accepts the imperatives and the logic of the code of responsibility, and who attempts to practice the Christian courage that Helps and his associates sought to inculcate in their readers.[22]

The issue of non-interference versus the acceptance of personal responsibility for the vulnerable is, of course, central to the conversation which takes place between the Hales and John Thornton in one of their first encounters in Milton-Northern. In this debate, Thornton takes what may be identified as the strong line of classical liberal thought. It is important to understand the implications of Thornton's changing ideas since it is through her narrative of his transformation that Gaskell indicates metaphorically the potential road that the unrevised liberal may follow. In his discussion with the Hales about the relations obtaining in the North between the 'masters and their men', Thornton uses arguments to defend his own practice which place him well within the dominant and respectable tradition of classical liberalism, with its vision of man as an essentially independent, private, and competitive being, the protection of whose interests is ensured by civil institutions and above all by the law.[23] Thornton believes firmly in justice. It is a belief which, as Gaskell will show, can work in different ways. While the machinery of justice may serve to endorse the rights of the self-centred individual, the concept of justice also comprises the notion of desert. And certainly, the potential for a change exists when one realizes, as Thornton will do when he considers the behaviour and circumstances of Higgins, that 'a person may deserve good if he does right' (as Mill later asserts in 'Utilitarianism',[24]) may, in fact, deserve a new chance in life. This idea also recalls, however, the age-old and insidious distinction between the deserving and the undeserving poor, a notion perhaps not entirely alien to Gaskell's depiction of the characters and subsequent fates of the workers Higgins and Boucher. Nevertheless, as Gaskell's account of Thornton's

---

[21] G. Simmons, *The Working Classes: Their Moral, Social and Intellectual Condition, with Practical Suggestions for their Improvement* (London: Patridge and Oakey, 1849), pp. 306–9.

[22] Hilary M. Schor argues in *Scheherezade in the Marketplace* that in this work Gaskell registers the restrictions on women's speaking out and resents them.

[23] See Gaus, *The Modern Liberal Theory of Man*, p. 7.

[24] 'Utlilitarianism', in *Collected Works*, vol. 10, p. 242.

'reformation' makes clear, there is in his change of attitude a 'diviner instinct' at work, and compassion or fellow-feeling is stronger than the influence of the 'mere reasonings of justice' (315).

In his 'unreformed' state, Thornton insists on his right to pursue his own good in his own way: 'We, the owners of capital, have a right to choose what we will do with it' (112). Thornton may assert that his 'theory is, that my interests are identical with those of my workpeople, and vice versa' (114), but his moral code, and the centrality it accords to rights and justice, assumes a 'disenchanted universe', a hostile world where the conflicts that prevail among separate, disengaged selves may be regulated only by the institutions of legality. The predicament of the Thorntons (mother and son) may be neatly summed up in a comment by Sheyla Benhabib who, in her recent critique of the code of justice and rights, has observed that 'the law contains anxiety by defining rigidly the boundaries between the self and other', but it 'does not cure anxiety, the anxiety that the other is always on the outlook to interfere in your space and appropriate what is yours, the anxiety that you will be subordinate to his will'.[25] The Thorntons believe that if the workers strike, it is for 'the mastership and ownership of other people's property ... they want to be masters and make the masters into slaves on their own ground' (110). Their fears of appropriation and subordination are based on a specific reading or interpretation of man's nature, as essentially grasping or selfish; of history, as the rise of an ever more anomic and compartmentalized society where independent males alone engage with one another; and of contemporary labour troubles, as yet another sign of revolutionary tendencies. For Gaskell such views are outdated, for moderate and rational change is underway: the significant change referring to the nature of working class movements, to their aims and strategies, which are symbolized in the novel by the victory of the reasoning and increasingly reasonable trades-union leader, Higgins, over the desperate, violent, and ill-fated worker, Boucher. That the one recognizes the supreme significance and responsibility of familial and communal bonds while the other does not, is clearly not casual. Like Margaret Hale, Higgins is the representative of a solidaristic, 'fraternal' view of social relations.

Thornton's views at the time of his discussion with the Hales, are however, entirely consistent with the classic tradition of rights, a tradition which is more concerned with individual dignity than with indigence. As Eva Feder Kittay and Diana T. Meyers have noted, according to such a viewpoint 'people are entitled to non-interference; they may not be entitled to aid, for the rights it recognizes morally equip people to take care of themselves while morally shielding them both from the demands of others and from the invasiveness of the state'.[26] In the cause of self-government, Thornton opposes both philanthropic benevolence and centralized state intervention, objecting strongly to 'Acts of Parliament and all legislation affecting [the] mode of management [at] Milton' (77). It is a credo to which he will remain true.

---

[25] 'The Generalized and the Concrete Other: The Kohlberg-Gilligan Controversy and Moral Theory', in Eva Feder Kittay and Diana T. Meyers (eds), *Women and Moral Theory* (Totowa, NJ: Rowman and Littlefield, 1987), p. 162.

[26] Kittay and Meyers, Introduction, *Women and Moral Theory*, p. 30.

For Margaret Hale there exists a notable contradiction between the reality of the factory system, hierarchic and authoritarian in its structure, in its expectations of dependence and obedience, and the moral code of the classical liberal capitalists which emphasizes independence and non-interference. The Hales cannot accept either his principles or practice. If Thornton's morality is based on the concept of rights, the moral vision of the Hales relies on the supremacy of duty. While the first is interpreted narrowly as involving above all the protection of interests, the second recognizes obligations to others, perceived as the natural expression of concern, a sentiment informing all meaningful or worthwhile social life.

The norms both father and daughter uphold are those of friendship, sympathy, and care. Their moral imperatives call for communication and trust so that conflict may be defused and not merely regulated. The Hales believe in connection, protection, and responsibility for the vulnerable, concerns shared by twentieth-century feminist philosophers, political theorists, and social psychologists. In portraying the social relations of Margaret Hale, Gaskell is able to suggest – just as Gilligan, Kittay, Meyers, and Benhabib have theorized – that the code of responsibility poses an important challenge to a rights-based morality; that it particularly reflects women's experience; and that its premises and principles need to be taken seriously, since, far from forming a reactionary movement, its adherents belong to a force for growth and change in the lives of individuals.[27] Margaret Hale's vision is – like that of the above-mentioned feminist thinkers – of lives interwoven and interdependent. To a considerable degree her identity is constituted by the idea of belonging to a community, so much so that her sense of purpose in life, on which her well-being depends, is bound up with her ability to understand and share the interests, problems and ethos of its inhabitants, first of the rural South, and later of the industrial North.

For Margaret Hale, it is clear, an ideal of care and cooperation, which entails the assuming of responsibility, provides a way of ensuring communication that can preserve connection in a world of conflict and competing interests. Yet in chapter after chapter Gaskell's narrative acknowledges as it investigates the difficulties of initiating, sustaining and developing dialogue; it identifies the many obstacles hindering meaningful talk, so that the novel proves just how problematic the business of communication can be. It takes all sorts of virtues – patience, honesty and perseverence– in order to speak in the right mode. Thus, for example, 'if speaking one's mind' may be deemed laudable– as when Higgins appreciates Margaret's frankly expressed perplexity with regard to union regulations ('I like her,' said Higgins suddenly. 'Hoo speaks plain out what's in her mind', 283), such frankness may equally be a sign of bad faith. Mrs Thornton takes 'fierce pleasure in 'speaking her mind' to

---

[27] See Carol Gilligan, *In a Different Voice: Pyschological Theory and Women's Development* (Cambridge, MA: Harvard University Press, 1982); and 'Moral Orientation and Moral Development', in *Women and Moral Theory*, pp. 19–36. On this topic see also in the same volume Diana T. Meyers, 'The Socialized Individual and Individual Autonomy: An Intersection between Philosophy and Psychology', pp. 139–53.

her 'victim', Margaret (304). But now the objective is not mutual understanding but rather the personal satisfaction that can derive from inflicting pain through a form of revenge.

Commenting on the necessity for forms of self-expression as a 'recipe for social change', Rosemarie Bodemheimer notes Gaskell's conviction that 'shifts and modifications of positions are assured through vigorous verbal clashes' (61). However, her reading fails to discuss the shift in Gaskell's own discourse as she explores the issue of the morality of interdependence. Thus Bodemheimer's account of Gaskell's ideal of adulthood seems to ignore one of the novel's major narrative strategies. Bodemheimer observes that 'Gaskell's revision of paternalism is a theory of interdependence that cuts across class lines by defining adulthood as an acceptance of responsibility for both dependence and dependents' (61). And she cites Margaret's statement that 'God has made us so that we must be mutually dependent' (169). However, while it is certainly correct that both character and author are convinced that for society to function properly it must recognize both the bonds of interdependence and the responsibilities inherent in them, the question of what constitutes adulthood, or the moral maturity of the self, is for Gaskell rather more difficult. Thus despite the judicious range in tone of Margaret's responses to Thornton during their discussion, despite their consistent reasonableness and transparent sincerity and conviction, it would be a mistake to assume that this represents the novel's views on the subject of a morality of individual responsibility. Margaret thinks she knows what adulthood involves. But as Gaskell's narrative demonstrates, at the stage she has reached at the time of her disagreement with Thornton (in Chapter 15), Margaret has not achieved either moral or psychological maturity. In fact, Gaskell anticipates the view of Carol Gilligan when she finds that unreflective adherence to the code of protection and responsibility does not correspond to the final stage in moral and psychological development.

From the Hales's lively discussions with Thornton it appears that they interpret the duties of interdependence as above all a question of offering good 'friendly counsel' or 'advice'. But Gaskell will twice place her heroine in a position where she has to face up to the problem of taking responsibility for the results of her own words of advice. The first time she is confronted by the dramatic predicament of Thornton as he faces the angry workers, a direct result of her words of advice: 'Go down and face them like a man. Save these poor strangers whom you have decoyed here. *Speak* to your workmen as if they were human beings. *Speak* to them kindly ...' (170, emphasis added). While some time later she takes full responsibility for protecting her brother, whom she has called back to England, when he is accosted by Leonards at the station. Gaskell's narrative, we find, insists on the costs that are part of the consequences of a firm commitment to a morality of altruism, which here entails unstinting protection of the vulnerable.[28]

---

[28] In the view of Judith Lowder Newton Gaskell 'celebrates the ideology of the women's sphere': *Women, Power and Subversion: Social Strategies in British Fiction* (Athens: University of Georgia Press, 1981).

Margaret's moral progress is a subject to which we will return later. First – and faithful to the order of events – let us turn to the question central to the readings of Catherine Gallagher and John Pikoulis,[29] of her influence on Thornton. The role she plays in his transformation is worth examining closely, for it is only when we do so that we can begin to see exactly what such a transformation signifies.

Clearly, Thornton's personal intervention during the riot at his mill – his endeavour to defuse the violence – would seem to be dictated by Margaret's urgings. But both now and later, when she advises Higgins to speak directly to Thornton rather then his overseer, what is significant is that Margaret's interference makes Thornton aware that he has options and what these choices mean. For it is in the process of making choices, according to both Gaskell and Mill, that the individual begins to strengthen his own powers of reason and his capacity to feel. As Mill was later to theorize in *On Liberty*: 'The human faculties of perception, judgement, discriminative feeling and mental activity, or even moral preference are exercized only in making a choice'.[30] On this occasion, as later when he decides not to press charges against the rioters and not to hold an inquest into the death of Leonards, Thornton avoids recourse to the processes of the law, and by such uncharacteristic instances of non-conformity causes surprise.

At time of the uprising, Thornton becomes aware not only of his responsibilities for his workers but also of the fact that he loves Margaret Hale. For differing reasons, Gallagher, Ganz, and Roberts find the convergence of the personal and social themes in this episode unfortunate. Following Mill and John Rawls, I will suggest, however, that the two are necessarily intimately related. Rawls has noted that it is a 'deep psychological fact' that 'the tendencies of our sentiments of love and friendship [are] aroused when others, with manifest intention, act for our good'.[31] In Margaret's gesture of protection, as she tries to shield Thornton from the violence of the crowd, the ideal at the heart of the code of responsibility is at one with the instinct, and is enacted in all its simplicity. Her behaviour at the time of the riot is – to use a Millian expression particularly appropriate in this context – that of a spontaneous individualist: one who is firmly, if naively, committed to her own moral code. And Thornton experiences 'strong feelings of admiration' for her – to adopt once more a Millian phrase (see below). However, that he is attracted and yet not dominated, is central to Gaskell's narrative strategies. These are designed to show first, that Thornton's development is an autonomous process, one in which he reforms his own character, and second, that

---

[29] John Pikoulis finds Margaret a strong, emasculating figure. She conquers Thornton, becoming his beloved, mentor and spiritual guide. The 'tyrant of his conscience', she marries 'not the master but a man created in her own image': '*North and South*: Varieties of Love and Power', *Yearbook of English Studies* 6 (1976): 176–93. In *The Industrial Reformation of English Fiction*, Catherine Gallagher argues that the source and nature of Margaret's power remain mysterious, ambiguous, contradictory.

[30] *On Liberty*, ed. Himmelfarb, p. 122.

[31] Gaus, *The Modern Liberal Theory of Man*, p. 128 and John Rawls, *A Theory of Justice* (Cambridge, MA: Harvard University Press, 1971), p. 494.

this reformation will naturally have important social implications. It is significant, then, that almost immediately after the riot the question of Margaret's lie to the police-officer, when she seeks to protect her brother from discovery, creates an estrangement between the two. Thornton, unaware of her brother's identity, is led to believe that she is attempting to keep secret a clandestine love-affair. Yet he still continues to believe that 'even with all her faults, [she is] more lovely and more excellent than any other woman' (300), and the excellence he discerns is clearly moral. Her mysterious behaviour means, however, that the dialogue between them is crucially interrupted. In a letter commenting on the process of the novel Gaskell explained that she had got to the part 'when they've quarrelled, silently, after the lie and she knows she loves him, and he is trying not to love her; and Frederick is gone back to Spain and Mrs Hale is dead and Mr Bell has come to stay with the Hales, and *Thornton ought to be developing himself* ...' (emphasis added).[32]

How, then, one might ask, is Gaskell's conception of autonomy rendered in Thornton's character development? For John Stuart Mill, 'we are exactly as capable of making our own character, if we will, as others are of making it for us'. And although the desire to change 'comes from external causes or not at all, experiences of the painful consequences of the character we previously had, or [from] some strong, feeling of admiration or aspiration',[33] a character may be said to be autonomous when, although stimulated by another, he perceives that there is a motive to change and acts upon that logic, inventing new ideals and objectives. The same kind of argument underlies, we find, Thornton's self-development, which is a gradual process that begins at the time of the riot and culminates with his becoming steward to the men's dining club. The turning point in this process is signalled by his changing relations to Higgins. Thornton has at first a reason to look upon Higgins as an enemy, a reason to refuse to hire the trade-union leader: he 'might as well put a firebrand into the midst of the cotton-waste' (309). But he finds in the man's virtue, a better one to trust him. Thornton is thus able to recognize and respond to reasons, to overcome his previous intransigence, prejudice, and old antagonisms, to disregard the discourse of conflict.

To a quite remarkable degree, Gaskell's narrative account of what is involved in making an autonomous choice is confirmed in, and corroborated by, arguments in Mill's later essay, *On Liberty* (1859). There Mill notes that the individual 'must use observation to see, reasoning and judgement to foresee, activity to gather materials for decision, discrimination to decide, and when he has decided, firmness and self-control to hold to his deliberate decision. And these qualities he requires and exercises exactly in proportion as the part of his conduct which he determines according to his own judgement and feelings is a large one'.[34] In her description of the crucial process whereby Thornton begins to change his attitude to the working man, Gaskell shows Thornton observing Higgins, being struck by his behaviour and subsequently obtaining

---

[32] Quoted in Uglow, *Elizabeth Gaskell: A Habit of Stories*, p. 366.
[33] *A System of Logic*, in *Collected Works*, vol. 8, pp. 840–41.
[34] *On Liberty*, ed. Himmelfarb, p. 123.

information about the man. But for Gaskell, as for Mill, the process of reflection must be linked to the possession of certain basic characteristics.

That John Thornton is endowed with a strong will is clear from the brief account he gives the Hales of his humble beginnings and struggle to become a manufacturer. The trouble is that Thornton's mentality is narrow. His attitudes, aspirations, and principles have been absorbed without reflection. They correspond and conform to those of his peers and especially to those of his mother, the incarnation of female strength but also of convention and prejudice. As a heteronomous agent, Thornton has accepted the image of himself created by others. Drawing in particular on the ideas of Rousseau, Mill and other New Liberal theorists argued that the individual may develop nonetheless if, in addition to the will or desire to change, he possesses certain innate capacities, of which love, fellow-feeling, and a sense of justice are the most important.[35] And it is precisely these qualities which Gaskell notes in her hero during the emblematic episode which marks his change of attitude to Higgins: 'But if he dreaded exposure of his tenderness, he was equally desirous that all men should recognize his justice' (314). What all this signifies, then, is that Thornton does not merely follow Margaret's axioms with the 'blind unreasoning kind of obedience' that he previously desired from his workers, but rather that his transformation is a realization of his own potential, so that, to adopt the words of Mill from *On Liberty*, his 'great energies [are] guided by vigorous reason, and strong feelings [are] strongly controlled by a conscientious will'.[36]

For Mill and Gaskell, personal 'reform' and social reformation go hand in hand. The end of the novel finds Thornton embarking on the kind of practical experiments in living that Mill was to advocate in *On Liberty*, creating a new space, neither public nor private, where a cooperative venture might concretely improve the conditions of the working classes, while initiating symbolically a form of class cooperation, hence anticipating the Millian belief that 'these developed human beings [may be] of some use to the undeveloped'.[37] Thornton is emphatic that this is not private philanthropy. The project is to be financed and organized by the workers themselves with a minimum of intervention on his part. It assumes – as does Mill in his *Principles of Political Economy* – that the introduction of autonomy into industrial relations might encourage workers to become self-directing, and more intelligent and developed individuals. Though subject to some criticisms by Higgins, the plan is of Thornton's own devising, and it never earns his mother's approval (351).

In a highly significant conversation with a certain Mr Colthurst, Thornton justifies his more experimental approach to social relations by insisting on the necessity for 'personal intercourse' that promotes greater understanding. Thornton's 'enlarged way

---

[35] See Gaus, *The Modern Liberal Theory of Man*, pp. 116–32. On Mill's conception of autonomy, see John Gray, 'Mill's Conception of Happiness and the Theory of Individuality', in John Gray and G.W. Smith (eds), *J.S. Mill, 'On Liberty' in Focus* (London: Routledge, 1991), pp. 194–207.
[36] *On Liberty*, ed. Himmelfarb, p. 135.
[37] *On Liberty*, ed. Himmelfarb, p. 128.

of thinking' substitutes for antagonism the prospect of interactive 'planning': 'I would take an idea, the working out of which would necessitate personal intercourse; it might not go well at first, but at every hitch interest would be felt by an increasing number of men, and at last its success in working come to be desired by all, as all had borne a part in the formation of the plan ...' (420). The kind of understanding he perceives as essential to good working relationships is in fact exactly the kind of understanding he tries to reach with Margaret Hale herself, engaging her finally in the discussion of what would be best for his own and his workers' future. And it relies on precisely the kind of judgement that is grounded in the particular form of sensibility that Benhabib has identified as constituting a powerful feature of Hannah Arendt's thought:

> The power of judgment rests on a potential agreement with others, and the thinking process which is active in judging is not, like the thought process of pure reasoning, a dialogue between me and myself, but finds itself always and primarily, even if I am quite alone in making up my mind, in an anticipated communication with others with whom I know I must finally come to some agreement. And this enlarged way of thinking, which as judgment knows how to transcend its individual limitations, cannot function in strict isolation or solitude; it needs the presence of others 'in whose place' it must think, whose perspective it must take into consideration, and without whom it never has the opportunity to operate at all.[38]

Margaret's influence on Thornton can be conceived as a kind of prodding that stimulates and activates the powers or sensibility required to make this 'moral conversation' work. It is the kind of sensibility that functions even when the self is quite alone, enabling the subject to hear the voices of those it has previously omitted from its conversations.

If Thornton's moral progress involves achieving the type of autonomy that can embrace an interactive mode of thought, in Margaret Hale's development coming to recognize the salience of authenticity in one's life is pivotal. What we are shown of Margaret's early history reveals an autonomous character, one who has worked out her moral ideas for herself. Though deferential in her attitudes to others – Edith, her Aunt Shaw, her mother and father– Margaret is never servile.[39] Her independence of judgement and critical faculty ensure that at all times Margaret is able 'to think her own thoughts'. And yet since the achievement of moral maturity, of which authenticity forms a key component, is an ongoing enterprise, this paragon of virtue, wisdom and beauty, is seen to be engaged at critical moments in an attempt at re-evaluation in order to 'regain power and command over herself' (319). And the novel suggests that this requires the mode of honesty, of honest self-scrutiny of how one is and how

---

[38] Hannah Arendt, 'The Crisis in Culture', *Between Past and Future: Six Exercises in Political Thought* (New York: Meridian, 1961), pp. 220–21; see Benhabib's discussion in *Situating the Self*, pp. 8–17.

[39] On this distinction see M.A. Friedman, 'Moral Integrity and the Deferential Wife', *Philosophical Studies* 47 (1985): 141–50.

one was and how one might be. It has to do with a conception of identity perceived in terms of self-worth and the abiding significance of one's values, where intregity and self-coherence are prime objectives.

But for Margaret Hale reclaiming an authentic self is no easy business. Margaret must express more respect for others while obtaining greater self-awareness and knowledge as a prerequisite for refashioning her own self-conception. Thus, although at the time of her arrival in Milton-Northern, Margaret is ever alert to what she considers infringements of her dignity (Higgins's invitation to his house, Thornton's first proposal), she fails to realize that putting into practice the ideals of responsibility and protection may lead to actions that impoverish her sense of integrity and self-respect. Both after the riot and after lying to the police inspector, Margaret suffers acutely. On the first occasion, though the loss of reputation is hard – her attempt to protect Thornton is interpreted as a shameless declaration of love – she can still cling to the sustaining belief that self-sacrifice is part of 'a woman's work' (247). But after the second episode, she finds no justification for her lie: she has demeaned herself and sacrificed something too important.[40]

Through what Bodenheimer calls her 'powerful pyschological intelligence', Gaskell accounts for her heroine's moral progress in terms that Carol Gilligan applies to women's pyschological development generally. Significantly, in Gilligan's view acquiring a sense of responsibility does not necessarily correspond to moral maturity, because the sacrifice of self inherent in the ideal of responsibility 'causes a disequilibrium' which initiates a transition from a concern with goodness to the concern with truth. Only in the final stage, when the individual realizes that 'relations are now understood to require the participation and interaction of integral selves rather than the sacrifice of self' is maturity reached.[41] Gaskell's heroine will experience just this kind of development or re-orientation to the good, a re-orientation towards what matters most. After the riot Margaret can console herself with the thought 'I did some good. But what possessed me to defend that man as if he were a helpless child!' (183). However, after lying to save Frederick there is no self-justification, only a profound and debilitating sense of falsehood: 'Of all faults, the one she most despised in others was the want of bravery; the meanness of the heart which leads to untruth. And here she had been guilty of it! ... No more contempt for her! – no more talk about the chivalric! Henceforward she must feel humiliated and disgraced in his sight' (292–3). Margaret feels anguish; her loss of authenticity contributes decisively to a significant loss of well-being. When morality appears to require the sacrifice of what we consider our most valuable part, then both Elizabeth Gaskell and George Eliot suggest, serious problems are bound to arise. Morality so conceived can indeed

---

[40] By contrast in Bodemheimer's account, 'Margaret's most significant experience is to become a human agent in her own right– a process that means living with the doubleness of her actions, like the men who act and decide in the public sphere', *The Politics of Story in Victorian Social Fiction*, p. 67.

[41] Introduction, in Kittay and Meyers (eds), *Women and Moral Theory*, pp. 7–8.

constitute 'a principle of narrowness in the thickness of ethical life'.[42] Ethics, on the other hand, involves creating the kind of meaningful life that finds a secure place for the fundamentals of well-being; while well-being demands an acceptable self-image and a way of life that can be justified.

In Gaskell's narrative, then, Thornton appropriately plays a central role in both phases of Margaret's psychological and moral awakening. For Margaret's moral maturity is the outcome of reflection not only upon truth and courage but also upon her pride. As Gaskell shows, pride is often ambiguous: a volatile mix of self-assurance and scorn. Hence, although Hume's 'due pride' or self-esteem is clearly a valuable asset – enabling Margaret to exert authority over lover, labourer, servant, and little boy alike – when it manifests itself as contempt, pride denies the Other self-respect and becomes a moral failing. In Margaret the propensity for contempt conflicts with the compassionate, sympathetic elements in her nature. Only when she comes to reflect on her own failings is she able to appreciate Thornton's generosity and strength, and feel gratitude and respect:

> She was smitten with a feeling of ingratitude to Mr Thornton, inasmuch, as in the morning, she had refused to accept the kindness he had shown her in making further inquiry from the medical men, so as to obviate any inquest being held. Oh! she was grateful! She had been cowardly and false, and had shown her cowardliness and falsehood in action that could not be recalled; but she was not ungrateful. It sent a glow to her heart, to know how she could feel towards one who had reason to despise her. His cause for contempt was so just that she should have respected him less if she had thought he did not feel contempt. It was a pleasure to feel how thoroughly she respected him. He could not prevent her doing that; it was the one comfort in all this misery. (278–9)

To the extent that Margaret is capable of protecting or rejecting what she comes to discover are significant facets of her self-conception, she is able to determine how authentic a character she will have. Thus in the course of her meditations, she eliminates the harmful, destructive element, the pride and scorn which had thwarted the full realization of her capacity to love and accept love, and thus to achieve a greater measure of inner harmony or coherence.

Margaret's re-evaluation of Thornton fits neatly, it might appear, into a popular novelistic tradition in which the heroine acquires deeper knowledge of the self and Other in pursuit of the wisdom that may bring fulfilment; a notable example being Elizabeth Bennet's recognition of her own errors and Darcy's merit in *Pride and Prejudice*. Yet it should be clear that Gaskell's more complex contextualization serves to articulate more complex ethical and social issues, and to express, moreover, a characteristically modern moral viewpoint. Symbolized in the web of relationships explored in the book is a conception of social relations that modifies or qualifies quite significantly current social and moral ideas, questioning both paternalist and classical liberal views. Gaskell's is a vision informed by the belief that the personal developments of individuals are necessarily interdependent, that the clash of ideas

---

[42] Geoffrey Galt Harpham, 'Language, History and Ethics', *Raritan* 7 (1987): 135.

is healthy, and that the differing and highly distinctive lives and personalities of members of society complement each other. The idea of gradual progress, to be achieved by mutually dependent developing individuals who are able to cultivate their higher natures through the interplay of variety of experience and diversity of thought, suggests deep affinities between the social thinking of Gaskell and Mill: Gaskell's narrative endorses Mill's belief that the 'multiform development of human nature, those manifold unlikenesses, that diversity of tastes and talents, and variety of intellectual points of view, which not only form a great part of the interest of human life but [which] by bringing intellects into a stimulating collision, and by presenting to each innumerable notions that he would not have conceived of himself, are the mainspring of mental and moral progression'.[43]

Both Gaskell and Mill uphold, then, the idea of a gradually developing society comprising human beings who are engaged in fully and variously developing or reclaiming what is good in themselves by the light of revised self-understandings. These individuals are morally and mentally vigorous. Able to reassess the validity of prevailing social and moral principles, they are alive to the implications of the ethical codes – of rights and responsibilities – that determine their own and other people's lives. Central to this moral and mental progression is the ever fuller realization of a nature which is at once more coherent and more independent; they are able to achieve significant measures of authenticity and autonomy, both essential facets of individuality. It is worth noting, however, that while in Mill's treatise the social matrix of individuality is largely unacknowledged, in Gaskell's narrative the individual's cultural tradition or chosen community is firmly established as a source of identity.[44] However recalcitrant this community might be, the attitude of Gaskell's exemplary individualists is at once critical and constructive, their approach to problems involves realizing, if not consensus, then some form of, or forum for, discussion and debate.

For these thinkers the attempt to achieve greater coherence and independence of spirit serves to guarantee the continuation of individual and social growth, promoting the kinds of experiments in living which they believed would mark a first step in the search for solutions to social problems. Hence, while community values or ideals should never impede the growth of individuality, the attainment of individuality, precisely because it involves the realization of the innate social nature of man, should contribute to the rise of a fairer society. That this kind of individuality lay for the moment within the grasp of the few – given all the Ediths, Fannys,[45] Aunt Shaws and Mrs Thorntons in North and South – was a concern that they also shared.

---

[43] Mill, *Principles of Political Economy*, in *Collected Works*, vol. 3, p. 209.
[44] See John Gray's critique of Mill's conception of individuality, 'Mill's and Other Liberalisms', in *Liberalisms: Essays in Political Philosophy* (London: Routledge, 1989), pp. 224–9.
[45] Note Gaskell's description of Fanny's thoughts: 'Fanny was not sure, from Mrs Slickson's manner, whether she ought to be proud or ashamed of her brother's conduct; and like all people who try and take other people's 'ought' for the rule of their feelings, she was inclined to blush for any singularity of action' (159).

Chapter 5

On Goods, Virtues and *Hard Times*

Dickens, Orwell decided, was a nineteenth-century liberal; a 'generously angry' writer, but one whose criticism was above all moral: 'in reality his target was not so much society as human nature'.[1] Since Orwell wrote, in 1939, not only has the ideological stance of Dickens's novel *Hard Times* continued to be the subject of critical controversy, but doubts have been raised as to whether his treatment of ethical issues can be taken as the expression of a coherent and consistent viewpoint.[2] In this chapter I begin by considering some long-standing objections to the novel before proceeding to identify what I take to be its most significant patterns of salience. These patterns, I will be suggesting, emerge more clearly when they are related to ongoing debates about the effects of liberalism, its elusive goods and strange virtues. I propose to examine *Hard Times* while bearing in mind recent reflections on the enduring features of liberalism, on its core tenets, principle concerns, and values. Current controversy continues to center on both the limitations and potential of this complex and multifaceted body of thought. Once we place *Hard Times* firmly within the context of the ongoing *critique and defence* of the moral and political implications of liberalism, we will find, I think, that more favourable claims can be made for both novel and novelist. Dickens's satire becomes more focussed.[3] Here I shall be arguing that if in *Hard Times* Dickens identifies certain distinctive strands of modern liberal theory and practice, then it is to gauge their impact on personal well-being broadly conceived. If two of the novel's main concerns are: What contributes

---

[1] 'Charles Dickens', in Sonia Orwell and Ian Angus (eds), *The Collected Essays, Journalism and Letters of George Orwell* (4 vols, London: Secker and Warburg, 1968), vol. 1, pp. 413–60.

[2] As Stephen Pulsford observes, 'there has never been critical consensus about Dickens' politics'. Pulsford provides a good summary of the different perspectives on this issue in 'The Aesthetic and the Closed Shop: The Ideology of the Aesthetic in Dickens's *Hard Times*', *Victorian Review* 21 (1995): 145–60. Pulsford concludes that 'the politics of *Hard Times* are ultimately not contradictory but unconstructive ... the novel can sense the institutions that infringe its own values, but not see its way towards practical solutions' (157). The tension within Dickens's thought is the subject of Nicholas Coles's 'The Politics of *Hard Times:* Dickens the Novelist versus Dickens the Reformer', *Dickens Studies Annual* 15 (1986): 145–79.

[3] For a discussion of the traces of liberal humanism within other works by Dickens see Vincent Newey, *The Scriptures of Charles Dickens: Novels of Ideology, Novels of the Self* (Aldershot: Ashgate, 2004).

to human flourishing? and, Has all that could be done to promote it been done? then Dickens's answer is not simply that what is largely missing from people's lives and hence required is amusement and/or affection, the goods granted paramountcy by the narrator. In this reading of the novel the range of Dickens's 'positives' is seen as far wider in scope, encompassing both life goods and a fundamental good, a constitutive good – the good will. In *Hard Times* the good will powers a vitally effective moral life.

Approaching Dickens's novel from the perspective of a (contested) liberal ethic, we can set about overturning both of Roger Fowler's oft remarked and damaging claims. In the first place, according to Fowler, Dickens 'attacks an unmanageably large and miscellaneous range of evils (utilitarianism in education and economics, industrial capitalism, abuse of unions, statistics, bad marriage, selfishness, etc.); ... he mostly oversimplifies them ...; [and] is unclear on what evil causes what other evil'.[4] One of the problems with this criticism is that it fails to conceptualize adequately the issues Dickens is addressing, and hence cannot trace the relations between these 'evils'. Two of the topics mentioned are misrepresented, we find, as 'industrial capitalism' and 'bad marriage'. While in the first case, Dickens is concerned with the illiberal practices of capitalists who self-advertise themselves as liberals, in the second, he points up the lack of opportunities for divorce, and this in a society in which independence and freedom are key issues. Divorce is still a class privilege, a liberty denied to the dispossessed majority. The last item in the list, 'selfishness', could be replaced by or reformulated as 'a concern for self-interest', the unlovely character trait that liberalism condones. For Dickens, the liberal discourse of character can breed strong (as regards determination) but strange offspring. The other 'evils' mentioned by Fowler, with the exception, of 'trade unionism' are part and parcel of the manifold problems associated with the widespread influence of liberal utilitarianism.[5] What the trade union 'abuse' highlights is the threat to the key values of liberalism that is posed by an increasingly important source of power. All these issues have some bearing, then, on the subject of the relations between liberty and liberalism, on the complex problem of the dangers to and the limits of Victorian liberalism.

Secondly, Fowler asserts that Dickens's 'proposed palliatives are feeble, misconceived in terms of purely individual initiatives and responsibilities and sentimentally formulated' (106). Fowler is not alone in denigrating Dickens's 'remedies', and other critics have found the other 'solutions' that their readings come up with equally untenable. For Catherine Gallagher, *Hard Times* would appear to suggest that the ideal family is a model for a deeply fractured society. But the novel itself then reveals doubts about this project and ultimately 'the job of reforming

---

[4] Roger Fowler, 'Polyphony and Problematic in *Hard Times*', in Robert Gittings (ed.), *The Changing World of Charles Dickens* (Totowa: Barnes and Noble, London: Vision Press, 1983), pp. 91–108.

[5] Robert Newson maintains that the criticisms of 'Benthamism' in the novel are made from a utilitarian standpoint: *Dickens Revisited* (New York: Twayne, 2002), p. 132.

society falls on Sissy's slight shoulders'.[6] According to Raymond Williams, *Hard Times* withdraws into personal feeling, exalting a childish innocence that 'shames the adult world, but also essentially rejects it'.[7] A better understanding of Dickens's combined ethical and ideological enterprise may be gained, however, if, eschewing the widespread preoccupation with 'solutions' and 'reforms', we conceive of his novel as revealing the need for a variety of essential 'goods' that pertain to both personal and public spheres.

Modern critics have generally not been greatly impressed by what they take to be Dickens's vision of the moral personality. Barbara Hardy's assessment that Dickens's picture of 'domestic proficiency and concentrated virtue has happily dated' may be taken as representing what many readers have continued to feel.[8] As an ideal, the Angel of the House is, unsurprisingly, unpopular, and perhaps this accounts for a failure to examine in any detail Dickens's articulation of the moral personality, of the moral economy of the psyche. The question is, however, whether either angels or self-sacrificing saints are really to the point. Arguably the issue that interests Dickens here is not What makes for saintliness? but What are the ingredients that together ensure effective moral agency? Typically, Dickens's moral exemplar or model is described simply as a noble innocent whose happiness consists in spreading joy around her and in satisfying the needs of others.[9] Of the various aspects of moral character that might engage the attention of the moral analyst (motives, perception, judgement, attitudes, emotions, commitments, ideals, intention, self-conception), it would appear that for Dickens the salient elements are impulse, instinct, and inclination.[10] Here I shall try to show that Dickens's picture of the psychological make-up of the moral personality is

---

[6] According to Catherine Gallagher, *Hard Times* embodies the contradictions of the paternalist metaphor it is keen to promote. It is, in Gallagher's opinion, 'fraught with ambiguities'. 'Up to its very last page, *Hard Times* is a book that simultaneously flaunts and discredits its metaphoricality, calling into question both the possibility of paternalist reform and the validity of its own narrative practice': *The Industrial Reformation of English Fiction*, pp. 155, 166.

[7] *Culture and Society: 1780–1950* (New York: Harper and Row, 1966), p. 109.

[8] Barbara Hardy, *Charles Dickens: The Later Novels* (London: Longman, 1968), p. 10.

[9] Thus F.R. Leavis: 'Sissy stands for vitality as well as goodness – they are seen, in fact, as one; she is generous, impulsive life, finding self-fulfilment in self-forgetfulness – all that is the antithesis of calculating self-interest ... the life that is lived freely and richly from the deep instinctive and emotional springs [is contrasted with] the thin-blooded, quasi-mechanical product of Gradgrindery': *The Great Tradition*, London, 1948, reprinted in George Ford and Sylvère Monod (eds), *Hard Times* (New York: W.W. Norton, 1966, 1990), p. 344.

[10] Patricia Ingham argues that feminine value, as opposed to femaleness, inheres in those innocent characters who have the magic ingredient of 'plasticity when faced with the needs of others: a "true" woman, as opposed to a female in her natural state is necessarily "a mother"': 'Nobody's Fault: the Scope of the Negative in *Little Dorrit*', in John Schad (ed.), *Dickens Refigured: Bodies, Desires and Other Histories* (Manchester: Manchester University Press, 1996), pp. 107–8.

more complex; that by adopting the technique of repetition with variation, involving different combinations of key psychic elements, Dickens constructs a neat typology of moral character, and points up the right relationship between the different human capacities that are essential both to moral agency and to a 'thick' or robust identity.

Pre-eminent among the significant features of the morally competent are capacities for accurate perception and lasting emotive attachments or commitments, and these are foregrounded in his strategies of representation. Each of these categories is crucially, and more or less explicitly, related to the will. A good will is foundational, the bedrock of an effective moral personality.[11] This being the case, the strict relation prominent liberals postulated between the impetus to further self-interest and the will becomes problematic. For Dickens, it was essential to re-affirm the function of the will as a moral source, an empowering force for the good; a force which is manifest in the quality and fitness of the moral response to others. This reading will reject views which sustain that in this novel Dickens is proposing or endorsing spiritual exaltation, moral rigourism, benign paternalism, or the self-defeating resort to privatism or self-sacrifice. Here Dickens's narrative is taken to be the expression of a troubled liberal: a liberal whose misgivings embrace on the one hand disregard for basic liberal standards, principles and goods in social life, and on the other, the pretensions, complacency, narrowness, obtuseness, the limited moral vocabulary and vision of hegemonic liberal capitalists and theorists. Dickens's polemic attests to a conviction recently expressed by Richard E. Flathman that 'liberals and liberalism are forever in need of ideas and images that protect and invigorate, disturb, disrupt and refashion their thinking and its arrangements and practices'.[12]

*

'Mankind is clueless about how to live, what to do'.[13] The idea that liberal theory provides no answers to the key questions: What is the purpose of life or what are the

---

[11] According to George Levine 'Through most of his earlier work, he had celebrated exuberantly the powers of innocence, of good intentions, of change of heart, although he had always been uneasy about strong will. In *Little Dorrit*, there is far more uneasiness, and no celebration ... the power of the will was indeed in question, where the voluntaristic model of behaviour was put to the test': '*Little Dorrit* and Three Kinds of Science', in Joanne Shattock (ed.), *Dickens and Other Victorians: Essays in Honour of Philip Collins* (Basingstoke: Macmillan, 1988), pp. 9–10.

[12] Richard E. Flathman, *Willing Liberalism: Voluntarism and Individuality in Political Theory and Practice* (Ithaca: Cornell University Press, 1992), p. 15.

[13] Stephen Holmes sums up the anti-liberal position of philosopher Alasdair MacIntyre in a way that strongly recalls the concerns of Dickens in *Hard Times:* 'Vital social relations have been desiccated by arid individualism. A warm, solidary, and emotionally satisfying communal order has yielded to a chilly, egoistical, and morally hollow one. The social faculties of prelapsarian souls have been grievously damaged by Western rationalism. Generosity, friendship, and joy have nearly vanished. Niggardliness and misery are all-pervasive. Idyllic normative consensus has been supplanted by sickeningly endless

ends of life? What are the goods that we should be seeking and that constitute a good life, a life of well-being? finds expression in the novel in the predicament of Louisa Gradgrind. Asked by her father whether she will accept the marriage proposal of the blustering bully Bounderby, Louisa voices for the first, but not the last, time one of the novel's major preoccupations: 'what does it matter?'. Her statement/question articulates the modern sense of inner emptiness, of weariness, the idea that nothing is worth doing. Gradgrind's response is typical of the man: though not totally uncaring, he looks to his theory to provide an answer. His theory favours radical detachment, viewing life and life's decisions from a purely universal or abstract point of view; and he is either unable or unwilling to suggest a course of action involving the 'aspirations and affections'[14] that might offer some prospect of personal fulfilment. In Gradgrind's version of liberal utilitarianism, reason – here represented as mental clarity, austere disengagment and instrumental efficacy – has attained the status of an end in itself. It has become a hypergood. But commitment to a hypergood is, as Dickens realised, highly problematic in that it usually determines the whole direction of one's moral orientation; encouraging an exclusivity of moral vision, it limits the focus of action.

Life goods should be abundant and diverse.[15] What the citizens of Coketown lack are various life goods that can satisfy basic human needs and confer dignity and self-respect. Certain of these goods belong to the social or political sphere, where principles regulate the relations that connect people from different walks of life, people possessing unequal shares of power like Bounderby and Blackpool. Dickens underscores dramatically the need for values which with hindsight we have come to view as central to the theories of liberalism as it was evolving in this period. Toleration or forebearance, open-mindedness, freedom of speech, and mutual respect, the goods which protect the dignity of the individual, promote understanding among people, and preserve social harmony and order, are in short supply in the grim world of *Hard Times*. The governing classes, represented by Gradgrind and Bounderby, have erred in so far as they have failed to live up to traditional liberal ideals.

It is obvious then that Dickens shares doubts about prevailing social codes and practices with Elizabeth Gaskell. But Dickens's approach to the issue of contemporary liberalism and its effects differs in significant respects from that of *North and South,*

---

disagreement. Thick preindustrial forms of social identity have been replaced by thinner and more universal ones. As a result *mankind is clueless how to live, what to do.* "Modernity" has few if any redeeming features, according to the tenets of "deprivation history" in this, its purest form': *The Anatomy of Anti-Liberalism* (Cambridge, MA: Harvard University Press, 1993), pp. 89–90, emphasis added.

[14] All page references in the text are taken from David Craig (ed.), *Hard Times for These Times* (Harmondsworth: Penguin, 1969), p. 136.

[15] Particularly relevant to an understanding of the role of goods in the ethical life is Charles Taylor's essay 'The Diversity of Goods', in Amartya Sen and Bernard Williams (eds), *Utilitarianism and Beyond* (Cambridge: Cambridge University Press, 1982), pp. 129–44.

which was written at the same time. In Gaskell's articulation of the often embattled exchanges between her male and female characters, John Thornton and Margaret Hale, the ideals of classical liberalism are expounded and subjected to critique. The novel's account of the debating, revising, experimenting and risk-taking that underlie productive social relations suggests that Gaskell's views can be reasonably aligned with the new liberal thought of J.S. Mill. *Hard Times,* on the other hand, dramatizes the power, the influence, the need for, and the limits of, key liberal notions, while it is also envisions the practice of 'community" values and virtues and explores some of the implications of certain 'communitarian' forms of life.

It is the firm conviction of modern communitarian thinkers, like Alasdair MacIntyre, that the community model provides its members not only with essential life goods (security, solidarity, fraternity) but also, and significantly, with a robust sense of personal identity, with a 'thick' self that is firmly rooted in his or her environment and capable of affection and empathy. By cooperating in community projects and sharing community ideals and practices, alienation, loneliness, and anxiety – the psychological distemper to which the liberal is prone – is kept at bay. The self flourishes when nourished on a diet of intimacy and care, when it finds purpose and direction in commitments to the well-being and aims of community members. But for liberal theorists like Stephen Holmes this cosy picture of community life is unreal, implausible. It fails to fill in the shadows, the dark side of solidarity. So where communitarians stress the therapeutic gains of communal life, liberals translate 'embeddedness' into restriction and restraint and find that the liberal goals of personal freedom and individuality are ditched in the cause of belonging.[16]

As the critics Catherine Gallagher and Rosemarie Bodemheimer both point out, the model of the cohesive family, whether extended or compact, constitutes for Dickens a locus of much that is worthwhile and admirable in social life.[17] Yet it is equally the case that the novel insists on the difficulties involved in 'belonging'. As a social idea the circus stands for communal practices set in contrast with the aggressively libertarian drives of all those characters for whom the family counts for little or nothing (Bitzer, Bounderby, and Tom Gradgrind). Potent images of the collective action of the circus folk (as a tower of strength, demonstrating mutual interdependence, as a welcoming refuge for the abandoned Sissy, as a repository of stories of developing family life)

---

[16] The literature on this topic is vast, among the many and important works are those by Michael Walzer, 'The Communitarian Critique of Liberalism', *Political Theory* 18 (1990): 6–23, Will Kymlicka, *Liberalism, Community and Culture* (Oxford: Clarendon Press, 1989), and Stephen Holmes, 'The Permanent Structure of Antiliberal Thought', in Nancy L. Rosenblum (ed.), *Liberalism and the Moral Life* (Cambridge, MA: Harvard University Press, 1989), pp. 159–82.

[17] Catherine Gallagher, *The Industrial Reformation*, pp. 160–61; Rosemarie Bodemheimer *The Politics of Story in Victorian Social Fiction* (Ithaca: Cornell University Press, 1988), pp. 199–202. There is no celebration of the moral potential of the family in *Little Dorrit,* as Patricia Ingham has shown in 'Nobody's Fault', in Schad (ed.), *Dickens Refigured*, pp. 98–116.

imply that this kind of family-community provides an intimate moral dimension where nurturing and sustaining is an habitual practice, where certain virtues, such as loyalty, trust, and love, endure and abound. These are the virtues, the moral imperatives, that Sissy has learnt in the circus and finds impossible to unlearn later in Gradgrind's world. But it is Sissy herself who relates to Louisa a story – of her early life with her father – that is, at one and the same time, an account of loyalty and attachment and love, and of what happens when one ceases to 'fit into' the group.

Moreover, just as Sissy's father's sense of failure and shame compels him to leave his community, so does Stephen Blackpool's open dissent mean that he is expelled from the working-class community of Coketown. Stephen's experiences highlight the costs of solidarity when unity is obtained through conformist bigotry. 'Private feelings must yield to the common cause' (175), maintains the obnoxious Slackbridge. And among the workers of Coketown, the shared goals and values of the community and the association to which they belong require 'severe conditioning and control',[18] eccentricity of behaviour or thought, differences of outlook, are not tolerated. It is this insight that distinguishes Dickens, the journalist, who actually went to the North of England to investigate the mechanisms of working-class solidarity, and who reported on the peace and concord he found there, from Dickens, the theorist, who wrote *Hard Times*.[19] The trade-union scenario in the novel is the representation of Dickens's liberal fear of the use of the concentrated power of associations to incubate fanaticism and promote 'insidious and individuality-diminishing influence'.[20] At the trade-union meeting Stephen experiences at one and the same time the force of community pressure and the loss of a fundamental liberal good. Indeed, twice Stephen is effectively deprived of the right to freedom of speech by those with the power to curb his prospects of earning a livelihood, both the trade-union leader and the factory owner. In analogous scenes, Slackbridge and Bounderby invite Stephen to speak out, to express his own views. Though Slackbridge does so only grudgingly after demands from the workers. But when Stephen refuses to endorse their opinions their vindictive reactions – they are both able to punish him, the trade-union leader significantly 'silencing him' – make a mockery of the idea of freedom of expression or discussion. Furthermore, just as Bounderby has the power to say whatever he likes, however outrageous, with impunity, so can he to all effects and purposes dissolve his marriage bonds when he pleases. Stephen, on the contrary, is denied any prospect of gaining the liberty to remarry and hence create a family of affect.

The long suffering Stephen challenges Louisa's special status as the character whose condition of deprivation is most disabling. Desolate and despondent, both

---

[18] Nancy L. Rosenblum points out that 'the idea of a self constituted by communal forces can point to severe social conditioning and control that is all the more efficient if it operates through self-discipline': 'Pluralism and Self-Defence', in Rosenblum (ed), *Liberalism and the Moral Life*, p. 219.
[19] 'On Strike', *Household Words*, 11 February 1854: 553–9.
[20] Flathman, *Willing Liberalism*, p. 8.

appear for the first time voicing similar desires, desires 'to see' that are effectively needs: 'Wanted to *see* what it [the circus] was like', (57) Louisa tells her father. 'Yet, I don't *see* Rachel, still' (103), says Stephen (emphasis added). Let us turn, then, to questions relating to the nature and function of perception and of a closely connected moral category, the will.

*

In *Hard Times* modes of perception generate theme and design. Out of the act of seeing, or desiring, or failing, or refusing, to see, a network of connotations develops, structuring the novel at the levels of plot and theme, connecting, often by means of the trope of *peripeteia,* or ironic reversal, scenes represented sequentially.[21] We may consider briefly some of the implications of a few notable examples. At the very beginning of the novel, Gradgrind forcibly prevents Tom and Louisa from watching the circus, judging the whole set-up a dangerous distraction, only in 'Whelp-hunting' to be compelled to see Tom dressed up in circus garb; now a tragi-comic figure, his son acts a farcical role in a farcical ending to a ridiculous system. Tom's disguise is meant to help him avoid capture for the crime he has committed. In the planning of this crime, Tom Gradgrind sets Stephen to watch the bank and so attract suspicion. But, while in the same building, Tom is being closely watched himself by Bitzer. In both cases the same self-interested motives prompt the 'watchful' activities. Then there is Mrs Sparsit who sees in her imagination a 'mighty staircase' down which Louisa Gradgrind moves inexorably towards disgrace and shame. Mrs Sparsit 'kept unwinking watch and ward over' Louisa. She follows Louisa when she takes flight from her husband's house only to lose sight of her at the crucial moment Louisa turns in the direction of her father's house. Despite not having seen which way Louisa went, such is Sparsit's faith in her knowledge of Louisa (paralleling Bounderby's presumed knowledge of his workers) that she recounts the wrong story to Bounderby. The moment marks the beginning of her own fall 'from her pinnacle of exultation into the Slough of Despond' (281). Rather than making any attempt to understand the 'real' Louisa, Sparsit lets her uncontrolled and unsympathetic imagination provide her with one insight too many. Thematically, perception functions therefore in ways that are crucial to Dickens's conception of moral personhood. In such a compressed or schematic work the activity of the eyes is rarely merely descriptive, but expresses instead a precise attitude, a state of responsiveness that is more often than not ethical in its implications.

---

[21] David Lodge observes that the use of peripeteia contributes to the 'didactic, illustrative import of the story'. But he does not discuss the ways in which this device allows Dickens to develop the thematic concerns of the novel: 'How successful is *Hard Times*?', reprinted in George Ford and Sylvère Monod (eds), *Hard Times* (New York: W.W. Norton, 1966, 1990), pp. 384–5.

In a Dickensian physiognomy typically the eyes are telling. One thinks for example of the oft-remarked 'pityful and plaintive look' of Amy Dorrit (Bk 1, ch. 7,) or the 'glaring' and 'staring' that characterizes the revolutionaries in *A Tale of Two Cities*. The aggression liberated in the look resurfaces in *Great Expectations*, where the narrative dwells on 'the collision and conflict of looks' that signal states of mastery and submission. In that novel, as Steven Connor has shown, 'Pip's growth to maturity can be seen partly in terms of his move to the position of spectator, rather than that of spectacle'.[22]

Throughout Dickens's work the amazingly rich imagery of observation is thoroughly exploited for its polyvancy. Adam Z. Newton discerns in *Bleak House* 'a continuum of looking' which arcs through the text. In this earlier novel Newton finds a pattern of 'one-sided specularity' which contributes to the creation of a narrative dynamics of secretiveness and exposure.[23] This dynamic of contrarieties, which belongs to the 'common action' that the text calls 'following', might be invested with moral implications. But according to Newton it is in the business of telling and listening that the ethics of *Bleak House* are inscribed. The 'watchful' state of many a character in that narrative may be contrasted to 'the lazy gaze' that is a characteristic – as David Trotter has noted – of the essentially harmless activity of Dickens's idle men: those who in *Nicholas Nickleby* and *Martin Chuzzlewit* stare rather than interpret or attend. It may be that their idleness, suggests Trotter, 'constitutes an implicit reproach to narratives which endorse strenuous self-making'. At times Dickens's phenomenology of perception 'scrupulously avoids any gesture at naked and aggressive existence', which makes for a moment of 'blissful unconcern' (206): a moment experienced as time-off from the ethical, a salutary interlude for both author and reader when nothing very much matters.[24]

In *Hard Times* the body language that talks loudest is that of the eyes, and the messages they send are indubitably indicative of moral stature or sensibility. Characters are differentiated and defined by their varying capacities for the discernment or understanding that in moral situations may be achieved through 'a just and loving gaze', an 'act of attention' that is undistorted by prejudice or malice.[25] They watch,

---

[22] Steven Connor, *Charles Dickens* (Oxford: Basil Blackwell, 1985), p. 128.

[23] Adam Zachary Newton, *Narrative Ethics* (Cambridge, MA: Harvard University Press, 1995) p. 257.

[24] David Trotter, 'Dickens's Idle Men', in Schad (ed.), *Dickens Refigured*, pp. 200–17.

[25] Iris Murdoch's penetrating discussion of the nature of moral agency may serve as a gloss for Dickens's concerns in this novel: 'As moral agents we have to try to see justly, to overcome prejudice, to avoid temptation, to control and curb imagination [one thinks of Sparsit] to direct reflection. Man is not a combination of an impersonal rational thinker and a personal will. He is a unified being who sees, and who desires in accordance with what he sees, and who has some continual slight control over the direction and focus of his vision ... the chief enemy of excellence in morality ... is personal fantasy: the tissue of self-aggrandizing, and consoling wishes and dreams [like those of Bounderby and Gradgrind] which prevents one from seeing what there is outside one'. From *The Sovereignty of Good* (London: Routledge, 1970), pp. 40, 59.

gaze, strain their eyes, have trusting eyes, or hawk's eyes or dark eyes of the mind; or the mind itself is capable of looking over and beyond [the tempter's distracting smile]; they look carelessly out, keep a sharp look out, use cunning scrutiny, steal looks remarkable for their intense and searching character, glance anxiously, look to, desire to look on, possess marvellous acuteness of countenance, stare, glimpse, peep or envision. And all the manifold modes of perception involved are certain short cuts to a reading of the inner self, a key element in the expression of desire, attitude, moral responsiveness.

Exemplary in this respect are the ways in which Sissy Jupe is perceived by the Gradgrinds. Early on in the novel at Louisa's request Sissy begins to relate the story of her life with her father. Tom, who enters the room stares at them both but then does not care enough about Sissy even to look at her again. He is totally unmoved by her story, viewing others instrumentally as means for achieving his own ends, and Sissy, it seems, is useless to him. But both Louisa and Bounderby have their uses, and his repeated demand that Louisa 'look sharp for Bounderby' (101), is at one and the same time a command that Louisa disregard Sissy and hurry to find Bounderby.

Gradgrind is certainly not manipulative in this way, but, as in his dealings with his daughter, he fails to pay sufficient attention to the person before him. Worshipping the hypergood Reason, Gradgrind has installed in the place of 'gods as great as itself' 'a grim Idol, cruel and cold, with its victims bound hand to foot, and its big dumb shape set up with *a sightless stare*, never to be moved by anything but so many calculated tons of leverage' (223, emphasis added). Averting his gaze at crucial moments, Gradgrind misses the signs related by the eyes.

Louisa, however, closely regards Sissy as she tells her story, evidently trying to understand what her life was like; she comes to feel compassion for Sissy; and then significantly, moves towards her: 'Louisa saw that she was sobbing; and going to her, kissed her; took her hand, and sat down beside her' (100). Her attentiveness followed by her caring response – given emphasis in the text by the mention of several separate and yet linked actions – parallels Sissy's own watchful attention and opening towards Louisa at the moment of her greatest need. 'Accurate moral perception is a good in its own right, but like other goods it is so only ceteris paribus', writes Lawrence Blum.[26] And his observation takes us precisely to that aspect of Dickens's narrative that merits greater attention: the modes he adopts to articulate his ideas about the relation of perception to other psychic capacities that pertain to moral personhood. Louisa 'would have been self-willed ... but for her bringing-up' (57), her father thinks with satisfaction. She has lost her willfulness, but the vital power of her will ('the animating source', 'essential to spirited, challenging and hence engaging' human life)

---

[26] Lawrence A. Blum, *Moral Perception and Particularity* (Cambridge: Cambridge University Press, 1994), p. 34. Blum acknowledges his 'intellectual debt' to Iris Murdoch, whose views are discussed in his book.

has not been impaired. [27] Appropriate moral responsiveness is, the novel implies, a function of necessary connections being made between a good will, good perceptions, and the empathy that goes with the capacity to care. But before focussing closely on the ways in which Dickens's narrative strategies engender ideas and elaborate his argument on this subject, I should like to consider a few influential and contrasting points of view relating to the controversy surrounding the significance of the will at the time Dickens was writing his novel.

*

Edward Tagart, the officiating minister at the Unitarian chapel in Little Portland Street, which Dickens attended regularly, had become by the 1850s a close friend. During the period when Dickens was preparing *Hard Times,* Tagart, a scholar of some repute, was at work on a defence of John Locke against those who accused the philosopher of having propagated atheistic views. Earlier, in 1843 – the year Dickens sent note of his 'earnest and grateful feelings for your eloquent and charming discourse of last Sunday' [28] – Tagart had published an introduction to a reprint of the renowned sermon the Cambridge Platonist Ralph Cudworth had preached in 1647 before the House of Commons. In both works passages are devoted to the disposition of the will.

'There is nothing in the whole world able to do us good or hurt, but *God* and our own *Will*; neither riches nor poverty, nor disgrace nor honour, nor life nor death, nor Angels nor Divels; but Willing or Not-willing, as we ought to do'.[29] 'As we ought to do': the terminus to Cudworth's statement on the significance of the will and its unique role in promoting the good, is crucial. How ought we to will? or what ought the will to be like? Cudworth feared and condemned 'the *blind, dark, impetuous Self will*' (102). He, like the other Cambridge Platonists, held that only those Christians who had power over their own wills, who, moving the mover, could direct this energy to virtuous ends (and above all to complying with God's will or commandments), could live happily and be said to be free.[30] In *Hard Times*, as we shall see, a similar antithesis or contrast between an 'anarchic' will obedient above all to impulse or inclination, and a will that is vital but in crucial respects subject to control and restraint, informs and shapes characterization at a fundamental level.

---

[27] Flathman, *Willing Liberalism*, p. 11.
[28] Charles Dickens, *The Letters, The Pilgrim Edition*, vol. 3, ed. Madeline House, Graham Storey and Kathleen Tillotson (Oxford: Clarendon Press, 1974), p. 449.
[29] Ralph Cudworth, *A Sermon Preached Before the House of Commons*, printed and sold by the Unitarian Association, 1843; all references cited are from the version edited by C.A. Patrides in *The Cambridge Platonists* (London: Edward Arnold, 1969), p. 99.
[30] Cudworth's fellow Neoplatonist John Smith maintained in 'The Excellency and Nobleness of True Religion' that 'The Second *Property or Effect of Religion,* whereby it discovers its own *Nobleness* ... is this, That it restores a Good man to a just power and dominion over himself and his own Will, enables him to overcome himself, his own Self-will and Passions, and to command himself & all his Powers for God ... There is nothing in the

In proposing the writings of Ralph Cudworth to his Victorian readers and listeners, Tagart reaffirmed the salience of the power of the good will in moral life, thus disputing the influential Augustinian belief in the fundamentally corrupt nature of the human will. But by so doing Tagart not only offered an argument against Saint Augustine, he also engaged in discussion with John Stuart Mill. In the same year in which Cudworth's sermon was republished by the Unitarian association (which attracted many prominent liberals to its meetings), John Stuart Mill argued in his *System of Logic* that 'Volitions are not known to produce anything directly except nervous energy'.[31] Mill's was an attempt, according to Tagart, 'to reduce the will to the level of physical sciences', and he was clearly greatly angered. In his book on Locke, Tagart engaged in direct combat, reasserting his belief in the primacy of the will in personal and social life:

> Be it what it may, be it the direct product of volition, still the indirect or ultimate products are far more important; nay, the only products of any importance; nervous action being a very insignificant and subordinate part of the phenomena dependent for existence upon the human will …. The pleasures and pains, the happiness or misery of inappreciable multitudes for long periods of time have been and may continue to be affected by the states of an individual will, commingled with other assisting conditions. All the interests of our intellectual, moral and social being are wrapped up, so to speak, in its character and agency.[32]

But arguably, far more damaging to the moral status of the will as well as pernicious to attempts at self-understanding, were the widely diffused convictions of the great liberal's father, James Mill. In Cudworth's sermon the 'Self-will' inspires loathing. In James Mill's matter-of-fact analysis this is clearly not the case. When disciplined and directed, the 'Self-will' has a valuable role to play. Prompting enterprise, it is the necessary spur to self-improvement of a social and economic nature, and hence the moving force behind national prosperity. 'It is indisputable', claimed James Mill, 'that the acts of men follow their will, that their will follows their desires; that their desires are generated by their apprehension of good and evil; in other words by their interests'.[33]

Liberalism has taught us that both political economy and justice require that every man has a right to pursue his own self-interest, albeit within certain well-defined bounds. The modern liberal apologist Richard E. Flathman argues that: 'developing, pursuing, and satisfying interests and desires are positive goods, are characteristics that deserve to be valued, protected, and promoted. They are made central to conceptions

---

World so boisterous as a man's own *Self-will*, which is never guided by any fixt or steddy Rules, but is perpetually hurried to and fro by a blind and furious impetus of *Pride and Passions* issuing from within it self'. See Patrides, *The Cambridge Platonists*, p. 162.

[31] *A System of Logic* in J.M. Robson (ed.), *Collected Works of John Stuart Mill* (Toronto: Toronto University Press, 1973), vol. 7, p. 362.

[32] Tagart, *Locke's Writings and Philosophy Historically Considered* (London: Longman, Brown, Green and Longmans, 1855), p. 139.

[33] James Mill, *Essay on Government*, 1828. See Steven Lukes *Individualism* (Oxford: Basil Blackwell, 1973), pp. 82–3.

of individuality, of equality, and of freedom, and hence are fundamental to a society suitable to human beings as liberals had come to conceive of them. We are not to apologize for our "desirousness" and "interestedness"; we are to insist upon them'.[34] And insist upon them is precisely what Bitzer does. In the chapter entitled 'Philosophical' Bitzer lays bare his motives for wishing to arrest Tom Gradgrind. 'I wish to have his situation, sir, for it will be a rise to me, and *will do me good*' (303, emphasis added). Like any good liberal where questions of justice are concerned, Bitzer acts, not in the spirit of rancour, but from a position of detachment: 'You seem to think that I have some animosity against young Mr Tom; whereas I have none at all. I am only going, on the reasonable grounds I have mentioned, to take him back to Coketown' (304). Bitzer may well be right on all counts. Nevertheless, there seems little to like in him, or little that might qualify as good. Yet Dickens has endowed him with many virtues: liberal virtues. Fully versed in the laws of political economy, independent, self-disciplined, prudent, courageous, conscientious, and industrious, Bitzer is determined to get on. As a description of our ambivalence towards the archetype that Bitzer represents, Iris Murdoch's, in *The Sovereignty of Good*, can hardly be bettered:

> how familiar to us [he is] ... the offspring of the age of science, confidently rational ... He is the ideal citizen of the liberal state, a warning held up to tyrants. He has the virtue which the age requires and admires, courage .... The sovereign moral concept is freedom, or possibly courage in a sense which identifies it with freedom, will, power. ... Act, choice, decision, responsibility, independence are emphasized in this philosophy of puritanical origin and apparent austerity. It must be said in its favour that this image of human nature has been the inspiration of political liberalism. However, as Hume once wisely observed, good political philosophy is not necessarily good moral philosophy. (80–81)

Hard Times is the expression of Dickens's agreement with Hume.

Bitzer does not just live by liberal tenets, however; he is, as it were, the abstract individual at the very centre of the classic theory of individualism. Demanding his rights and respect for contracts (the 'bargain' made for his schooling) detached in outlook and pursuing his solitary quest for independence, advancement, and profit, Bitzer stands for all that liberalism's critics hold to be most deleterious. In the view of MacIntyre, Sandel et al., the self for whom these are the values that count can only be thin, insubstantial, volatile.[35] *Hard Times* anticipates their accusation: Bitzer is 'colourless' and 'transparent', Bounderby, 'blustery', a lot of hot air, while Harthouse 'drifts'. With the drifting Harthouse we return firmly to the subject of the will; for within the novel's comprehensive moral discourse Harthouse's is the personality that is vitiated by a wanton will.

---

[34] Richard E. Flathman, 'Liberalism and the Human Good of Freedom', in Alfonso J. Damico (ed.), *Liberals on Liberalism* (Totowa, New Jersey: Rowman and Littlefield, 1986), pp. 82–3.
[35] Alasdair MacIntyre, *After Virtue: A Study in Moral Theory* (London: Duckworth, 1981), pp. 216–21.

*

In his admirable introduction to *Little Dorrit,* the novel composed immediately after *Hard Times,* Lionel Trilling observed that in that novel: 'The whole energy of the imagination ... is directed to finding the non-personal will in which shall be our peace'.[36] More recently, Harold Bloom has commented on the centrality of the will throughout Dickens's fiction, but has expressed doubts about Dickens's belief that there can be different kinds of will. 'The aesthetic secret of Dickens appears to be that his villains, heroes, heroines, victims, eccentrics, ornamental beings, do differ from one another in the kinds of will that they possess. Since that is hardly possible for us, as humans, it does bring about an absence of reality in and for Dickens.' It is Bloom's opinion that Dickens refuses 'to offer us any accurately mimetic representations of the human will'.[37] On Dickens's view, what is undeniably real is the immanent sustaining power of a good will. But 'purposive' self-wills and wanton wills are also characterized and encapsulated in the dynamics of his narrative, albeit in a somewhat rudimentary manner. And it looks promising for Dickens's theory that a close fit can be traced between his narrative account of the operations of the will and the acute and rigorous analyses of the will developed recently by philosopher Harry Frankfurt. For both Dickens and Frankfurt 'the character of a person's will constitutes what he most centrally is ... the boundaries of his will define his shape as a person'.[38]

To begin at the beginning, Frankfurt observes in *The Importance of What We Care About*, that 'Reason has usually been regarded as the most distinctive feature of human nature and the most sharply definitive'. And of course the (problematic) Gradgrindian educational project is based on this Enlightenment intuition. 'I believe, however', continues Frankfurt, 'that volition pertains more closely than reason to our experiences of ourselves and to the problems in our lives that concern us with the greatest urgency'.[39] On this view the state of an agent's will in a crucial factor in that person's sense of who she is and what she can achieve: 'the volitional necessities that bind a person identify what he cannot help being... Just as the essence of a triangle consists in what it must be, so the essential nature of a person consists in what he must will. The boundaries of his will define his shape as a person'. In Frankfurt's lucid exposition of his voluntarist thesis, we have – I suggest – the underlying premise upon which Dickens's moral typology of character is constructed. 'Suppose', observes Frankfurt:

---

[36] Lionel Trilling, Introduction, *Little Dorrit* (Oxford: Oxford University Press, 1953), p. xv.
[37] Harold Bloom, Introduction to *Charles Dickens* (New York: Chelsea House, 1987), p. 4.
[38] 'On the Necessity of Ideals', in G. Noam and Thomas E. Wren (eds), *The Moral Self: Building a Better Paradigm* (Cambridge, MA: MIT Press, 1993), p. 24.
[39] Harry Frankfurt, *The Importance of What We Care About* (New York: Cambridge University Press, 1988), p. viii.

that someone has no ideals at all. In that case, nothing is unthinkable for him; there are no limits to what he might be willing to do. He can make whatever decisions he likes and shape his will just as he pleases. This does not mean that his will is free. It means only that his will is anarchic, moved by mere impulse and inclination. For a person without ideals, there are no volitional laws he has bound himself to respect and to which he unconditionally submits. He has no inviolable boundaries. Thus he is amorphous, with no fixed identity or shape.[40]

As an illustration of Frankfurt's conception of a 'rational wanton', Harthouse, the languid aristocrat from beyond Coketown, is nothing short of exemplary. 'What distinguishes the rational wanton from other rational agents', observes Frankfurt, 'is that he is not concerned with the desirability of his desires themselves. He ignores the question of what his will is to be'[41]. Pursuing whatever course of action he is most strongly inclined to pursue, Harthouse clearly 'does not care which of his inclinations is strongest'. Harthouse the libertine is free. He is free from all ties, free to come and go as he pleases, free to choose his occupation, free to change his mind. But such freedom is not an unambiguous good; 'since nothing is necessary to him, there is nothing that he can be said essentially to be'.[42]

Where Harthouse's wanton will is simply 'anarchic', moved by mere impulse and inclination, the good will, as personified in Sissy and Rachel, is at once free *and* constrained. Among the most important characteristics of the two women are their capacities for loving and caring; and it is a characteristic of this love that it willingly accepts the ties that are thereby created. The Platonic preacher Cudworth, in the sermon to which we have already referred, described the paradoxical nature of this love with great clarity: 'Love is at once a Freedome from all Law, a state of purest Liberty, and yet a Law too, of the most constraining and indispensable Necessity'.[43] In Dickens's novel, the 'natural restraint' that the good will, susceptible to love, imposes on the loving contrasts with the 'system of *unnatural* restraint' (165, emphasis added) that Gradgrind has forced upon his children. Once taken into the Gradgrind household, Sissy becomes subject to the same oppressive system, the same bombardment of facts: 'It hailed facts all day long so very hard, and life in general was opened to her as such a closely-ruled cyphering book, that assuredly she would have run away, *but for only one restraint*' (95, emphasis added). The 'restraint' that prevents Sissy from running away is precisely the kind of 'necessity' to which Frankfurt refers in his study on the will: 'About certain things that are important to him, a person may care so much, or in such a way, that he is subject to a kind of necessity .... To the extent that a person is constrained by volitional necessity there are certain things he cannot help willing or that he cannot bring himself to do'.[44] Sissy's desire for freedom – 'her

---

[40] Frankfurt, 'On the Necessity of Ideals', pp. 24–5.
[41] Frankfurt, *The Importance of What We Care About*, pp. 16–17.
[42] Frankfurt, 'On the Necessity of Ideals', p. 25.
[43] Patrides, *The Cambridge Platonists*, p. 125.
[44] Frankfurt, 'On the Necessity of Ideals', p. 20.

strong impulses ... to run away" – is effectively overruled by a stronger desire which is related to what she most cares about, and that is her father. The source of the power that compels Sissy to remain with the Gradgrinds, is none other than her own will. It is 'lamentable', records the narrator ironically, that 'this restraint was the result of no arithmetical process, was *self-imposed* in defiance of all calculation ...' (95, emphasis added). Underlying Dickens's description of Sissy's predicament is the notion that her action is free in so far as it involves this decisive moment of assent or repudiation, when the power governing the will assents to or refuses to consent to the proposed impulse. This decisive moment constitutes a commitment of the true self which is rooted in her deepest desire.

Sissy stays in Coketown, as both her own good nature and the plot require, to play a saving role in the lives of the Gradgrind children. The sustaining relationship she offers Louisa at the moment of her breakdown is replicated in the story of Rachel and Stephen. But in developing his dramatic interpretation of the powers of the will in the scene where Rachel saves both Stephen and his wife, Dickens's account becomes at once more complex and enigmatic, and undoubtedly for some readers more problematic. Although with regard to the plot, the scene in Stephens's house is virtually irrelevant, thematically, it is centrally important, bringing together in a unity of interconnection Dickens's ideas on the moral efficacy of good perceptions, firm commitments and a vital will. Unlike Sissy's 'just and loving gaze', however, Rachel's 'act of attention'[45] belongs to a different ontological order, for Rachel is asleep at the critical moment in which Stephen's wife reaches out for the poison.

Rachel, we learn, has hurried to Stephen's house in response to a message that someone needed 'looking to'; both looking at and looking after. To Stephen and the reader she articulates the nature of her motivation in coming in terms of commitment: her ready response to the call was made in the cause of a friendship formed long before. Urging Stephen to sleep, she tells him she will 'watch' over his wife. Rachel's capacity to care and moral competence is contrasted at every turn with Stephen's moral helplessness, expressed repeatedly in his need to see her: ' "Let me see thee ..... Let me see thee .... Let me see thee .... I can never see thee better than so ...' (122). Stephen's fears are transformed into his monitory nightmare, in which, 'subject to a nameless, horrible dread', he can neither see 'one pitying or friendly eye', nor 'look again' 'on Rachel's face or hear her voice'. Waking up he realizes that Rachel has fallen asleep and watches as his wife reaches out for the poison. But 'Dream or reality, he had no voice, *nor had he power to stir*' (emphasis added). Stephen is powerless, his will to act immobilized by his conflicting feelings for his wife: 'he was motionless and powerless, except to watch her' (124). But Rachel awakes and acts. Her action can only be interpreted in terms of clairvoyance; Rachel possesses insight, the profound, even mysterious, capacity for perception or knowledge which, when combined with the commitment that comes from caring, powers the will.

---

[45] Key terms in Murdoch's conception of the moral personality: *On the Sovereignty of Good*, p. 34.

Dickens's delineation of moral personality highlights its vital, assertive nature, a nature which gains resolution through adherence to a Christian morality of love, faith and hope. Through his representation of effective moral agency, Dickens registers his distance from all those who, like John Stuart Mill, found the Christian ideal 'essentially a doctrine of passive obedience'.[46] Sharing the neoplatonic dislike of Quietism, Dickens endows his liberators with a life-enhancing energy and resilience. In his moral agents, opposing characteristics are paradoxically reconciled; innocent and mature – in the responsible giving of care and attention – spontaneous and self-disciplined, they are both free and yet obedient.

---

[46] *On Liberty*, ed. Himmelfarb, pp. 112–13.

Chapter 6

Anatomizing Excellence: *Middlemarch*, Moral Saints and the Languages of Belief

Boldly voicing her disgust with 'fearful, delicate, dainty ladies', Dixon, the heroine's servant in Elizabeth Gaskell's novel *North and South*, suggests that the cult of femininity is to blame for the lack of saints in the modern world (415). In Dickens's novels angels abound; and males, like Stephen Blackpool of *Hard Times* attribute saintliness to those females, like Rachel or Sissy, who are capable of acute moral perception and responsiveness to the needs of others. In the Prelude to *Middlemarch* George Eliot identifies Saint Teresa's saintliness with her great act of institutional and spiritual reform, a manifestation of moral excellence apparently inconceivable in the nineteenth century. So how do we recognize a modern saint? What qualities does she possess? And what can act in place of the 'social faith' that according to the narrator of *Middlemarch* in earlier times spurred the saint to accomplish great good? That Dorothea Brooke is proposed by George Eliot as a likely candidate for moral saintdom seems obvious. It is less obvious whether by the end of the novel she can be seen to have reached such glorious heights. In the opinion of one of Dorothea's neighbours, the mordant Mrs Cadwallader, Dorothea suffers from a 'constitutional disease' that makes her obstinate 'in her absurdities' (84–5).[1] Absurd at times she may be, but more significantly, Dorothea misses her vocation 'to make her life greatly effective', and her lack of worldly recognition, of influence and acclaim, is generally read as signalling failure.[2]

In this chapter I will be exploring the novel's notions of moral competency and moral excellence and their relation to eudaimonia. Given the novel's unmistakeable emphasis on virtue, what significance, it may be asked, are we to attribute to notions

---

[1] All references to the novel in the text are taken from the Penguin Edition, Harmondsworth, 1965, reprinted, 1981, ed. W.J. Harvey.

[2] For example, Jerome Thale asserts that '*Middlemarch* is, specifically, a novel about vocations, and Lydgate and Dorothea fail because they have not taken the measure of the world in which they are to work as medical reformer and as modern St Theresa': *The Novels of George Eliot* (New York: Columbia University Press, 1959), p. 144. Barbara Hardy claims that 'Dorothea's strength lies in aspiration, not in action or creation': 'Public and Private Worlds', in Harold Bloom (ed.), *George Eliot's Middlemarch* (New York: Chelsea House, 1987), p. 45. According to Kathleen Blake, '*Middlemarch* shows that not to shape the world is to be shapeless oneself': see '*Middlemarch* and the Woman Question', in Bloom (ed.), *George Eliot's Middlemarch*, p. 55.

of personal welfare? For many a critic of Eliot's ethics, this novel implies that for its heroine a good life – or rather the best life – is quite simply a life spent doing good; factors which are conducive to personal well-being are just not salient. I shall be suggesting here that the text supplies reasons for supposing that a rival view is developed: that, as with Elizabeth Gaskell, a good life is perceived to be a life full of energetic and 'beneficent activity', but it is also one in which a heroine should flourish. Mutually satisfying or *genuinely* intimate relationships are pivotal: it is important – for instance – that a heroine enjoy her partner's enjoyment of herself; she should be able 'to repose on [his] delight in what she was' (516.) That this is a highly desirable form of gratification takes Dorothea Brooke most of the novel to realize. (Unlike Margaret Schlegel who early on in her narrative appreciates being appreciated by some one both enterprising and caring.) Moreover, a prime requirement in a good life is a sense of inner coherence or 'wholeness'. And it seems that, just like John Stuart Mill, Eliot believed that a person who felt this lack of inner harmony would find sustained moral endeavour virtually impossible to pursue.

Nowadays moral excellence is not only difficult to achieve, it is difficult to identify, to understand and even to admire. In what has become a classic on the subject, philosopher Susan Wolf claims there are two types of moral saint – the rational (who sacrifices her own interests to her moral ideal, and who 'feels the sacrifice as such') and the loving (whose happiness is strictly bound up with making others happy) – but finds that both kinds of saint and the saintly life she lives are likely to be unappealing, perhaps even disturbing. It is Wolf's contention that the moral saint is not someone we would much care for and that the 'saintly' life is at odds with our post-romantic ideals of a life of personal fulfilment, a life of many and varied goods. When moral concerns dominate the self will suffer, will in all likelihood lack individuality or authenticity. 'Saintliness', in Wolf's view, is incompatible with 'roundness', and moral perfectionism is an unsatisfactory ideal given that the saint in pursuing her moral project will necessarily have to sacrifice the non-moral interests and skills that contribute to a richly developed character.[3]

George Eliot's idealist, Dorothea Brooke of *Middlemarch*, has (initially) much the same goals as Wolf's would-be rational saint as she strives to achieve a higher mode of life and feeling. In common with Wolf, Eliot realizes this commitment is going to give rise to apprehensions. Thus neighbours think of Dorothea as strange or alarming, and even friends find her 'fanatical', while the reader's attitude to Dorothea's fervour cannot but be influenced by an ironic view of her marriage prospects which signifies Eliot's own perplexity . However, where Wolf's major concern is with lack of *roundness*, what most preoccupies Eliot is *wholeness*: a sense of wholeness is essential – it would appear – to a life of 'being well and doing well in being well'. In the young Dorothea Casaubon, Eliot devises a picture of what a moral saint might be like, examines it thoroughly, admires some characteristics, but dismisses it as a flawed ethical ideal. In *Middlemarch*, I shall argue, Eliot's vision of what it is good

---

[3] Susan Wolf, 'Moral Saints', *Journal of Philosophy* 79 (1982): 419–39.

to be involves considerations as to what makes a life cohere and hence contributes to a state of flourishing. For Eliot a good life exhibits a harmony between values and motives; there is a strict connection between what one believes in or values most and the reasons that motivate one's behaviour. In other words, built into the foundations of her definition of a good life is the requirement that good be achieved in an integrated way.[4] But for George Eliot's heroine realizing this kind of harmonious state of self-fulfilment will be an arduous and at times agonizing business.

*

Of (moral) saints we have high expectations, though what we expect and admire may differ.[5] Eliot's heroine can be seen to meet many of the requirements of conventional notions of saintliness: she strives for self-perfection, responds to pain with fortitude, takes an exceptional interest in the welfare of others, and feels deeply and compassionately for those in distress. Eliot explores the implications of such actions even as she suggests that saintliness involves something extra, a special kind of faith, an enduring capacity for 'perfect' trust. Put in such a way Eliot's views may gain some of the clarity of Wolf's, but any reading of her novel which investigates its moral concerns must sooner or later acknowledge that those critics who claim the novel is confused or contradictory have good reasons for doing so.[6] The roles Eliot attributes to the narrative voice indubitably complicate as they animate her moral discourse. As in *Adam Bede*, Eliot's narrator expounds a didactic rhetoric of the emotions (asserting, for example, that 'our good depends on the quality and breadth of our emotion', 510), while holding a brief for the supreme value of vocation. If we are to be able to distinguish between the novel's conceptions of morality and what looks like morality but is not, and between morality and exceptional goodness or moral saintliness, it will help, I suggest, to background the passions and desire and take a closer look at the ways in which forms of belief function in the novel.

---

[4] So avoiding the schizophrenia that Michael Stocker identifies in modern ethical theories. Stocker's is an attempt to get philosophers to think more about significant psychological states; in particular he notes that 'one mark of the good life is a harmony between one's motives and one's reasons, values and justifications'. Stocker's critique is levelled at those theories that have concentrated on notions of duty, rightness and obligation: 'The Schizophrenia of Modern Ethical Theories', reprinted in R. Crisp and M. Slote (eds), *Virtue Ethics* (Oxford: Oxford University Press, 1997), pp. 66–78.

[5] For views that disagree with Wolf on the nature of the moral saint see R.M. Adams, 'Saints', *Journal of Philosophy* 81 (1984): 392–401, Lawrence Blum 'Moral Exemplars: Reflections on Schindler, the Trocmes, and others', in *Moral Perception and Particularity* (Cambridge: Cambridge University Press, 1994), and Owen Flanagan, 'Prologue: Saints' in *Varieties of Moral Personality: Ethics and Psychological Realism* (Cambridge, MA: Harvard University Press, 1991).

[6] For different reasons, this is the viewpoint of Richard Poirier and J. Hillis Miller, see '*Middlemarch*: Chapter 85: Three Commentaries', *Nineteenth-Century Fiction* 35 (1980): 448–53.

Dorothea Brooke is endowed with the kind of distinctive character traits that impress as the expressions of a forceful personality; outspoken, impulsive and energetic, fortunately – unlike Eliot's heroes Felix Holt and Daniel Deronda – she is not given to long speeches of an edifying nature. That such a vibrant personality runs great risks of being suppressed and subsumed, becomes ever more apparent as the story of her married life with the scholar Casaubon unfolds. Dorothea's marriage presents her with many an occasion to exercise her finest qualities just as it affords Eliot the opportunity to explore the complexities of influential notions of goodness. The key moral question as to whether Dorothea is to be taken as an exemplar of great virtue becomes compelling the moment the dying Casaubon requests his wife 'to apply herself to do what [he] should desire' (518) even after his death. This is the moment when the issue has to be faced and the reader must decide whether the motives or reasons which so often have determined Dorothea's behaviour – her great compassion and sense of duty, together with her remarkable powers of endurance – are qualities which make for moral saintliness. It seems as if Dorothea will comply with her husband's request for her continuing and total dedication to his monumental project after his death, a project in which she no longer believes. But are her reasons for doing so good ones? In her intricate rendering of Dorothea's mental state George Eliot conveys Dorothea's bewilderment and distress. In response to critics who recoil at what they take to be a puritanical morality that condones the repression of the vital self, Jeanie Thomas claims that we are meant to find Dorothea's pyschological suffering unacceptable.[7] But I would add that we are also expected to evaluate the ideal of (female) virtue as a nice mix of sympathy and self-suppression, which Dorothea effectively embodies at this time, and by making use of ideas supplied by the novel itself find it fundamentally flawed.

At stake then is a crucial moral question: Can the selfless action Dorothea is contemplating doing be judged to be right or ethically desirable? Does it in fact conform to her own idea of what is 'right and best', which, as Casaubon has realized, fires her powers of devotion (517). Significantly, Dorothea asks herself this question

---

[7] See Jeanie Thomas, *Reading Middlemarch: Reclaiming the Middle Distance* (Ann Arbor: UMI Research Press, 1987), p. 10. Among the many readings that view Eliot as a stern moralist prescribing an ethos of duty and self-renunciation see, for example, Walter Allen, *George Eliot* (New York: Macmillan, 1964), p. 95, John Holloway, *The Victorian Sage: Studies in Argument* (London: Macmillan, 1953), p. 126, John Halperin, *Egoism and Self-Discovery in the Victorian Novel: Studies in the Ordeal of Knowledge in the Nineteenth Century* (New York: Burt Franklin, 1974), p. 161 and U.C. Knoepflmacher, *Religious Humanism and the Victorian Novel: George Eliot, Walter Pater and Samuel Butler* (Princeton: Princeton University Press, 1965), p. 84. Calvin Bedient criticises George Eliot's 'puritanical' morality which condones the repression of the vital self. For Bedient, Eliot also proposes the negation of such a position, but unwittingly. See *Architects of the Self: George Eliot, D.H. Lawrence, and E.M. Forster* (Berkeley: California University Press, 1972), pp. 36–44.

but does not anwer it: 'Was it right, even to soothe his grief – would it be possible, even if she promised – to work as in a treadmill fruitlessly? ... [T]here was a deep difference between that devotion to the living, and that indefinite promise of devotion to the dead ... his heart was bound up in his work only: that was the end for which his failing life was to be eked out by hers' (520–21). During her emotional turmoil, it is the image Dorothea conjures up of herself that comes to assume most relevance. In the finely nuanced portrayal of her mental struggle, one thought becomes dominant, the thought that she cannot inflict pain on her husband: 'she was too weak, too full of dread at the thought of inflicting a keen-edged blow on her husband, to do anything but submit completely... She saw clearly enough the whole situation, yet she was fettered: she could not smite the stricken soul that entreated hers'. It is at this much discussed point in the novel that we get the narrator's comment: 'If that were weakness, Dorothea was weak' (521–3).[8] Dorothea's unbounded pity, we are to infer, is debilitating yet to be prized. It brings to mind a previous example of the narrator's admiration for Dorothea's 'resolved submission' to Casaubon, an act energized when 'the noble habit of the soul re-asserts itself' (464). Now, the narrator's rhetoric again seems to assume and convalidate a view of the moral issue in terms associated with the images in which Dorothea in her anguish has come to conceive it: refusal=defiance=violence=strength. Either, it seems, she must accept the role of (noble) victim, 'doomed to submit', or of aggressor and harm the 'stricken soul'. But so far she is unable to 'resolve' or decide either way.[9]

In delineating her heroine's moral predicament, George Eliot insists on the fact that Dorothea can see the whole situation clearly – that there is no view of marriage duties that impose such an obligation on her to help Casaubon, that all such labours are moreover futile – but what Dorothea does not, apparently cannot, try to see clearly is herself. What she sees is the stark vision of herself as aggressor, smiting Casaubon. And this vision is mesmerizing. All moral meaning, all sense of self, resolves itself into this nightmare image. That self-representation may play a vital role in moral action is acknowledged by philosopher Jonathan Dancy: 'In the most extreme cases,

---

[8] Susanne Graver argues against the views of Sandra M. Gilbert and Susan Gubar (*The Madwoman in the Attic: The Woman Writer and the Nineteenth-Century Literary Imagination* [New Haven: Yale University Press, 1979]), that there is no tension between the novel's rhetoric and its plot with regard to this episode: 'The doctrine of living for others is examined so thoroughly as to reveal how it miscarries even when one attempts to practice it as an ideal'. See *George Eliot and Community* (Berkeley: California University Press, 1984), p. 206.

[9] As Professor Ken Newton has suggested to me, there are parallels between this scene and the scene where Mary Garth is requested by Featherstone to burn one of his wills (ch. 33). Both women are subjected to the pressure of an unreasonable man. However, Eliot does not examine Mary Garth's motivation in any depth because there is no mental conflict, and her integrity is never under threat at the crucial moment. Significantly, it is only later that she questions 'those acts of hers which had come *imperatively* and excluded all question in the critical moment': p. 353, emphasis added.

the [moral] dilemma is what it is because it involves the question of what sort of person one will be'.[10] Yet Dorothea's image of herself as assailant is a monstrously distorted one – the product of a conflictual relationship that has given birth to painful fancy and continual fear. Her dilemma thus points up the potential for disaster that inheres in a motivational process in which self-conception or representation becomes the decisive factor.[11]

What has got totally lost as Dorothea's thoughts focus on this vision of herself – what indeed is missing from the text at this point – is something Eliot has already indicated as crucial to her heroine's sense of self: a firm belief in and desire for 'what is perfectly good', the pursuing of which makes life worth living (427). Kierkegaard expresses such an idea in the following terms: 'Eternally speaking, there is only one means and there is only one end: the means and the end are one and the same thing. There is only one end: the genuine Good: and only one means: this, to be willing only to use those means which genuinely are good – but the genuine Good is precisely the end'.[12] In *Middlemarch,* at this moment of crisis, there is no 'reaching forward of [Dorothea's] *whole* consciousness towards *the fullest truth, the least partial good*', which the novel has noted is a defining characteristic of her moral personality (235, emphasis added). An article by J.A. Froude on Spinoza published in the *Westminster Review* of 1855, points up the crucial link that according to Spinoza must exist between conceptions of the good and well-being:

> While we are governed by outward temptations, by the casual pleasures, the fortunes or misfortunes of life, we are but instruments, yielding ourselves to be acted upon as the animal is acted on by its appetites, or the inanimate matter by the laws which bind it – we are slaves ... So far, on the contrary, as we know clearly what we do, as we understand what we are, and *direct our conduct not by the passing emotion of the moment, but by a grave, clear and constant knowledge of what is really good,* so far we are said to act – we are ourselves the spring of our own activity – we desire the *genuine well-being* of our entire nature. (emphasis added)[13]

---

[10] Jonathan Dancy, *Moral Reasons* (Oxford: Blackwell, 1993), p. 124.

[11] Elizabeth Ermath discusses the moral implications of George Eliot's representation of the clergyman Farebrother's self-conception in *Realism and Consensus in the English Novel* (Princeton: Princeton University Press, 1984), pp. 235–6. Farebrother alerts Fred to the folly of his ways, thus acting in Fred Vincy's interest rather than his own; as a result, Fred avoids losing Mary's affection, which Farebrother had hoped to win for himself. Ermath comments that 'By recognizing the presence in himself of two distinct motives, Farebrother is able to keep control of himself, literally to maintain his identity'. Clearly, desiring to be true to his best conception of self is a good reason, but the novel seems to suggest that there is a nobler, less fallible, motive involving a belief in something external to the self. This conviction is reserved for Dorothea.

[12] Sören Kierkegaard, *Purity of Heart is to Will One Thing*, trans. and with an introduction by Douglas Steere (London: Collins, 1961), p. 177.

[13] The passage is quoted by Hilda M. Hulme, ' The Language of the Novel: Imagery', in Barbara Hardy (ed.), *Middlemarch: Critical Approaches to the Novel* (London: Athlone Press, 1967), p. 119.

George Eliot remarked of this article that although she did not agree with Froude's own views she thought his account of Spinoza's doctrines admirable. For Eliot clearly there is a disharmony between Dorothea's deep-rooted belief in and desire to discover 'what is perfectly good' and the reasons, the emotions of fear and pity, which now seem likely to motivate the actions that will have such a critical effect on her life, on her well-being. The moral incoherence which necessarily ensues from such a mismatch, from this unresolved conflict, is made manifest in the text in the fragmentary speech characterizing Dorothea's mental and physical breakdown. If we are to assess the alternatives facing Dorothea in Eliot's terms then any momentary relief afforded Casaubon by Dorothea's promise must constitute a 'partial good' when set against Dorothea's damaging loss of integrity or wholeness of consciousness.[14] Paradoxically, it seems that Dorothea's great qualities are, in this case, the wrong qualifications for 'saintliness'. Such a martyrdom as Dorothea faces has no meaning, no genuine good can come of it, and George Eliot contrives Casaubon's timely death.[15] If, as Dorothea affirms during her conversation with Will Ladislaw, the poet, however imbued with sensibility he may be, needs to produce poems to qualify as such, so, George Eliot recognizes, does the saint need not only faith, but faith that in shaping her actions is productive of a (great) good.

To claim that in *Middlemarch* beliefs ground the moral personality is to run counter to a strong tradition of criticism that emphasizes the vital role of the passions in Eliot's conception of character.[16] In the words of Quentin Anderson: 'she knew and could show that every idea is attended by a passion; that every thought is a passional act' (247). The readings of K.M. Newton, Barbara Hardy, Paris and Anderson all suggest that the moral thrust to good is a function of some kind of emotion and that it is more often than not inextricably linked to the satisfaction of a personal need, so that the action thus prompted is to be considered fundamentally egoistic in its motivation. To

---

[14] Hence Bernard J. Paris's statement that Eliot insists 'upon other men as the objective sanction of morality and upon living for others as its end is the rock, as it were, upon which her religion of humanity is built', fails to do justice to the complexity of Eliot's moral vision as portrayed in this scene: *Experiments in Life: George Eliot's Quest for Values* (Detroit: Wayne State University Press, 1965), p. 248.

[15] Carol Christ discusses the implications of such 'providential' deaths in 'Aggression and Providential Death in George Eliot's Fiction', *Novel* 9 (1976): 130–40.

[16] Thus M.C. Henberg: 'Motivation, Eliot believes, comes from the feelings alone, and the ethical task is to educate our feelings by imaginative 'experiments in life', unflinching projections of the actual likely consequences of our actions': see 'George Eliot's Moral Realism', *Philosophy and Literature* 3 (1979): 22. Likewise emphasis is given to the role of the emotions in Eliot's fiction in the following works: K.M. Newton, *George Eliot, Romantic Humanist: A Study of the Philosophical Structure of her Novels* (London: Macmillan, 1981), Barbara Hardy, '*Middlemarch* and the Passions', in Ian Adam (ed.), *This Particular Web: Essays on Middlemarch* (Toronto: Toronto University Press, 1975), pp. 3–21, Paris, op. cit. and Quentin Anderson, 'George Eliot', in Boris Ford (ed.), *Middlemarch, From Dickens to Hardy* (Harmondsworth: Penguin, 1958), pp. 274–93.

quote Anderson again: 'human behaviour is now seen as a set of symbolic gestures expressive of individual needs and desires' (289). Desire, the emotions, beliefs; in her ambitious imaginative engagement with the phenomenology of motivating states, Eliot attempts to render transparent the complex springs of human action, the promptings of the inner life, developing an elaborate account of motives that is quite novel in her fiction. But what is striking about her understanding of what makes motivation moral are its significant points of contact with and departures from dominant theories. An idea of the development occurring in her thought may be gained by even a brief look at the language of belief found in her earlier historical novel *Romola*. Whereas in *Romola* the narrator emphasizes the saving power of 'energetic belief' in enabling the heroine to find a way out of despair and engage in meaningful acts to aid the suffering, in *Middlemarch* this precise explanatory expression is absent from the text; probably because George Eliot realized that it was not in fact sufficiently explanatory of moral motivation.

From the moment Casaubon prevents further discussion of Dorothea's seemingly inexplicable decision to give up riding by asserting that: 'we must not inquire too curiously into motives ... they are apt to become feeble in the utterance ... we must keep the germinating grain away from the light' (44), the novel directs a strong light on motives. Given that much is made of Dorothea's impetuous generosity of feeling, the role played by principled belief in Eliot's account of moral motivation may appear surprising. In the 'great' Kant's view (as Eliot referred to him) the moral agent's will responds purely to principles, reasons which are understood to be generally applicable.[17] Kant's cognitive theory of motivation in which practical reason and self-control are elements of central importance – in so far as they are the distinguishing features of the moral self – has been modified recently in ways that strike resonances when read alongside Eliot's text. In this revisionist view 'moral reasons are purely cognitive states, but they are beliefs which we would not have unless we already had a concern for others. On this account the moral reasons do not require the presence of independent desires in order to motivate, since the independent desires are needed at an earlier stage. The desires are not among one's reasons for acting, though they are necessary for one to have the reasons one has'.[18] Such a reworking of Kant has significant implications as regards our view of the moral agent. If the mental rigour or detachment essential to the practice of the Kantian moral principle has provoked repugnance in critics, the capacity to feel and care for others required by this revised

---

[17] In a letter to her friend Sara Hennell of 19 July 1854, Marian Evans referred to 'the great Kant': quoted by Rosemary Ashton, in *George Eliot: A Life* (London: Hamish Hamilton, 1996), p. 112. G.H. Lewes and George Eliot continued to acquire books on Kant for their library. Among these were the books on Kant now in Dr Williams's Library in London, see *The George Eliot-George Henry Lewes Library: An Annotated Catalogue of their Books at Dr Williams's Library, London*, ed. William Baker (New York: Garland, 1977).

[18] Dancy, *Moral Reasons*, p. 10.

Anatomizing Excellence: Middlemarch, Moral Saints and the Languages of Belief

Kantianism must condition favourably our response to the actor. In short it gives us a strong reason to admire.[19]

In Eliot's novel a disposition to care – a ready sensibility to appreciate the needs of others – plays an active part in the moral personality; and the character of Lydgate appears exemplary in this respect. As the novel repeatedly illustrates, Lydgate's capacity to provide the kind of care that comes from caring makes him a good doctor. Eliot's portrayal of Lydgate's mental state at the time he aids the ailing Bulstrode, highlights the importance of his recognition that he is first and foremost 'a Healer'. But her description of exactly how he 'checks' 'resentful hatred' for Bulstrode, and gets into the frame of mind that makes for a moral action links two elements that do not usually go together in accounts of moral agency. Lydgate, as one who has developed a valuable instinct or propensity which is bound up with the duties of a social role that is a determining feature of his identity, belongs in a special category of moral agent. His ability to 'check' his repugnance for Bulstrode is owing to his awareness of 'that *instinct* of the Healer which *thinks* first of bringing rescue or relief to the sufferer' (781, my emphasis). The phrasing of the motivational structure implies then that the thrust to action, of which Lydgate himself is conscious, comes from an instinctive reflex that channels his thoughts in the appropriate direction. Lydgate finds himself automatically thinking of helping. And once he has had the thought the outcome, the action, is inevitable. To recognize the situation for what it is, is to feel bound by it to act, to be motivated to act on this recognition:

> ... Lydgate felt sure there was not strength enough in him [Bulstrode] to walk away without support. What could he do? He could not see a man sink close to him for want of help. He rose and gave his arm to Bulstrode, and in that way led him out of the room; yet this act, which might have been one of gentle duty and pure compassion, was at this moment unspeakably bitter to him. It seemed as if he were putting his sign-manual to that association of himself with Bulstrode ... Poor Lydgate, his mind struggling under the terrible clutch of this revelation [that 'the town knew of the loan, believed it to be a bribe, and believed that he took it as a bribe'] was all the while *morally forced* to take Mr Bulstrode to the Bank .... (783–4, emphasis added)

Lydgate feels he is 'morally forced' to act. In adding these two words to an account of Lydgate's moral reasoning, which already suggests a lack of conviction, George Eliot completes her assessment: Lydgate is a human being acted upon, not a complete initiator of his actions. His motives lack the conviction or firm belief that comes

---

19   On this dilemma see M. Stocker: 'What is lacking in these theories is simply – or not so simply – the person. For, love, friendship, affection, fellow feeling, and community all require that the other person be an essential part of what is valued': 'The Schizophrenia of Modern Ethical Theories', in Crisp and Slote (eds), *Virtue Ethics*, p. 71. Marcia Baron seeks to dispel such doubts in 'On the Alleged Moral Repugnance of Acting from Duty', *Journal of Philosophy* 81 (1984): 197–219. Baron argues that a Kantian does not have to be preoccupied with morality rather than people.

from a choice freely or resolutely made. Kant makes the point that 'if the practice of virtue were to become a habit the subject would suffer loss to that *freedom* in adopting maxims which distinguishes an action done from duty'. Thus, it is one's duty to confirm or re-affirm resolutely one's duty; one's fidelity or adherence to one's moral principles: 'Virtue can never settle down in peace and quiet with its maxims adopted once and for all but, if it is not rising, is unavoidably sinking'.[20] The novel denies Lydgate the accolades of moral heroism. Lydgate is the only one present at the meeting to act, yet his mechanical response calls into question the appropriateness of any admiration we might feel.

As the novel draws to its close, Dorothea – in a scene which is clearly to be compared and contrasted with that of her earlier moral dilemma – also perceives an opportunity to help someone, in this case Lydgate's wife, Rosamond. And she must also check strong feelings – this time of anger and scorn – if the crucial moral action is to get underway. Here it is worth noting, first, that Dorothea doesn't just 'check' her feelings, she 'overcomes' 'the tumult' of emotion, though it must be admitted that the time span is longer. In Eliot's complex account, in Chapter 80, of the process that ensures Dorothea's movement from her cold bedroom and the solitude of her anguish to a fervent embrace with Rosamond, the emotions or feelings are recognized as vital forces, but forces that must sometimes be mastered. Furthermore, although desire certainly plays a crucial role in the motivational process, Dorothea's desire is no simple inclination or impulsive feeling but is of a special nature: it contains a belief. It is an 'informed' or 'idealized desire',[21] which involves a prior belief in a rational ideal, in this case the standard of 'perfect Right' or Justice as Fairness and Mercy. Thus as she wakes to a 'new condition', as she feels 'liberated' from her terrible conflict, Dorothea 'yearned towards the perfect Right, that it might make a throne within her and rule her errant will' (846). Dorothea desires that her will might be constrained by the authority of a great good, an ideal of justice. Another way of putting this would be in the Kantian terms that are appropriate to the whole passage. Dorothea is able to commit herself to finding a way of acting that would be just and fair, and she does so by ensuring that her will is good because governed by a principle which is fit to be a moral law.[22] It is the thought of an ideal – her own ideal of Right – that empowers Dorothea to ask herself 'what should I do?'. The many references to 'all the

---

[20] Mary J. Gregor (ed.), *The Metaphysics of Morals* (Cambridge: Cambridge University Press, 1991), pp. 209–10. Kant observes that 'the true strength of virtue is a *tranquil mind* with a considered and firm resolution to put the law of virtue into practice. That is the state of *health* in the moral life ...': p. 209.

[21] For an analysis of this concept see Michael Smith, 'Realism', in Peter Singer (ed.), *Ethics* (Oxford: Oxford University Press, 1994), pp. 170–76.

[22] Kant holds that 'Whatever is derived from the particular natural situation of man as such, or from certain feelings and propensities, or even from a particular tendency of human reason which might not hold necessarily for the will of every rational being (if such a tendency is possible) can give a maxim valid for us but not a law; that is, it can give a subjective principle by which we may act but not an objective principle by which we

active thought' that goes into determining what action 'should' be undertaken so that Dorothea can fulfil the 'obligation' laid on her by the three lives in contact with her own has further Kantian overtones, suggesting that as she reasons Dorothea is being self-determining, actively deciding to be bound by a conception of duty, and that it is the conception of 'obligation' alone which motivates. But, we note also that Eliot's revised cognitivism finds room in an important parenthesis for the idea that a desire for the well-being of others is a necessary *pre-condition* for moral motivation.[23]

> For *now* the thoughts came quickly. ((*It was not in Dorothea's nature...to sit in the narrow cell of her calamity, in the besotted misery of a consciousness that only sees another's lot as an accident of its own.*)) She began *now* to live through that yesterday morning *deliberately* again, *forcing* herself *to dwell on* every detail and its possible meaning ... She *forced herself to think* of it as bound up with another woman's life .... (845, emphasis added)

Thus within the narrative of the dynamics of moral agency which unfolds in the novel's present time – the time 'now' – we find an explicatory parenthesis which refers 'back' to Dorothea's habitual (and admirable) concern for others. Kant distrusts the efficacy of 'certain feelings and propensities', and requires a 'deliberate resolve': 'the capacity and considered resolve to withstand a strong but unjust opponent [impulses

---

would be directed to act even if all our propensity, inclination, and natural tendency were opposed to it'; thus the distinction between 'subjective ends, which rest on incentives, and objective ends, which depend on motives valid for every rational being': *Foundations of the Metaphysics of Morals* in *The Philosophy of Immanuel Kant*, trans. and ed. Lewis White Beck (Chicago: Chicago University Press, 1950), pp. 80–87.

Mary J. Gregor explains Kant's conception of ethical laws in the following manner: 'Ethical laws, on the other hand, will be those that arise directly in inner legislation, in which pure practical reason provides not only the law but also the constraint accompanying the law. Since this legislation is concerned with the moral goodness of our will, ethical laws will be conditions of "inner freedom", a state in which choice is free from the influence of the inclinations as such and open to that of our practical reason with its motive of duty': *The Doctrine of Virtue*, Part II of *The Metaphysics of Morals*, trans. and with an Introduction by Mary J. Gregor (Philadelphia: Pennsylvania University Press, 1971), pp. xx–xxi.

For Kant to act from duty is to act *from the thought* that one must act only according to maxims that can be universalized by the will. Of course Dorothea does not actually ask herself if her maxim could function as a universally applicable moral law. But the notion of the 'perfect Right' – the ideal of acting justly and fairly – which is to guide her will, is one which is fit to be a universal law.

23 Note that Kant remarks that there is 'no obligation' to have 'moral feeling' or 'love of one's neighbour', 'because they lie at the basis of morality, as subjective conditions of receptiveness to the concept of duty, not as objective conditions of morality'; thus these feelings do have a role in promoting receptivity but are not apparently necessarily crucial to the achievement of the moral action: Mary J. Gregor (ed.), *The Metaphysics of Morals*, p. 200.

of nature or natural inclination] is *fortitude* (*fortitudo*) and, with respect to what opposes the moral disposition within us, *virtue*'.[24] Likewise in Eliot's text, Dorothea *deliberately* forces herself to think and then to achieve the 'calm resolve' that will enable her to determine (freely) what to do. Dorothea is capable of this resolve – this calmly deliberate engagement of the will – coming at last to a decision to return to Rosamond that necessitates a great deal of self-control. Though often near to breaking point, it will take her through her emotionally fraught encounter.

Eliot's treatment of moral motivation might seem to confirm our impression that Dorothea's beliefs and the acts that they instigate are to be taken as evidence of her exceptional moral goodness – her saintliness. However, for a Kantian – and this reading suggests that Eliot underwrote key elements of Kant's moral theory – the capacity to adhere to Kantian moral precepts is proof of morality but no more. It provides a system of action-guiding principles by which all can apparently abide.[25] Those who do so may be virtuous but not necessarily saints.

*

Attitudes to Eliot's characters are inevitably conditioned to a considerable degree by the nature of the beliefs that orient their lives. If Mary Garth earns respect for her belief in the duty of gratitude which informs her loyalty to Fred and her family, the response to Ladislaw's conviction that 'the best piety is to enjoy, when you can' (252) is always likely to be mixed. Of all the varied discourses of belief articulated in *Middlemarch* there is one often beginning with the words 'it is fitting' that Eliot finds disquieting and compelling.

Traditionally, the concept of 'what is fitting' involved the perception of an appropriate match between the nature of the person and their circumstances that was taken to correspond to some eternal standard of right or of naturalness. The eighteenth-century philosopher Samuel Clarke provides a lucid exposition of key ideas of this theory: there are 'the same necessary and eternal different Relations that different things bear to one another', and a 'consequent Fitness or Unfitness of the Application of different things or different Relations one to another ... these eternal and necessary differences of things make it fit and reasonable for Creatures so to act; they cause it to be their Duty, or lay an Obligation upon them ...'. In Clarke's view, determining wherein lies the fitness of things requires the rational agent 'to act in constant conformity to the eternal rules of Justice, Equity, Goodness and Truth' as ''tis very unreasonable and blameworthy in Practice, that any Intelligent Creatures ... should either negligently suffer themselves to be imposed upon and deceived in Matters of Good and Evil, Right and Wrong, or wilfully and perversely allow themselves to

---

[24] Mary J. Gregor (ed.), *The Metaphysics of Morals*, p. 186.
[25] In her critique of Kantian ethics Elizabeth Anscombe claims that the idea of 'legislating for oneself is absurd': 'The concept of legislation requires superior power in the legislator': 'Modern Moral Philosophy', reprinted in Crisp and Slote (eds), *Virtue Ethics*, p. 27.

be over-ruled by absurd Passions, and corrupt or partial Affections, to act contrary to what they know is Fit to be done'.[26]

Always a problematic morality,[27] in *Middlemarch* the ubiquitous discourses of fitness have become emptied of any moral meaning. They are now expressions of convenience, impersonal words masking personal aspirations or desire, and of which they are the rationalization.

'What can the fitness of things mean, if not their fitness to a man's expectations?' (163). The narrator's ironic comment highlights the presumption in Fred Vincy's confident assumption that he will get what he has done nothing to deserve. Fred believes that it is appropriate given that he possesses the tastes and manners of a gentleman that he should inherit the Featherstone fortune. The clergyman-scholar Casaubon believes that there is 'a fitness' or it is fitting that '[Dorothea's] ardent and self-sacrificing affection [should] round and complete the existence of [his] own' (73). Dorothea will make his life 'whole'. This time the irony is missing. Later contemplating his imminent death, Casaubon does not stop to ask himself whether it is reasonable, just or fair, that his young wife continue, as he urges her to do, his arduous and abstruse intellectual labours. Nor do notions of what is fitting prevent him from adding the infamous codicil to his will. Of even greater expectations is the evangelical banker Bulstrode, who, faced with the ruin of his hopes for spiritual and social eminence, believes that 'it must be more [fitting] for the Divine glory that he should escape dishonour' (742). But presumption is again punished, and Eliot ensures that shame and disgrace, through the medium of a rambling Raffles, await the man whose original sin is – significantly – a betrayal of 'feminine trustfulness' (666).

If in the novel the language of fitness signifies assumptions and opinions – degraded forms of belief – about the *correctness* or appropriateness of relationships or situations, the discourses of trust deal with *goodness*. In *Middlemarch* those capable of trust possess a willingness or readiness to believe in the virtues of others, which is itself virtuous. It is a morality that making for vulnerability requires a kind of inner strength like courage to sustain it.

The capacity to trust is a characteristic of the hard working Caleb Garth, who was 'not distrustful of his fellow men when they had not proved themselves untrustworthy' (264). Though far from well-off, he makes a loan to Fred Vincy. His trust is based on a belief that Fred will be as scrupulous as himself. He is willing to count on Fred's reliability; and his trust is thus, in this instance, specific. When Fred fails to pay back the loan on time and Caleb Garth reveals his doubts about Fred to his daughter – 'I'm afraid Fred is not to be trusted, Mary' – his lack of confidence in Fred does nothing to dent the astute Mary's constancy and loyalty, and this despite her vexation voiced when she sees him next that Fred seems 'fit for nothing in the world that is useful'

---

[26] 'Discourse upon Natural Religion', in *British Moralists; Being Selections from Writers Principally of the Eighteenth Century*, ed. L.A. Selby-Bigge (New York: Dover, 1965), vol. 2, pp. 3, 12, 13. See also J.L. Mackie, *Hume's Moral Theory* (London: Routledge and Kegan Paul, 1980), pp. 15–16.

[27] See Selby-Bigge (ed.), *British Moralists*, vol. l, pp. xxxiii–xxxv.

(288–90). Fred may be caring, but he is as yet insufficiently careful: '[Fred] means better than he acts, perhaps. But I should think it a pity for anybody's happiness to be wrapped up in him ... And so should I, father, said Mary ... Fred has always been very good to me; he is kind-hearted and affectionate, and *not false*, I think, with all his self-indulgence' (290–91, emphasis added). Fred's untrustworthiness is acknowledged with regret; but father and daughter try to see his character whole; his unreliability is perceived as a critical but not fatal flaw of character.

Unreliable, but not 'false', just as there are different types of untrustworthiness so are there different kinds of trust. The 'perfect' trust knows no boundaries: this 'indefinite' or 'over-trust' 'extends beyond the limits of reason' or hard 'external fact' and is accompanied by complete confidence.[28] This trust is invested with good; it is a form of generosity that confers great value on the recipient; it is life-enhancing and empowering. It is the kind of belief that imparts self-esteem for it involves not simply an assumption as to the reliability of the subject so perceived but, more seriously, constitutes an affirmation of his fundamental goodness, his moral worth, his good will; it is a belief that 'you cleave to what you believe to be good'.[29] As a firm belief there is no conditional element in the thought; there is no opening for doubt, no provision for the possibility of failure. At the time he is implicated in the sudden demise of Raffles, Lydgate waits in vain for a sign from Rosamond that she possesses this kind of trust in him: 'If she has any trust in me – *any notion of what I am*, she ought to speak now and say she does not believe I have deserved disgrace' (814, emphasis added). This is the 'perfect' trust that Dorothea has in Lydgate, Ladislaw, and, at the start of her marriage, in Casaubon. As Eliot's contrast in the attitudes of Dorothea and Rosamond makes clear perfect trust is grounded not in feelings – which are derivative – but in the conviction that one's fundamental beliefs about what is right and good are shared and constitute the grounds for action. For Dorothea, without that conviction 'spiritual emptiness and discontent' (516) ensue.[30]

Whereas Casaubon, set hard against Dorothea's ideals of justice, is unable to live

---

[28] According to Elizabeth Ermath, George Eliot is working with a conception of trust that is of minimal value and somehow functions strategically: 'All the novels deal with the politics of trust, that is with those strategies for maintaining at least provisional agreement in a world characterized by misunderstanding and clashes of will': *Realism and Consensus in the English Novel*, p. 253.

[29] The phrase is taken from a letter Marian Evans wrote to her friend Sara Bray, admonishing her for her lack of trust: 'If we differ on the subject of the marriage laws, I at least can believe of you that you cleave to what you believe to be good, and I don't know of anything in the nature of your views that should prevent you from believing the same of me'. The letter is cited by Rosemary Ashton in *George Eliot: A Life*, p. 138.

[30] George Eliot makes Dorothea short-sighted, and observes that she is hasty in her trust (48), and asks 'what believer sees a disturbing omission or infelicity?' (74). Karen Jones expresses the same idea in 'Trust as an Affective Attitude', *Ethics* 107 (1996): 12. This account of trust emphasizes the importance of feelings of optimism but plays down the significance of belief.

up to her 'perfect' trust, Will Ladislaw, it appears, carelessly destroys her trust in him, and she experiences great misery. In George Eliot's plot, the climax of the increasingly intimate relations between Will and Rosamond prepares the trap of circumstances – Dorothea is shown into the wrong room, and is literally closed in by a table – in which she is caught. But there is another 'place' in which Dorothea must not remain entrapped: the Slough of Despond cited in the epigraph of the previous chapter.[31] It belongs to Dorothea's moral greatness, then, that she is not crushed by despair, nor touched by cynicism. Unlike Lydgate her 'resolution is [not] checked by despairing resentment' (814). Dorothea emerges from her experience of betrayal, still believing in and determined to use her own moral powers, and confident of the capacity of others to preserve their integrity (wholeness of character) and to respond to her goodwill.[32] This is the 'overtrust' that William James, like George Eliot, perceives as central to saintliness: 'We find that error by excess is exemplified in every saintly virtue', James observes.

> The saints, existing in this way, may, with their extravagances of human tenderness, be prophetic ... Treating those whom they met, in spite of the past, in spite of all appearances, as worthy, they have stimulated them to *be* worthy, miraculously transformed them by their radiant example and by the challenge of their expectation ... The saints are authors, *auctores*, increasers, of goodness ... The world is not yet with them, so they often seem in the midst of the world's affairs to be preposterous. Yet they are impregnators of the world, vivifiers and animators of potentialities of goodness which but for them would lie forever dormant. It is not possible to be quite as mean as we naturally are, when they have passed before us. One fire kindles another; and without that over-trust in human worth which they show, the rest of us would lie in spiritual stagnancy.[33]

Supreme value has been attached to trust more recently by Aurel Kolnai: 'the attitude of trust ... unless it is vitiated by hare-brained optimism and dangerous irresponsibility, may be looked upon, not to be sure as a starting-point and the very basis, but perhaps as the epitome and culmination of morality'.[34]

If James's remarks seem most relevant to the effect Dorothea has on Will and

---

[31] Hence this reading contrasts with that of David Carroll, who finds that at this point Dorothea's 'trust in human nature is shattered'. See '*Middlemarch* and the Externality of Fact', in *This Particular Web*, pp. 73–90.

[32] Herbert Morris observes that 'We operate with a conception of worth of human beings that leads to our esteeming more highly those who are not just moral persons but morally wise persons. They have ... not been crushed by what they have confronted, but have emerged, victorious, capable, despite and because of knowledge [of betrayal] of affirming rather than denying life': *On Guilt and Innocence* (Berkeley: California University Press, 1976), p. 161.

[33] *The Varieties of Religious Experience: A Study in Human Nature* (London: Longmans, Green and Co., 1920), pp. 340, 358.

[34] Aurel Kolnai, 'Forgiveness', in *Ethics, Value and Reality: Selected Papers of Aurel Kolnai* (London: Athlone Press, 1977), p. 223.

Rosamond, what Kolnai has to say points up the crucial difference between morality and moral saintliness, or the moral outlooks of Farebrother and Dorothea. When they both learn of the suspicions that Lydgate may have been bribed by Bulstrode, Farebrother, noted for his selflessness, kindness, and compassion, is pained but has his doubts; he cannot be 'confident' (full of faith) that Lydgate has not fallen below himself. He knows that 'character is not cut in marble' (790). Dorothea's energetic speech emphasizes the fact of her belief: 'You don't believe that Mr Lydgate is guilty of anything base. I will not believe it. Let us find out the truth and clear him' (784–5). At which point the reader may make his assessment of character on the basis of the following inferences – Dorothea believes that it is possible (for Lydgate) to conserve integrity despite strong temptation, whereas Farebrother, who has actually proved in his relations with Fred and Mary, that his own integrity can survive such a trial, is nevertheless not prepared to believe that others are equally capable.[35] Dorothea has no doubts, her great virtue, her 'overtrust', which prompts the risky action that is anathema to the hesitant males who surround her, is an irrepressible expression of her identity, and accordingly the manifestation of the great gap that exists between 'the moral saint' and the lesser mortals of *Middlemarch*.[36]

*

Dorothea's trust allows Lydgate to recover his self-esteem and the respect of others that is crucial to his well-being. Yet the novel's delineation of Lydgate's afflictions is characterized by a tension which reflects an uncertainty as to what at this moment matters most to him; for at this point the novel offers two possibilities: what counts is his exalted sense of purpose or, alternatively, his sense of personal honour or reputation. The difficulty in accomodating both elements in an account of what is of most concern to him at this time becomes apparent in the disjunction that signals the divide between the thoughts of narrator and subject. Lydgate's inner turmoil finds him becoming 'violent and unreasonable', and in the narration the reason given for this state of anguish is the 'blight on his honourable ambition'. The expression 'honourable ambition' sums up neatly what for Lydgate would be a double good: a sense of purpose that promises to lead to something that is good in itself – the success of his medical research – but which will also enhance his reputation. Clearly, for the narrator it is precisely the promotion of 'the intellectual life – the life which has a seed of ennobling thought and purpose' – which is of greatest value, which is in fact 'supreme' (793). In the narrator's interpretation of Lydgate's predicament it is the potential loss of this vital sense of purpose, of what drives this superior way of life – a way of life which has become threatened by 'the soul-wasting struggle with worldly annoyances' – that

---

[35] On the question of how we are to read Farebrother's character see also n. 11.
[36] Revelant here is Laurence Lerner's criticism of criticisms of Eliot's ethics in 'Dorothea and the Theresa-Complex' in P. Swinden (ed.), *Middlemarch* (London: Macmillan, 1972), pp. 225–47.

is to be understood as the prime reason for his grief. The narrator's explication of Lydgate's failure is informed then by a perfectionist vision, one conceived in terms of a chief good whose pursuit will (additionally) ennoble the soul.

However the report of Lydgate's own feelings as well as his meditations given immediately after the narrator's comment, do not substantiate this view. Lydgate's thoughts of the 'hateful fatality' that comes as a 'blight' on his 'honourable ambition' focus, we find, on the issue of honour as (ordinary) reputation lost. What seems to matter most to him is the sense of 'wounded honour' that derives from the accusation, the slur, of 'baseness'. It is this which fills him with despair rather than the struggle against the 'worldly annoyances' (or debts) that impede the fulfilling of his noble vocation:

> *He felt himself becoming violent and unreasonable as if raging under the pain of stings... Everything that had happened to him there seemed a mere preparation for this hateful fatality, which had come as a blight on his honourable ambition, and must make even people who had only vulgar standards regard his reputation as irrevocably damaged ...* For he was very miserable. Only those who know the supremacy of the intellectual life – the life which has a seed of ennobling thought and purpose within it – can understand the grief of one who falls from that serene activity into the absorbing soul-wasting struggle with worldly annoyances.
> *How was he to live on without vindicating himself among people who suspected him of baseness?* (791–2, emphasis added)

At this point, then, Lydgate shares with Rosamond, Ladislaw and the Bulstrodes, a common fear; the idea of social disgrace, of reputation lost, which is not simply annoying but potentially devastating. It is in large measure due to Dorothea that Lydgate is able to regain the respect of others. Like Dorothea herself, he comes only through the harsh experience of incomprehension and distrust to appreciate fully the good that derives from the belief that others have in oneself. Thus although the narrator seems insufficiently aware of this development, both characters come to make a right estimate of this belief, this esteem, as a *foundational* good in life, one that is crucial to well-being. The explanatory power of the narrator's perfectionist ethics, an ethics of individual endeavour and accomplishment, of talents well-exercised in the cause of self-improvement, thus fails to match the evidence of narrative experiences that serve rather to prioritize an ethics of welfare, an ethics whose prime concern is with human need or with what is foundational in human life. From the perspective of well-being, 'of doing well in being-well', it is sociable living and intercourse, and in particular, the respect and esteem that are part of desirable personal relations that assumes paramountcy. Above all, reciprocal emotional engagement and appreciation are prized because this mutual approving regard is central to the mental well-being that is ease of mind.

Of the goods that the novel considers fundamental to well-being, it is the *gift of intimacy* involving the deliberate sharing of important experiences, that becomes the dominant motif of the last chapters. Genuine intimacy is manifest in the communication of caring that comes through certain forms of contact and that is by nature selective or exclusive. Thus the narrative's final thematic movement is determined by the challenges that characters have to confront if intimacy – a state in which sorrow may be shared or 'the vibrating bond of mutual speech' may be enjoyed – is to be accomplished or restored. Intimacy longed for, gained or re-established – albeit of varying degrees of candour or confidence or complicity – between Dorothea and Rosamond, Dorothea and Will, the Bulstrodes, the Brooke sisters and the Lydgates provides the unifying motif that will bring the various stories to their close. The terrible isolation that characters endure or impose on others has often been emphasized. But in the last Book the physical and mental distance between them is constantly observed, insisted upon, as is the touch and especially the look, both vital expressions of intimacy, that denote the attitude of caring which can bring relief from solitude.

Thus Mrs Bulstrode, on hearing of her husband's disgrace, locks herself in her room, while he waits in anguish below. Later, however, 'resolving' not to leave him alone, she puts 'one hand on his ... and the other on his shoulder'...

> He raised his eyes with a little start and looked at her half amazed for a moment: her pale face, her changed mourning dress, the trembling about her mouth, all said, 'I know'; and *her hands and eyes rested gently on him.* (808, emphasis added)

To Lydgate in his despair, it is as if he and Rosamond 'were adrift on one piece of wreck and looked away from each other' (814). After Dorothea's visit, Rosamond looks into his eyes and shows a (somewhat languid?) concern for him for which he is 'thankful':

> 'But has she made you any less discontented with me?'
> 'I think she has,' said Rosamond, *looking up in his face.* 'How heavy your eyes are, Tertius – and do push your hair back.' He lifted up his large white hands to obey her, and felt thankful for this little mark of interest in him. (858, emphasis added)

Finally, Will learns from Rosamond that Dorothea now knows exactly what happened between them, but wonders nevertheless whether intimacy can be regained, whether they can ever return to '*a world apart*, where the sunshine fell on tall white lilies, where no evil lurked, and *no other soul entered*' (862, emphasis added). When Will and Dorothea meet again the actual distance between them is registered, until the play of hand upon hand begins. Even so confidence and closeness are delayed, and Dorothea realizes that '*if he would have looked at her* and not gone away from her side ... everything would have been easier' (870, emphasis added). At this point, Dorothea opts for and achieves what Eliot realizes she cannot do without: the complicity or private communication embodied in look, touch, and word, that belongs to mutual understanding and deep affection. Life with Will Ladislaw provides Dorothea Brooke with the 'beneficent activity which she had not the doubtful pains of dicovering and marking out for herself' (894). If Dorothea achieves a full life, a life of 'doing well in being well', it is as part of a lively and companionate relationship, with a man who enables her 'to repose on his delight in what she was' (516). In fact one could go further and see this as one of the most desirable of unions: as with that of John Thornton and Margaret Hale, this is marriage conceived as a passionate and enterprising alliance.[37] New families are made and old ones saved as in the Finale the narrative voice distances the reader by a shift of perspective to 'after-years'. To the end the narrator pursues her grand theme of vocation. Yet the satisfactions attendant on the difficult achievement of genuine intimacy, that constant striving after 'complete union', which in the final chapters ensures delight or consolation, can be experienced as constituting a successful narrative challenge to the rueful note registered in the rhetorical closure to the tales of the noble but frustrated ambitions of those 'who lived faithfully a hidden life' (896).[38]

---

[37] For a fascinating discussion of how eighteenth-century gentry couples portayed their marriages to the world see Amanda Vickery, *The Gentleman's Daughter: Women's Lives in Georgian England* (New Haven and London: Yale University Press, 1998), pp. 59–72.

[38] For an interpretation that views the ending as highly problematic see D.A. Miller, 'George Eliot: The Wisdom of Balancing Claims (*Middlemarch*)', in K.M. Newton (ed.), *George Eliot* (London: Longman, 1991), pp. 187–97.

Chapter 7

The Magic in *Mentalité*: Hardy's Native Returns

One of the most impressive features of Thomas Hardy's novel *Far From the Madding Crowd* was, in the opinion of the critic Ian Gregor, the passionate nature of the language of love. In Gregor's eloquent words: 'again and again we are made aware of surges of feeling, arising precipitately, and ransacking language for their expression'.[1] There is great love, too, in Hardy's subsequent work, *The Return of the Native*, of 1878, or so we are supposed to believe. As Hardy's idealistic reformer, Clym Yeobright, takes a (short) break from his educational project, 'his sound and worthy purpose', he sets about wooing the enigmatic Eustacia Vye, a woman who appears to him at first both as a 'melancholy mummer' and 'a romantic martyr to superstition'.[2] To Clym at the time of his infatuation words do not come easily: 'They remained long without a single utterance, for no language could reach the level of their condition: words were as the rusty implements of a by-gone barbarous epoch, and only to be occasionally tolerated' (254). Clym Yeobright cannot find the right words, the new words, to express his new feelings. But whatever the limitations of the language of love, the most passionate language in the text, the reader may well come to feel, is that of hate, as Yeobright, about to strike Eustacia Vye, now his wife, desists and resorts to verbal violence instead. At this moment his is a 'barbarous' language indeed. In a dramatic scene, which few critics have chosen to dwell upon, Yeobright seizes upon the available evidence as signs of his wife's guilt. He puts the worst interpretation upon her actions; he is convinced that she is the cause of his mother's death. A contemporary of Hardy might have had some problems understanding Eustacia, she is after all fairly unconventional. But the novel comes up with explanations that serve as justifications for her strange ways. Most likely the reader will find there are sufficient reasons to exonerate her.[3]

A cultivated reader of the time might well wonder, however, whether one could ever

---

[1] *The Great Web: The Form of Hardy's Fiction* (London: Faber and Faber, 1974), p. 51.
[2] All references are to the Penguin Edition, Harmondsworth, 1978, edited and with an introduction by George Woodcock: p. 238.
[3] According to Robert Langbaum in the novel we are provided with a moral and a psychological reading of her character. According to the moral reading Eustacia 'makes a wrong moral choice ... according to the psychological reading [she] is a victim of circumstances'. See *Thomas Hardy In Our Time* (London: Macmillan, 1995), pp. 95–111.

find a satisfactory explanation – find the precise reasons – for Yeobright's troubling behaviour.[4] Neither at the time he confronts his wife, nor later, does Yeobright grasp the implications of his speech-acts. Anticipating the theories of French sociologist Gaston Bouthoul, Hardy's narrative uncovers the connections between language employment and cultural survivals or aspects of *mentalité*. Crucially, in this novel there is no unmaking of certain connections revealed in potent speech-acts; there is no undoing of their damage. It was the view of Hardy's contemporary, philosopher F.H. Bradley, that a man's 'common heritage', the ideas and sentiments expressed in the language of his childhood, 'stamps' his mind 'indelibly'. Published two years before the novel made its appearance, Bradley's *Ethical Studies* made the trenchant claim that 'when [an individual] can separate himself from that world, and know himself apart from it, then by that time his self, the object of his self-consciousness, is penetrated, *infected*, characterized by the existence of others'.[5] What seems to have left its mark on Hardy is just this idea of the possible *contagion* of one's cultural heritage.

Having in a series of fascinating chapters illuminated 'the custom[s] of the country' or community, Hardy moves centre-stage a character whose ethical idealism might endow his life with meaning at the same time as it is intended to enrich the lives of others. 'Mother, what is doing well?' Yeobright asks on his return to Egdon Heath. His own ideal can be understood in terms of a search for fulfilment that somewhat paradoxically involves personal loss: 'He wished to raise the class at the expense of individuals rather than individuals at the expense of the class. What was more, he was ready at once to be the first unit sacrificed' (230). Yeobright will give up his job in Paris, and abjuring material gain and comforts work strenuously on his educational project. In striving to realize his aim, Yeobright creates an opportunity for the exercise of his own talents, for the realization of an apparently worthwhile goal which will confer satisfaction and sense of self-fulfilment. He may expect to gain the pleasure that is the feeling of 'self-realizedness', and that obtains, F.H. Bradley had suggested, from finding an appropriate role within one's community.[6] However, in order to understand what happens to 'thwart and spoil' a life driven by good intentions we must peruse the dynamics of his relationships with those with whom he is most intimate, those whose happiness is closely bound up with his own.

Yeobright's 'darkened understanding', we discover, means that at critical moments he fails to achieve the moral competence that is manifest in appropriate action: he lacks the lucid responsibility that underlies self-direction. Failing to take the initiative at crucial times, Yeobright fails those closest to him: his mother and his wife. If, like the wanderer on the Heath, the reader of this novel, is looking for 'complete

---

[4] Edward Neill notes that 'In this novel Hardy is a connoisseur of 'faultlines' which indicate divisions in society, and between persons, but also within them': *The Secret Life of Thomas Hardy* (Aldershot: Ashgate, 2004), p. 43.

[5] F.H. Bradley, *Ethical Studies* (2nd edn, Oxford: Clarendon Press, 1927), p. 172, emphasis added.

[6] See F.H. Bradley's discussion of this form of pleasure in 'Selfishness and Self-sacrifice' in *Ethical Studies*, pp. 260–62.

effects and explanations', then he or she might start by attending to the influence of a place and culture on one of the 'more thinking among mankind'. But they might also consider the repercussions of the sensibilities *and* insensibilities that define this 'modern type' of man.

*

From the first page of the first chapter when Hardy's hypothetical furze-cutter attempts to read the sky and the earth and thus come to a decision as to his best course of action, the act of interpretation is viewed as a significant – and we may come to the conclusion that it is perhaps *the most significant* – moment in human life: 'Looking upwards, a furze-cutter would have been inclined to continue work; looking down, he would have decided to finish his faggot and go home' (53). For the characters in Hardy's novel, as for the (imaginary) labourer, interpreting means having to get to grips with the way things look. It means trying to establish the truth by deciphering the available information, making sense of signs, sounds, appearances: all the elements manifest at a moment in time that have some crucial bearing on one's own life, and which provide a reason for what one might do next. However, the evidence provided by Nature in this place and at this time is simply contradictory: 'while day stood distinct in the sky', 'the heath wore the appearance of an instalment of night'. In this place, the signs cannot be trusted to produce an unambiguous answer to the question of what to think, and hence how to act. Yet paradoxically it is only at these mysterious times that a special kind of knowledge emerges, when 'the great and particular glory of the Egdon waste' can be understood: for 'nobody could be said to understand the heath who had not been there at such a time', only then can 'its complete effect and explanation' be discerned (53).

This text insists on our compulsive curiosity, on our constant and obsessive need to make sense of our surroundings, on our quest for 'explanations' or meaning.[7] Now we will want to know the 'true tale of the heath'. But the kind of understanding we are most interested in acquiring relates, it would seem, to an elusive phenomenon. For the ideal reader of this novel can scarcely help but wonder about the effect of the moods of the heath on the moods of those with a 'subtler and scarcer instinct': this is the instinct which belongs to 'the more thinking of mankind' (54–5). These individuals will instinctively feel themselves in harmony with this primitive place; they will feel its fascination and will moreover want to become part of it, merge with it, by donning the raiment appropriate to the landscape, for 'we seem to want the oldest and simplest human clothing where the clothing of the earth is so primitive' (56). For the modern mind, 'the mind adrift on change', this primitive world has a strong appeal: as it exerts it pull so does it gives a sense of stability, a necessary

---

[7] For a wide-ranging approach to the problem of the need to create meaning in an impersonal world see Vincent Newey, *Centring the Self: Subjectivity, Society and Reading from Thomas Gray to Thomas Hardy* (Aldershot: Ashgate, 1995).

'ballast'. Clym Yeobright's return to the heath and his merger with the earth through manual labour thus 'appears at first a major access of power: a re-entry into a state of primordial warmth'.[8] At times Clym attains the kind of peace of mind or well-being that is 'positive and profound'.[9] In what other ways this place will exert its power, what other effects this primitive world might have on 'the more thinking of mankind' will only be revealed much later in the narrative through the language of passion. As the bonfires start to light up on Egdon Heath the reader's view of this primitive world must find space to accomodate not only impressive aspects of Nature, but also the timeless rituals of an ancient culture.

As Chapter One closes, a road is discerned that traverses the lower level of the heath, and in Chapter Two an old man is to be seen walking along it. With this appearance of 'Humanity ... upon the Scene', the search for explanations and the business of interpretation begins in earnest. From the beginning of Chapter Two the attempt to find explanations – satisfactory or satisfying – gets well underway as characters strive to come up with credible reasons, as they try to to discern the meaning of a set of circumstances. Such urgent endeavour constitutes in this narrative a major organizing principle, crucially creating and informing action and event, and structuring the process that is plot.

Now, we find, it is not only Nature that has to be understood. Characters are from the start shown to be engaged in grasping and interpreting the meanings that underlie individual actions and social practices. The narrator has to guess at the old man's occupation. The old man himself is sure of the meaning of his fellow traveller's red appearance, but curious as to what he has in his cart. While we read that 'the natural query of an observer would have been, Why should such a promising being as this have hidden his prepossessing exterior by adopting that singular occupation?' (59). There is a great deal that is obscure on Egdon Heath, and the urge to interpret these phenomena, to find 'an intelligible meaning' is described as 'natural', 'instinctive'. Thus on first glimpsing the form of Eustacia 'the *first instinct* of an imaginative stranger might have been to suppose it the person of one of the Celts who built the barrow ... It seemed a sort of last man among them, musing for a moment before dropping into eternal night with the rest of his race' (62, emphasis added). Like those of the 'imaginative stranger', interpretations seem at times to issue forth spontaneously. In this case such involuntary readings are simply immediate responses to the tales that have fed the imagination. In trying to make sense of a phenomenon some readings just are compelling, it would appear. But what does the idea of interpretive constraint entail? Hardy's thoughts about how individuals go about making sense of the circumstances in which they find themselves leads to the issue of how far one can control one's interpretations. And this means considering the impact of a particular social and cultural matrix. If Hardy's characters have little control over the way in

---

[8] Andrew Radford, *Thomas Hardy and the Survivals of Time* (Aldershot: Ashgate, 2003), p. 93.

[9] J.C. Dave, *The Human Predicament in Hardy's Novels* (London: Macmillan, 1985), p. 52.

which they interpret the evidence before them it follows that the influences which come into play are critical. One of Hardy's prime concerns in this novel is with the factors that operate in or shape the business of interpretation, with the influences that go into the determination of meaning. The mind is at times so plastic or so permeable to its cultural imprint, Hardy suggests, that it readily and imperceptibly absorbs 'diseased' notions: insidious ideas can become so firmly embedded at some level of the consciousness as to become virtually ineradicable. And this brings to the fore the problem of responsibility, of the kind of responsibility one might have for interpretations, or misinterpretations, that are, as it were, 'forced' upon one. In *The Return of the Native* Hardy reviews the problem of the conditions that inhibit autonomous thought and the practice of self-direction.

*

For the narrator interpreting the landscape of Egdon Heath means searching for an 'intelligible meaning' from which may derive a state of aesthetic or intellectual 'satisfaction' (56). But more than satisfaction may hang on getting the reading right. When the lovely, lonely, and dissatisfied Eustacia Vye views Hardy's hero from afar, she is soon encouraged by signs both real and imaginary to feel that she is destined to form a happy union with him. Confidently interpreting both his appearance and his bearing, she attributes to him refinement of character and gentility. Willfully misreading his intentions, she convinces herself that he can be persuaded to leave the heath. Once they are married the consequences of interpreting words, deeds, looks, gestures and silences is nothing if not serious. Eustacia's interpretion of Mrs Yeobright's question as to whether she has received a gift of money from Wildeve (her previous lover) sets the plot on its course towards tragedy. Her interpretation of the older woman's words is too acute; she comes up with a reading that she would have done better to suppress. For Eustacia construes Mrs Yeobright's inquiry as an accusation that she has been receiving 'dishonourable presents' (302) from Wildeve after her marriage. From this point onwards openly expressed hostility divides the two women. What may strike the reader as somewhat ominous is Clym Yeobright's response to his wife's account of the meeting. As he tries to understand exactly what happened between them, as he endeavours to discover the precise 'meaning' of his mother's words, his own words betray a desire to attribute guilt to one or the other. Thus his first question 'How could she have asked you that?' is followed swiftly by 'O, there must be some misapprehension. *Whose fault was it* that her meaning was not made clear?' (307, emphasis added). What might have been thought of as a terrible misunderstanding has become a matter of wrongdoing.

At the time Mrs Yeobright makes her valiant attempt to heal the breach between herself and her son and his wife, the well-being of all three hangs on the interpretation of a face at a window. The reader's own interpretation of events will most likely exonerate the first misinterpreter – Eustacia – when she fails to open the door to Clym's mother. Her reluctance to do so is explained by her feelings – her dislike and unease, her determination not to have to face the mother's hostility. 'But how can I open the door to her, when she dislikes me – wishes to see not me, but her son? I won't open the door!" she exclaims to Wildeve. But the narrative of events can hardly be misinterpreted: the reader can account for Eustacia's crucial mistake. When Mrs Yeobright knocks a second time both Eustacia and Wildeve gather the same information and interpret it in the same way: 'They could hear Clym moving in the other room, *as if disturbed by the knocking*, and he uttered the word "Mother"' (346, emphasis added). Eustacia's misinterpretation of what is happening in the next room is described in such a way as to suggest that this is no wilful act of self-deception: '"Yes – he is awake – he will go to the door," she said, with a breath of relief. "Come this way. I have a bad name with her, and you must not be seen. Thus I am obliged to act by stealth, not because I do ill, but because others are pleased to say so"' (346).

Yet it is equally the case that Eustacia's interpretation provides her with a reason to persist in the kind of conduct that is most in keeping with her feelings. She grasps at a reading of circumstances that enables her to circumvent any thought of what she ought to do. Her reading is compelling because it is so convenient. Some interpretations are, it would seem, simply irresistible. When, previously, Eustacia had asked Mrs Yeobright how she could have 'suspected me of secretly favouring another man for money', Mrs Yeobright's reply implies that she, too, acted under some kind of compulsion: 'I could not help what I thought' (304). Her words suggest that she was not free to act otherwise, that she had no choice; she had no control over what she thought.

For all the power of her assumptions, Mrs Yeobright does nevertheless – as we have seen – make the effort to achieve a reconciliation. But the start of her visit of good will signals another failure: a failure to engage in the necessary interpretive act when it is vital to do so:

> Thursday, the thirty-first of August, was one of a series of days during which snug houses were stifling, and when cool draughts were treats … In Mrs Yeobright's garden large-leaved plants of a tender kind flagged by ten o'clock in the morning: rhubarb bent downward at eleven; and even stiff cabbages were limp by noon.
>
> It was about eleven o'clock on this day that Mrs Yeobright started across the heath towards her son's house, to do her best in getting reconciled with him and Eustacia, in conformity with her words to the reddleman. (337)

As Mrs Yeobright sets out she ignores the eloquent signs of nature, the wilting flowers, that proclaim that she has chosen the wrong day, or the wrong time of day, to visit her son and daughter-in-law. This failure to read is subsequently compounded by what can only be called a hermeneutic disaster. For her interpretation of what happens when she gets to the cottage and finds the closed door and sees the face at the window, is fatal. It is fatal to herself. Hurrying away, she has disappeared by the time Eustacia decides to open the door.

After her death, an opportunity for some kind of reconciliation between Yeobright and his wife requires a re-interpretation. Such an initiative on Yeobright's part may well be interpreted by the reader as a sign of his capacity to change; seemingly, he can now think new thoughts and move on. Reflecting on Eustacia's manner when he had accused her of receiving a lover in the cottage, Yeobright becomes convinced that there were after all 'no signs of dishonour', and hence that 'an absolutely dark interpretation of her act towards his mother was no longer forced upon him' (410). No longer acted upon, no longer 'forced' to interpret in a certain manner, Yeobright makes an attempt to contact his wife. But the upshot is odd: if this taking of the initiative means that Yeobright can envisage a new, positive, active, role for himself, so too does his letter writing testify to his vision of himself as a man whose words have been determined by another. Looking to the future, he still clings to a self-justifying version of what happened in the past. This is an appraisal that will exonerate him of responsibility – responsibility for his own (cruel) words:

> MY DEAR EUSTACIA, – I must obey my heart without consulting my reason too closely. Will you come back to me? Do so, and the past shall never be mentioned. I was too severe; but O, Eustacia, the provocation! You don't know, you never will know, what those words of anger cost me *which you drew down upon yourself.* (412, emphasis added)

These words have in fact left a strong impression on Eustacia's mind. His language still resonates, making all thought of a new start problematic. For Eustacia re-interpreting his discourse may not be possible, for at the moment of violent confrontation Yeobright accused her of being a witch.

*

Lionel Trilling noted in *Beyond Culture* that culture furnishes an individual with 'his *categories and habits of thought,* his range of feeling, his idiom and tones of speech'.[10] In Hardy's first version of the novel the reader was left in no doubt at all as to the category in which to place Eustacia Vye. In her initial appearance, Eustacia – then called Avice – was altogether more sinister. Indeed, 'she was to have suggested a satanic creature supernatural in origin'.[11] Given to ready anger and strange bursts of laughing, when pierced by Susan Nunsuch's needle, Avice utters 'three most terrible screeches'.[12] The violence of the deed may be dreadful, but so too, the reader may feel, is Avice's reaction. Equally significant, in the early version of chapter VII we find the narrator's comment/description that 'had it been possible for the earth and mankind to be entirely in her grasp ... there would have been the same sudden changes from fair to foul, from foul to fair ...'. Here the allusion to the incantations of the three witches in Macbeth, suggests that the narrator is in full agreement with the peasant chorus that 'Avice Vye [was] a witch'.[13] In Paterson's view such a loaded reading of Avice's character was no longer admissable once Hardy began to feel

---

[10] 'Preface to *Beyond Culture*' (1965), in *The Moral Obligation to be Intelligent: Selected Essays,* ed. and with an introduction by Leon Wieseltier (New York: Farrar, Straus, Giroux, 2000), p. 551, emphasis added.
[11] See John Paterson, *The Making of the Return of the Native, University of California Publications: Studies in English* 19 (Berkeley, 1960), p. 17.
[12] Paterson, *The Making of the Return of the Native,* p. 25.
[13] Paterson, *The Making of the Return of the Native,* p. 18.

increasing sympathy for her. Sympathy may come into it, but I would suggest that Hardy's rewriting of Eustacia had to happen for another reason. The change in her representation was required somewhat paradoxically as a result of the development in Hardy's conception of his 'hero'. This rethinking involved not only the major theme of Yeobright's 'modern' predicament and idealism – his attempt 'to argue upon the possibility of culture before luxury to the bucolic world' – but this reconfiguration of Eustacia would have important consequences, Hardy realized, with regard to the moral issue of Yeobright's responsibility for the deaths of his mother and his wife.

John Paterson's account of Hardy's rewriting points up some of the implications of the change taking place in the construction of Yeobright's character:

> There is some evidence, certainly, that the role of humanitarian reformer that Clym was called upon to play was not an altogether natural extension of his personality. 'The humblest walk of life would satisfy him,' Hardy was to report, 'if it could be made to work in with some form of his culture scheme'. Originally, however, [Hardy] ascribed to him a markedly different motive, a motive less suggestive of the humanitarian than of Hamlet – Clym wanted to be free not to educate the masses but 'to think his own thoughts'.[14]

Paterson does not comment on the small but significant revision of the revision: in the passage he cites from Hardy's manuscript 'some form of culture scheme' replaces the earlier phrase 'some form of education scheme'. While other changes which relate to Eustacia also served to indicate the especial significance that 'culture' had come to assume in Hardy's conception of these lives. Thus Hardy was to add to an expression of Eustacia's fear that she might be supplanted by a rival the phrase 'some woman far beneath herself in culture'.[15] In short, if Eustacia's cultivation was to act as an attraction for Yeobright above and beyond her beauty, providing him with an additional motive to stay on the Heath, Yeobright's own 'culture' project provided Hardy with a thematic principle of great ironic potential. Here was his point of departure for what was to become a multifaceted inquiry into the power and meaning of 'culture'. Significantly, what was subsequently deleted from the text: the words that Clym wanted 'to think his own thoughts', is now present in the novel not as a statement of this character's intent, but as an issue that is bound up with the problem of the function of culture. For the question the text poses is precisely: To what extent can Yeobright be said 'to think his own thoughts?' and hence be held responsible for the actions which derive from them? The textual changes made are particularly important with respect to our reading of Hardy's hero's interpretations of his wife's behaviour at the time of his mother's death. Given the original unfavourable bias of the text towards Eustacia, Yeobright's hostile attitude to his wife at this point would have been unremarkable, indeed, perfectly understandable. It would have signalled a convergence of all major viewpoints: Clym's enmity conjoining with the suspicion of the other characters, and with the dislike of the narrator *and* the reader. But in the final version of the novel, the

---

[14] Paterson, *The Making of the Return of the Native*, p. 65.
[15] Paterson, *The Making of the Return of the Native*, p. 85.

many changes made to the representation of Eustacia should mean that the reader's attitude to her may even be sympathetic. And hence Yeobright's accusations and what they reveal of his way of thinking should strike us as problematic. But what we should also find problematic, I shall argue, is his long-accepted status as a suffering exemplar of the modern consciousness: of the 'more thinking among mankind'.

*

In the final version of the novel the reader is invited to picture Clym Yeobright as the anguished possessor of 'modern perceptiveness'. Here is a man separated by a 'long line of disillusive centuries' from the 'Hellenic idea of life' (225). Clym Yeobright cannot recapture the Hellenic 'zest for existence', and the observer reads in his face his vision of life 'as a thing to be put up with'. Without a doubt Hardy's Victorian contemporaries would have had no problems finding connections here with the governing themes of Matthew Arnold's influential text *Culture and Anarchy*, which was published nine years earlier, in 1869.[16] The 'mental luminousness' (194) which Yeobright lacks corresponds precisely to the '*unclouded clearness of mind*, [the] *unimpeded play of thought*' that was 'the uppermost idea' with Hellenism according to Arnold (128, emphasis added). In his well known essay *Culture and Anarchy* Arnold is concerned to outline the differences between what he terms the two major 'disciplines' or 'forces' of Hebraism and Hellenism. These cultural movements function for Arnold not only as comprehensive systems of knowledge, but also as inspirational models which provided mankind with designs for living well and especially for thinking well. Indeed, the aim of both kinds of culture was to foster specific states of mind. Hebraism strives to inculcate 'strictness of conscience', supplanting the 'spontaneity of consciousness' that characterized Hellenism at its best. In Arnold's words 'as Hellenism speaks of *thinking clearly*, seeing things in their essence and beauty, as a grand and precious feat for man to achieve, so Hebraism speaks of becoming conscious of sin, of awakening to a sense of sin, as a feat of this kind' (131, emphasis added). With the cultural predominance of Hebraism, thought is infused by the notion of sin, and achieving mental clearness hence becomes a challenge. The danger, which finds an echo in the title to Chapter 2 of Book the Fifth of Hardy's novel, 'A Lurid Light Breaks in upon a Darkened Understanding', is articulated in Arnold's repetition of the admonitory words of Bishop Wilson: 'take care that your light be not darkness' (126).

Culture figures in Arnold's text not only as a mode of thinking but also as a special kind of knowledge garnered from different periods and writers. The province of an intellectual elite, it is 'the best' that has been thought. This is clearly in Hardy's words, 'Knowledge of a sort which brings wisdom rather than affluence' (230); it is the knowledge which supplies the content of a modern proselytizing vision. In this sense culture contributes to, and is the sign of, private accomplishment or enrichment, and

---

[16] 'Culture and Anarchy: An Essay in Political and Social Criticism (1867–69)', in Stefan Collini (ed.), *Culture and Anarchy and Other Writings* (Cambridge: Cambridge University Press, 1993), pp. 53–187.

as such it is to be contrasted with a public realm of common assumptions and ideas. This distinction between knowledge as the basis of self-cultivation, and knowledge as grounding common thought and practice has been applied to the novel. If critics have agreed on one thing, it is that Yeobright's exile in Paris, his education and idealism, his private accomplishment which has contributed to his 'developed consciousness', have cut him off from his original culture – the realm of common knowledge and practices to which he returns.

Clym's idealism, a 'kind of high rationality', means for Bruce Johnson that 'he loses touch with the living vitality of his own culture'.[17] For Ian Gregor, Yeobright's is a 'sophisticated consciousness;' 'he is part of the evolving consciousness of the age', one who 'can admit into Wessex a world beyond its boundaries, and, in so doing, can inoculate it against the quaint'.[18] In Terry Eagleton's analysis of modes of imagery, Yeobright is seen to be 'trapped at [a] point of agonized tension between the complexities of developed consciousness and the thwarting constructions of an immediate material context'.[19] Beginning with a discussion of contemporary anthropological theories of stages of knowledge, Patricia O'Hara goes on to argue that *The Return of the Native* is concerned with the 'intellectual progress of the race'. The novel shows Hardy contrasting 'primitive perception and habits of mind' with Clym Yeobright's 'modern rationalism'. According to O'Hara, 'While the rustics may be agents of unchanging human impulses, they are also represented as impediments to progress. The cultural space they inhabit is, so to speak, eons away from that of Clym Yeobright and the narrative consciousness that tells his tale'.[20] 'The narration,' claims O'Hara, 'is equivocal in its judgement of each' (155–6). In *Darwin's Plots* Gillian Beer focuses on the Native's predicament from the perspective of Darwin's theory of evolution and its impact on Hardy's thought; and her topic is 'the near impossibility of return': 'In an evolutionary order it is not possible to choose to return to an earlier state'. Yeobright's desire to educate the other inhabitants makes him 'an invader – an alien force which disrupts and changes'.[21] Here I would like to suggest that all the readings mentioned share a common failing in so far as they foreclose upon a question that is of prime interest to Hardy in this work. And that question is: How does an individual's thought world respond to or connect with his culture?

That the writing of Matthew Arnold has a particular relevance to Hardy's views on such a subject is clear. Terminating his essay on Hellenism and Hebraism, Arnold suddenly switches to the perspective of the individual member of society. If he is to

---

[17] Bruce Johnson, 'Pastoralism and Modernity', in H. Bloom (ed.), *Thomas Hardy's The Return of the Native* (New York, Chelsea House, 1987), p. 128.
[18] Gregor, *The Great Web*, p. 80.
[19] Terry Eagleton, 'Thomas Hardy: Nature as Language', *Critical Quarterly* 13 (1971): 155–62.
[20] Patricia O'Hara, 'Narrating the Native: Victorian Anthropology and Hardy's *The Return Of the Native*', *Nineteenth-Century Contexts* 20 (1997): 147–63.
[21] Gillian Beer, *Darwin's Plots: Evolutionary Narrative in Darwin, George Eliot and Nineteenth-Century Fiction* (London: Routledge and Kegan Paul, 1983), p. 254.

emerge from the confusion that has arisen from the clash of the two cultural systems and get 'a clue to some sound order and authority' then the individual needs, Arnold claims, 'to go back upon the actual *instincts and forces which rule [his] life*, seeing them as they really are, connecting them with other instincts and forces, and enlarging [his] whole view and rule of life' (137, emphasis added). Surveying his own time, Arnold finds that the culture of Hebraism continues to function as a conditioning 'force'. But Arnold is convinced that it is a power which need not condition us entirely *if* we see both our instincts and our culture 'as they really are'. For Arnold culture constitutes both a mental phenomenon, 'an inward condition of the mind and spirit', and an ideational frame or boundary which can be transcended, it would appear, by the intellectually active who, partially (?) immune to any ill effects, can travel both backwards and forwards capturing what is valuable in the thought of past and present cultures, strenuously making 'the effort to see things as they really are'. The Arnold who finishes his essay on such an optimistic note has resolved for himself an earlier troubling thought. But it is a thought which continues to perplex Hardy:

> It is all very well to talk of getting rid of one's ignorance, of seeing things in their reality, seeing them in their beauty; but how is this to be done when there is something which thwarts and spoils all our efforts? This something is sin ... under the name of sin, the difficulties of knowing oneself and conquering oneself ... become ... a positive, active entity hostile to man. (131)

Despite his extensive reading of modern socialist tracts, Hardy's returning Native is, we shall see, highly susceptible to the 'force' of Hebraism, to the power of the idea of guilt or sinfulness. But we find traces of another influential contemporary text within Hardy's narrative. In the opinion of anthropologist E.B. Tylor, writing only three years after Arnold, culture embraces a far wider range of phenomena.[22] In his famous definition culture or 'civilization' is a whole way of life in which the individual is seemingly enveloped: it is a 'complex whole, which includes knowledge, belief, art, laws, morals, custom, and any other capabilities and habits acquired by man as a member of society'.[23] For Tylor, the picture of man's relation to his culture is complicated by the so-called 'doctrine of survivals'. Survivals, according to this theory, bring the past into the present, but it is a past which is often emptied of meaning, for survivals may be 'worn out' customs (144) or 'fossilized' myths (20).[24] According

---

[22] On the importance of Tylor's work to Hardy see Andrew Radford, *Thomas Hardy and the Survivals of Time*.

[23] E.B. Tylor, *Primitive Culture : Researches into the Development of Mythology, Philosophy, Religion, Language, Art and Custom* (2 vols, London: John Murray, 1871), vol. 1, p. 1.

[24] The narrator comments in the novel on the difference between a 'mere revival' among traditional pastimes and a 'survival' which is carried on with a 'stolidity and absence of stir': 'the agents seem moved by an inner compulsion to say and do their allotted parts whether they will or no. This unweeting manner of performance is the true ring by which, in this refurbishing age, a fossilized survival may be known from a spurious reproduction': p. 178.

to Tylor, although traditional practices may continue and the words associated with them may be spoken, usually they lose their power to affect an individual's thought or emotions. But this is not always the case. If survivals are 'processes, customs and opinions' – the proofs and examples of an older condition of culture out of which a newer has evolved – their continuation may not simply be due to 'force of habit': if 'most of what we call superstition is included within survival', then some 'opinions' or 'ideas' may still act as vital forces 'for good and evil'.[25]

On Egdon Heath superstition has survived as a potent force, providing the Native with his *raison d'être*: superstition is precisely the justification for his 'culture' project. On hearing how Susan Nunsuch had pricked Eustacia with the stocking needle, 'Yeobright said quietly to his mother, "Do you think I have turned teacher too soon?"' Her words in reply are perceptive and prophetic, though she does not realise this, for her meaning is connected only with considerations of his social and economic status: '"It is right that there should be schoolmasters, and missionaries, and all such men," she replied. "But it is right, too, that I should try to lift you out of this life into something richer, and that *you should not come back again, and be as if I had not tried at all*"' (236, emphasis added).

Socially, the Yeobrights belong on a different level from the rest of the inhabitants of the Heath. Of Mrs Yeobright, the curate's daughter, the narrator notes that her sense of superiority came from her 'consciousness of superior communicative power' (83). Both Yeobrights might claim greater powers of understanding; their education has given them that modern trait – a more sceptical outlook on life. It is a healthy scepticism that is revealed in Mrs Yeobright's comment on Eustacia Vye: 'people say she's a witch but of course that's absurd' (221). Notoriously, however, as Hardy realized, superstition is insidious. Why else does Mrs Yeobright throw a slipper at the retreating figure of Thomasin leaving her house to be married to Wildeve? In Mrs Yeobright's remark the 'but' marks the contradiction in her thought. 'There, I don't believe in old superstitions, *but* I'll do it' (216, emphasis added). Mrs Yeobright's action is a sign of (partial) conformity; she participates in a custom of the place. As Tylor observed, 'the civilized mind still bears vestiges neither few nor slight of a past condition' (62).

Endeavouring to explain the underlying cohesion that is characteristic of culture as the 'whole way of living' of a place or community, Tylor quotes von Humboldt that 'Man ever connects on from what lies at hand' (17). On his return, Hardy's hero apparently has little to 'connect' him any longer to the heath folk. He has left Paris, refusing to stay 'with people who had hardly anything in common with myself'. But his conversation with the men gathered at the scene of the haircutting demonstrates their failure to understand his 'maning' (meaning), and he seems to have little in common with them either (229).[26] Yet connections there are, the narrative will reveal:

---

[25] Tylor, *Primitive Culture*, vol. 1, p. 15.
[26] According to Andrew Radford, 'Hardy employs Clym ... to investigate the idea of continuity as a thing treasured in itself. Through the returned native, Hardy suggests the dangers of a too exclusively civilized or analytical mode of mental life'. Clym's 'altruistic fantasy of educating the illiterate heathfolk constitutes a major threat to the "nearly

connections of which Yeobright is seemingly unaware. They are disclosed in the discourses which centre on Eustacia. In Hardy's well-structured plot Eustacia Vye is the object of two acts of cruelty separated in time by an interlude in which love but also misinterpretations are generated. In the first of the discourses Christian Cantle explains to the Yeobrights how Eustacia is wounded in church by Susan Nunsuch. In the second, she is subjected to Yeobright's physical and verbal aggression.

> 'Tis news you have brought us, then Christian?' said Mrs Yeobright.
> 'Ay, sure, about a witch … [Susan Nunsuch] 've waited for this chance for weeks, so as to draw her blood and put an end to the bewitching of Susan's children that has been carried on so long …'
> 'Tis a cruel thing,' said Yeobright ….
> 'Truly now we shall see if there's anything in what folks say about her' [said Humphrey]. (235–6)

Later in the day the conversation about Eustacia resumes when Sam the turf-cutter enters. At this point Mrs Yeobright expresses a view of Eustacia which is purportedly factual and yet manages to be if not openly hostile, then certainly ambivalent: 'I have never heard that she is of any use to herself or to other people. Good girls don't get treated as witches even on Egdon'. To which Yeobright replies 'Nonsense – that proves nothing either way'; then questioning Sam: 'Is this young *witch-lady* going to stay long at Mistover?' (237, emphasis added).

After Clym has married the young '*witch lady*' communication breaks down between both mother and son and mother-in-law and daughter-in-law, as we have seen. The mother dies and the son bitterly repents not having made the attempt to see her before she set out on her fatal journey to visit them. Then, in the chapter entitled 'A Lurid Light Breaks in upon a Darkened Understanding', Yeobright hears from Susan Nunsuch and her son that Eustacia saw his mother arrive at their cottage and yet the door was kept shut: 'Kept shut, she looking out of windows? Good heart of God! – what does it mean?' His reading follows on fast. Where Eustacia has been actively evil: 'You shut the door – you had a man in the house with you – you sent her away to die …'. He and his mother have become innocent victims of the evil-doer:

> 'Do you brave me? do you stand me out, mistress? Answer. Don't look at me with those eyes as if you would bewitch me again! Sooner than that I die ….'
> 'Call her to mind – think of her – what goodness there was in her: it showed in every line of her face! Most women [which clearly includes Eustacia], even when but slightly annoyed, show a *flicker of evil* in some curl of the mouth or some corner of the cheek; but as for her, never in her angriest moments was there anything malicious in her look'. (393, emphasis added)

---

perished" links between obsolete forms of life and those which generally prevail'. But it would also, claims Hadford, 'expunge the more unglamorous and baleful "instincts of merry England" … in particular the savage ignorance of Susan Nunsuch's black witchcraft': *Thomas Hardy and the Survivals of Time*, pp. 90–92.

What follows afterwards is extraordinary: savage and cruel, his words, which echo those of Christian and Humphrey, are meant to destroy as surely as the curse on Eustacia soon to be uttered by Susan Nunsuch: '*How bewitched I was!* How could there be any good in a woman that *everybody spoke ill of?*' (395, emphasis added). It is the appeal to '*everybody's*' opinion that gives Yeobright away. It provides the 'proof' not of Eustacia's guilt but of his own collusion or complicity: it signals a connection. 'Popularly,' noted Tylor in his discussion of the phenomenon of the 'evil eye', 'what *everybody says must be true,* what *everybody* does must be right'.[27] Eustacia's eyes are 'bewitching' – a word repeated twice – but it is not their seductive power Yeobright fears. Rather he suggests he has fallen victim to their malefic effect. His 'wild' words of condemnation are the expression of a consciousness still at some level in touch with its primitive origins.

> breaking down at last; and, shaking with sobs which choked her [Eustacia], sank upon her knees. 'O, will you have done! O, you are too relentless – there's a limit to the *cruelty of savages!* I have held out long – but you crush me down.' (395, emphasis added)

Significant patterns thus emerge in the speech acts in these scenes, connecting Yeobright to the natives, who are now (ironically) the bearers of knowledge and the arbiters of truth. But what can account for the close correspondences in these discourses? In *Physics and Politics,* the work of Hardy's famous contemporary Walter Bagehot, which was completed in 1876 two years before the novel, a theory is expounded as to the reasons for verbal affinities within communities. The human mind possesses an innate tendency 'to become like what is around it': 'the propensity of man to imitate what is before him [constitutes] one of the strongest parts of his nature'.[28] It is the view of Christopher Herbert that Bagehot 'stresses more forcefully than any other writer had so far the unconscious and the fundamental irrationality of the imitative instinct, and he very suggestively focuses on linguistic "style" as the essence of what is imitated. As he does so the rhetoric of magical transmission creeps into his argument'.[29] In an important passage Bagehot finds men powerless before the insidious influence of language: 'Most men catch the words that are in the air, and the rhythm which comes to them they do not know from whence; an unconscious imitation determines their words, and makes them say what of themselves they would never have thought of saying'.[30]

According to Bagehot, men have little or no choice, they are bewitched by words: 'we must not think that this imitation is voluntary ... Insensibly and as by a sort of magic, the kind of manner which a man catches eats into him' (92–6). Moreover, the theorist noted, 'unbelief far oftener needs a reason and requires an effort than

---

[27] Tylor, *Primitive Culture*, vol. 1, p. 12, emphasis added.
[28] Walter Bagehot, *Physics and Politics* (London: F. Morgan, 1876), p. 92.
[29] *Culture and Anomie: Ethnographic Imagination in the Nineteenth Century* (Chicago: University of Chicago Press, 1991), p. 141.
[30] Bagehot, *Physics and Politics*, p. 33.

belief. ... The mere presentation of an idea, unless we are careful about it, or unless there is within some unusual resistance, makes us believe it; and this is why the belief of others adds to our belief so quickly, for no ideas seem so very clear as those inculcated on us from every side' (94). Such a remark seems peculiarly relevant to what happens to Yeobright as he listens to the narrative of his mother's last painful moments (387–8). He may ask Susan Nunsuch 'what does it mean?' But he soon decides: there is no resistance to the idea that Eustacia intended to harm his mother, that she is a 'murderess', who should get 'the torment' she deserves. In the case of Clym Yeobright a propensity and 'magical' process 'makes him in the end what at first he [does not] seem' (96).

For the French sociologist, Gaston Bouthoul, such thought patterns or *mentalité* are part of the cultural identity of an individual from the very beginning of his life within a given community. They are moreover extraordinarily tenacious:

> Derrière toutes les différences et les nuances individuelles il subsiste une sorte de residu psychologique stable, fait de jugements, de concepts et de croyances aux quels adhèrent au fond tous les individus d'une même société. Cet ensemble constitue la structure mentale specifique de chaque civilisation. C'est ainsi que nous proposons de definir la mentalité du point de vue de la société ... La mentalité est le lien le plus resistant qui rattache l'individu à son groupe. L'éloignement ni l'exil ne suffisent à changer la mentalité même aprés plusieurs generations.[31]

If the theory of *mentalité* holds, the Native can never sever the bonds that connect him to the inhabitants of Egdon Heath, into whose society he was born. The imprint of his cultural heritage can never be erased. In the act of accusing Eustacia, Yeobright recreates or strengthens a connection, and this movement of his thought finds no hindrance in the form of a modern moral principle of fairness. There is no willingness to suspend judgement. Rather judgement is facilitated by a potent inclination or tendency to point the finger of blame: a default attitude of 'sin-awareness'. Someone must be guilty of his mother's death, and therefore someone must be punished. Indeed, Eustacia's own words spoken in response to Yeobright's onslaught, would seem to give weight to an Arnoldian interpretation of the Native's predicament: 'If to have done no harm at all is the only innocence recognized, I am beyond forgiveness', she asserts. '*But I require no help from your conscience*' (393, emphasis added). The 'strictness of conscience' that in Arnold's view characterized Hebraism, is manifest in what becomes in Yeobright almost an obsession with guiltiness and signs of sin. In Yeobright

---

[31] Gaston Bouthoul, *Les Mentalités* (Paris: Presses Universitaires de France, 1952) : 'Despite all the differences and individual nuances there remains a kind of stable psychological residuum, comprising judgments, concepts and beliefs, to which at bottom all individuals of the same society adhere. This cluster constitutes the specific mental structure of each civilization. It is indeed that which we propose to define as mentalité from the social point of view .... Mentalité is the strongest tie which attaches an individual to his group. Neither estrangement nor exile are sufficient to change mentalité even after several generations': pp. 30–31.

a concern for 'acting rightly' is displayed in a readiness to pass judgement, to identify and attack any instance of perceived wrongdoing. This is an outlook that infiltrates all too easily his heuristic endeavours. In striving to reconstruct what happened between his wife and mother during the angry exchange over the gift of the guineas, he displays an attitude that is ominously inquisitorial: 'whose fault was it that her meaning was not made clear?' (307) he demands of Eustacia. Later, awareness of his neglect of his mother before her death provokes an overpowering sense of sinfulness: 'I committed the guilt; and may the whole burden be on my head!' he says, as if invoking God's wrath (373). At the time of the confrontation when Eustacia speaks of his 'blunders' and 'misfortunes', which have been a wrong to her, Yeobright's reply, 'I don't know what you mean by that. Am I the cause of your sin?' (394) reveals just how profoundly the idea of sinfulness has 'engaged [his] spirit'.[32] It is an idea of immense influence, one that fashions a seemingly dominant attitude. Yeobright continues his diatribe asserting that 'Instead of *hating* you I could, I think, mourn for and pity you, if you were *contrite*, and would *confess* all' (393, emphasis added). Rather than explain, Eustacia must repent and be 'contrite', she must 'confess'. At this point we are surely meant to recall the words spoken between them on an earlier occasion and perceive the irony. At that earlier time, eager to interest her in his 'culture scheme', Yeobright states that he 'has come to clean away the cobwebs' that have given Eustacia her 'magical reputation' and asks if she will help him.

> 'I don't quite feel anxious to. I have not much love for my fellow-creatures. Sometimes I quite *hate* them.'
> 'Still I think that if you were to hear my scheme you might take an interest in it. There is no use in *hating* people – if you *hate* anything, you should *hate what produced them*.'
> 'Do you mean Nature?' asks Eustacia. (244, emphasis added) [33]

But she receives no reply.

Where Yeobright is silent, eminent writers on culture were forthright in their views as to the nature and strength of the 'forces' that 'produced' people. They participated in protomodernist debates on the self's fundamental nature as 'construct'. E.B. Tylor is convinced of the 'unity of nature' and the 'fixity of its *laws*'; so that 'our thoughts, wills and actions accord with *laws* as definite as those which govern the motion of waves' (2, emphasis added). In Tylor's account, the phenomena of culture – comprising communal knowledge, customs and superstitions – together constitute the most significant factor affecting the processes of human thought and behaviour. In Bagehot, the notion that man is passive before the power of language is affirmed in

---

[32] Arnold, 'Culture and Anarchy', p. 133.
[33] Maybe Eustacia has been reading Wordsworth's *Prelude*, Book VII, 1805–1806:
   Nor was it mean delight
   To watch crude Nature work in untaught minds;
   To note the laws and progress of belief;
   Though obstinate on this way, yet on that
   How willingly we travel, and how far!

The Magic in Mentalité: *Hardy's Native Returns* 159

a manner that can only be called uncompromising: 'He has lived in an atmosphere of infectious belief, and he has inhaled it' (93). The innate tendency to think and act alike is consolidated in 'the cake of custom', which represses individuality and originality. Of course changes can and do come about in styles of thought and meaning, Bagehot argues. The law of Natural Selection ensures and encodes the principle of variation, the disposition to change which is the 'principle of progress' (64). But when we look closely at the way individuals habitually operate we find that 'if you strengthen the motive in a given direction, mankind tend more to act in that direction'(10).

Matthew Arnold is somewhat more cautious, remarking that Hebraism and Hellenism are neither of them '*the law* of human development', rather they are each of them 'contributions to human development' (133, emphasis added). But this note of caution is absent from the discourse of Hardy's narrator: the Hellenic 'idea of life' is inappropriate, he asserts, 'as we uncover the defects of *natural laws*, and see the quandary that man is in by their operation'(225, emphasis added).

However, Yeobright's quandary lends itself to still further considerations, so that we may want to stress not only the role of a 'strengthened motive', but also the function of an absent motive. Yeobright's predicament is compounded by his failure to act in the right manner at the right time. His tragedy can be traced to his *un*spontaneity, to his blind inertia. On two occasions in waiting for them to come to him he misses the opportunity to save his mother and then his wife. The missing motive – the idea of duty or the feeling of love or compassion, the urgent desire for reunion – that can move the will and hence initiate action, is the most difficult to understand and explain. The desire to be reconciled reasserts itself in Yeobright, but not the desire *physically* to make the first move; and when the step is taken it is too late. The question that arises, and that Hardy leaves ambiguous, is whether we are to attribute Yeobright's immobility to self-absorption, to ambivalence, to male pride or inflexibility, to depleted reserves of sympathy. We can in any case picture Hardy's hero as simply unaware of the moral void before him: his is a sin of omission. At key moments Yeobright loses, to adopt the words of D.H. Lawrence, 'the incomprehensible initiative and control of the individual soul or self'.[34] So active and energetic a man is passive when it matters most: one of the 'more thinking' of mankind, fails to think hard enough about the well-being of those he has caused to suffer.

Yeobright's own words testify to a radical uncertainty as to 'what he is and what makes him so' (Bagehot, 3). There is a time when to Eustacia's remark that 'the world seems all wrong in this place', he can reply 'if we make it so' (354): it is a sturdy affirmation of a belief in self-direction, of the importance of – in Bagehot's words – 'independent and self-choosing thought'. Yet grasping at a reason to explain why he had set out too late to visit his mother, he 'insisted that he must have been horribly perverted by some fiend not to have thought before that it was his duty to go to her, since she did not come to him' (372–3). By the end of the novel he can at one and the same time accept responsibility for having (actively) 'driven two women to their

---

[34] Cited in F.R. Leavis, *Thought, Words and Creativity: Art and Thought in Lawrence* (London: Chatto and Windus, 1976), p. 46.

deaths' and suggest that, as the subject of a divine plan, he is some kind of victim: 'God has set a mark upon me' (464). Contrite but confused, in his state of despair Yeobright is perhaps understandably unclear about the nature of the influences to which he has succumbed, pressures from which neither his knowledge nor his strenuousness have saved him.

In the very last chapter of the novel, fervently devoted to his mother's memory, Yeobright admits that 'It was all my fault' (473). But the other natives clearly prefer other explanations: though his preaching in two languages, a 'simple language on Rainbarrow' and 'a more cultivated strain elsewhere' on 'morally unimpeachable subjects', is hardly a success – 'some believed him and some believed not', – 'everywhere he was kindly received, for the story of his life had become generally known' (474). The story of the Native that was, and still is, 'generally known' is the one that was interpreted at the time to his advantage'.[35] Within his community Clym's story grew, it seems, in the same way as the narratives that sprang up after the deaths of Eustacia and Wildeve: 'All the known incidents of their love were enlarged, distorted, touched up, and modified, till the original reality bore but a slight resemblance to the counterfeit presentation by surrounding tongues' (447). On Egdon Heath and elsewhere, the pursuit of meaning through narrative re-elaboration has meant that Yeobright's image retains its dignity; he is respected and even esteemed. Yeobright continues to be 'kindly received'. The respect he retains may be due in part to his perseverance in seeking a meaningful way of life. Sticking to his cousin's advice, and 'doing whatever will be most comfortable', Clym starts writing his sermons (469). These, he emphasizes, will never be 'dogmatic' (474); they will exemplify – it seems – the virtues of reasonableness. For Yeobright what satisfaction he can salvage is bound up, we may imagine, with the thought that he is finally serving *his* community.

---

[35] This more favourable appraisal finds support in F.H. Bradley's *Ethical Studies*: 'violent emotion may make it impossible for the person to keep two courses before him and decide – impossible to separate himself from the strain put on him, so as either to resist it or to identify himself with it. In such cases the agents can not collect themselves so as to will, and though with knowledge, yet with pain and feeling of guiltiness, as in a dream, they perform some act which is abhorrent to them, and which they impute to themselves with guilt, but which (provided always their fault has not led to it) the sober onlooker may be unable to impute to them, in their character of moral agent ... If there is no theoretical certainty of the future with a systematic principled character, how will it be when the habituated self involves contradictions? ... Many of us show selves to ourselves and the world, which are not the realization of another element which we take about with us, and which quietly, or it may be longingly, remains below the "floor of consciousness"; perhaps never to appear, perhaps to burst out in we know not what, in light or love, or in "dirt and fire"': *Ethical Studies*, pp. 46, 54–5.

Chapter 8

Howards End and the Confession of Imperfection

Irritated by being asked by his lover yet again whether he will marry her, the young clerk Leonard Bast launches into a description of 'the kind of man' he is: 'I don't take heed of what anyone says. I just go straight forward, I do. That's always been my way ... If a woman's in trouble, I don't leave her in the lurch. That's not my street. No, thank you. I'll tell you another thing too, I care a good deal about improving myself by means of Literature and Art, and so getting a wider outlook. For instance, when you came in I was reading Ruskin's *Stones of Venice*. I don't say this to boast, but just to show you the kind of man I am'.[1] Although the woman's response reveals her profound indifference to such ardent aspirations, there were others with whom Leonard Bast's words would resonate. In lining up his interests as evidence that he is not 'one of your weak knock-kneed chaps', Forster's character spoke directly to the heart and mind of another and certainly more interested lady – the philanthropist Helen Dendy Bosanquet, whose work of 1902, *The Strength of the People*, was concerned precisely with the ambitions of Bast's kind of person and with strategies for dealing with his weaknesses.[2]

Like so many others belonging to the 'lower orders', Leonard Bast appears poised on the very edge of the abyss, 'he could see it, and at times people whom he knew had dropped in and counted no more' (58). Bosanquet, too, worried about the prospects of such precarious lives. But there were ways, she was convinced, of warding off the dangers such people faced, of improving their chances of living a decent life.[3] It was essential to gain insight into the achievement of enhanced control over

---

[1] *Howards End* (1910), ed. Oliver Stallybrass (Harmondsworth: Penguin Books, 1973), p. 65; all references in the text are to this edition.

[2] Helen Bosanquet, *The Strength of the People: A Study in Social Economics* (2nd edn, London: Macmillan, 1903).

[3] Peter Widdowson and Daniel Born discuss the importance to Forster of other texts on the 'condition of England problem'; in particular, both focus on the ideas of Masterman. See respectively, *E.M. Forster's 'Howard's End': Fiction as History* (London: Sussex University Press, 1977) and Daniel Born, 'Private Gardens, Public Swamps: *Howards End* and the Revaluation of Liberal Guilt', *Novel* 25 (1992): 141–59. Anne Wright remarks that 'as an Edwardian "Condition of England" novel *Howards End* connects with contemporary non-literary discourse, and most obviously perhaps with C.F.G. Masterman's *The Condition of England* ... the book mapping out for us, by its narrative, the limitations

circumstances. Among reformers, what gave Bosanquet some claim to originality was her thesis that character building was strictly related to the possession of 'interests': if interests make for inner strength so it seems does inner strength make for better lives.

Underlying Bosanquet's optimistic theory was the belief, expressed most succinctly by philosopher, Bernard Bosanquet, her husband and fellow philanthropist, that 'character is the condition of conditions'.[4] Historian Stefan Collini has noted the ubiquity of discourses on 'Character' amongst leading political and economic theorists beginning with John Stuart Mill and continuing via Spencer and Green[5] through to Alfred Marshall.[6] Helen Bosanquet's own and oft' quoted authorities on the subject were Thomas Chalmers, Mill, William James and Alfred Marshall, of whose work she even ventured a criticism. A brief correspondence with the eminent economist ensued when she sent him a copy of the first edition of her book. His letter to her, published in the 1903 edition of her work, reveals that his views on the subject of weak character were equally intense. 'I think I agree with you in the main. I have always held', he wrote, 'that poverty and pain, disease and death are evils of greatly less importance than they appear, except in so far as they lead to weakness of life and character; and that true philanthropy aims at increasing strength more than at the direct and immediate relief of poverty' (vii). As Collini observes, one cannot help feeling that the evil of death was being somewhat underrated by this remark, but one cannot doubt the sincerity of Marshall's conviction that 'it was a central part of the economist's professional task to identify those forces which will help to build up "a strong and righteous character"'.

It was another kind of writer, however, who supplied Helen Bosanquet with the touchstone of Character: the same writer who supplied some of Forster's characters with their own ever elusive ideal. The twin capacity to 'see life steadily and to see it

---

and possibilities of life in England now': *Literature of Crisis, 1910–22* (London: Macmillan, 1984), pp. 23–6. For a recent analysis of the way the ideas of both Masterman and New Liberal theorists resonate within the novel see David Medalie, *E.M. Forster's Modernism* (London: Palgrave Macmillan, 2002).

[4] Bernard Bosanquet, 'Character and Its Bearing on Social Causation', in Bernard Bosanquet (ed.), *Aspects of the Social Problem* (London: Macmillan, 1895), p. vii–viii. See *The Philosophy of the State and the Practice of Welfare: The Writings of Bernard and Helen Bosanquet (Pioneers of Social Welfare)*, Introduction by David Gladstone (London: Routledge, 1996).

[5] For Green 'the good is character', and 'no one can convey a good character to another. Everyone must make his character for himself': T.H. Green, *Prolegomena to Ethics* (Oxford: Kraus reprint, 1969), sec. 332, p. 401. In Forster's novel Margaret Schlegel's experiences with Henry Wilcox would seem to bear out the truth of Green's dictum. For many critics Margaret is to be regarded as a failure precisely because she cannot change Henry Wilcox.

[6] Stefan Collini, 'The Idea of "Character" in Victorian Political Thought', *Transactions of the Royal Historical Society* 35 (1985): 29–50.

whole', the quality prized by Matthew Arnold in his 'Sonnet to A Friend' – became the goal to aspire to. For Bosanquet an individual's interests were the means by which this aim was to be achieved: some people see things always as 'disconnected scraps without meaning ... if we look for the factor which gives *the power to see things steadily and see them whole*, and which distinguishes the rational life from these chaotic wrecks, we shall find it in the "interests" of life as distinct from its appetites' (27–8, emphasis added). At one point, it seems that by 'interests' Bosanquet might mean 'commitments', more or less challenging plans or concerns imbued perhaps with a moral purpose: 'we feel we know nothing of [a new acquaintance] until we know his interests; for it is they which will rule his actions and make him in turn an interest to us. They are at once his clues through life, *and the bonds which unite him to other men*' (28, emphasis added). But as she develops her theme, what she has in mind would seem to be all those manifold elements that contribute to a lifestyle, that mixture of inputs which according to Bosanquet constitute the salient circumstances of an individual's habitual way of life. And the kind of lifestyle an individual creates for himself will apparently make all the difference to his behaviour when adverse conditions intervene; for 'it is the man himself, his wants and interests, that determine his circumstances'. Of his circumstances, almost all are, in Bosanquet's view, subject to the power of choice:

> It is the actual surroundings in which a man lives, the kind of house he inhabits, the people he associates with, the food he eats and the water he drinks, the education and recreation he enjoys, and the work he is obliged to do. This is what we mean by the circumstances which make a man what he is, and mould his life, whether he will or no, for good and evil. ... It is always the man in his selective activity who makes his circumstances, who chooses what his world shall be ... (43–4)

To the question whether Leonard Bast can be saved from the chaos of the abyss by his interests, whether they be Ruskin, Beethoven or walking by night, Foster's short answer would seem to be no. Neither his interests nor 'a bit of good luck' will, Bast thinks, help him 'see the universe': 'To see life steadily and to see it whole was not for the likes of him' (67). But luck does make a difference to Leonard's life. Bad luck, in the form of the enticing upper-middle-class Helen Schlegel, enters the life he was striving to improve via music by taking his umbrella, and some time afterwards exits from it leaving him to spend his last resources on an expensive hotel bill. Thereafter, it is downhill all the way; contingency and biology contributing most decisively to Leonard's downfall.

Foster, it appears, cannot share Bosanquet's faith that interests invariably provide the key to the 'development of the wider life' (41), empowering a man to choose what his world shall be (44). Whatever his interests, the lower-middle-class clerk struggles in vain to reach those goods which might make for a plausible sense of self-fulfilment, of well-being: 'Oh, it was no good, this continual aspiration. Some are born cultured; the rest had better go in for whatever comes easy' (67). Yet defining strong character and determining its potential influence or impact on ways of life is of interest to

Forster.[7] The two models he has in mind – we can call them conservative and liberal, or 'managerial' and 'perfectionist' – privilege different criteria or values from those adopted by Bosanquet. But both, growing out of the same fears of self-indulgence, degradation, irrationality and instability, privilege the notion of self-control. In Forster's novel self-control is clearly a valuable attribute, a key component in a good life: the kind of life his upper-middle-class heroines might reasonably aspire to.

Moreover, the language of 'interest/s', it is worth noting, pervades the novel; such 'interests' having reference to a variety of concerns which, we discover, inspire or evoke widely differing degrees of commitment. According to Margaret Schlegel interests are of immense importance: 'The only things that matter are the things that interest one' (68). It is one's interests which make life meaningful, that confer shape and substance – that give life its defining character. Indeed, the narrator wonders whether 'any emotion, any interest, once vividly aroused, can wholly die' (69). Unlike Bosanquet, however, the life style of Leonard Bast and his kind interests Forster only up to a point. His existence is of concern chiefly because he comes to represent a moral problem for Forster's middle-class heroine and middle-class reader: the problem of how much he *should* interest the Schlegels. At moments of high drama the question Margaret Schlegel has to answer is: Whose interests should be allowed to prevail?

On a structural level 'interests' contribute crucially to the creation and elaboration of plot. Leonard Bast is admitted into the world of the cultivated middle classes precisely because he counts as one of Margaret's interests: 'Would it be some young man or other whom she takes an interest in?' Aunt Juley asks Helen (45). Margaret 'found him interesting *on the whole*', we read; then reading on find the statement significantly qualified:' everyone interested the Schlegels on the whole *at that time*' (50, emphasis added). After Leonard has caused a 'vulgar' scene in front of Mr Wilcox and his daughter, Margaret tries to get them to understand that they – Helen and herself – are concerned for him, because something important is lacking in his life. 'He hasn't got the cosy home that you assumed. He needs outside interests' (151). Then at the novel's climax, Bast must be 'thrashed within an inch of his life' because, according to the Wilcoxes, it is in Helen's 'interests'(297). When Tibby unintentionally betrays the secret that will lead to Leonard's death it is because: 'he was not enough interested in human life to see where things will lead to' (303). Interests or the lack of them do indeed come to have a powerful impact on actions. Whether, as Bosanquet suggests, they can make for a crucial form of 'bonding' – the bonding which can unite people from different classes – is a question the novel will explore.

Forster's novel shares with Bosanquet and other reformers, I have suggested, a fascination with defining inner strength. Whether Leonard can be said to have a

---

[7] By contrast, in Michael Levenson's reading of the novel 'character is essentially a mode of aesthetic response ... that human responses vary so greatly poses perhaps the chief difficulty of the novel: the heterogenity of modes, the diversity of styles, tones and manners': *Modernism and the Fate of Individuality: Character and Novelistic Form from Conrad to Woolf* (Cambridge: Cambridge University Press, 1995), pp. 80–81.

strong character is of continuing interest to the Schlegels. Bast is hard to pin down, however, and their opinion of him changes. The last word on the subject spoken by their brother, Tibby, seems to decide the question in his favour. By now homeless, Bast has had the courage to refuse a substantial money gift from Helen, and is deemed 'somewhat a monumental person after all' (252). What they do not know is that although Bast is no longer capable of holding down a job of work, he has become very good at manipulating his relations into giving him money. Exploiting their fear of scandal, he controls their purse strings ever more effectively. The strength that Forster identifies in Leonard is the strength of character of which Helen Bosanquet makes no mention: it is a strength that may be morally problematic. Like Margaret, in this respect – who tries to get clear of the Basts at Oniton in order to shield Henry Wilcox – he endeavours to protect someone he has taken reponsibility for, even if this is to the detriment of others. 'Unmarried, Leonard would never have begged; he would have flickered out and died. But the whole of life is mixed. He had to provide for Jacky, and went down dirty paths that she might have a few feathers and the dishes of food that suited her' (310). 'The whole of life is mixed': Forster may raise a moral issue that Bosanquet cannot consider, but there are times when the narrator simply refuses to take a stand.

In Bosanquet's view a man's choice of house is an especially telling factor among the circumstances that in turn make him what he is or what he will become. 'A man's preferences not only influence his choice of home and locality; they will actively modify that home and locality to his liking if they are not already what he prefers. It is wonderful how short a time it takes for the home to become the mere reflection of the family that lives in it ...' (46). Does the home reflect the character of the family or the family take on some of the character of the home? In Helen Schlegel's first letter to her sister we find that contrary to her expectations, Howards End, the home of the Wilcox family, has loads of character. Quite without the distractions of ornamentation, there is no superficiality about it. Solidly built, it still retains many of its original features, and hence is genuinely charming. Impressed by the house, she is all too impressed by the character of its owner. Willingly relinquishing under his influence the liberal ideals of tolerance and equality that had seemed to occupy a prime place among her commitments, Helen abandons all sense of who she is/was. But this 'abandonment of personality' comprises nothing less than the abandonment of that hard-to-be-won achievement, the exercise of autonomous thought: the manifestation of inner strength that was so highly prized by that great instigator and promoter of liberal ideals, John Stuart Mill. In reviewing how such a thing could happen Helen/Forster describes the defeat in terms of pure self-indulgence; it is a loss of control that culminates in her sexual advances to Paul Wilcox. As she listened to the words of the 'sound man of business' attacking social reformers, Helen leaned back 'luxuriously among the cushions' of the Wilcox motor car; she liked 'giving in to the Wilcoxes', she 'liked being told that her notions of life were academic'; she 'rejoices' as the Schlegel 'fetishes' are overthrown by the exponent of the 'robust ideal' (38).

The Robust or managerial ideal of Strong Character may appear appealing, has indeed in the abstract a great deal to recommend it, as Margaret Schlegel argues throughout the novel. In practice, however, as she will find out, it has the built-in danger of what might be called a quantitative defect. Put simply, it can be overdone. When that happens strength becomes strenuousness,[8] rigour becomes ruthlessness, and assertion becomes aggression. The results can be fatal. Hence the male casualties at the end of the novel.[9]

The ability to control or manage, whether it be the business of marriages, or deaths, or large organizations, this is the quality that both reveals and 'breeds character', Margaret claims as she talks to Helen about her experiences. 'There's grit in it' (41). The expression is only one of the many that associate strength of character with control, with being able to command effectively: 'Their hands were on all ropes' thinks Margaret. It is a phrase that recurs. When Leonard Bast pictures the Schlegels and the other members of their family 'all, all with their hands on the ropes', passing up 'the narrow rich staircase at Wickham Place, to some ample room', it seems to him that this command over the good things of life has been achieved effortlessly, is indeed a matter of luck. 'Some are born cultured; the rest had better go in for whatever comes easy' (67). Henry Wilcox, proud of what he has managed to achieve in business, also conceives of this success in the same terms: 'he felt that his hands were on all the ropes of life, and that what he did not know could not be worth knowing' (138). Such control goes hand-in-hand with a wonderful sense of self-confidence that contrasts sharply with Leonard Bast's debilitating unease and painful attempts at getting 'upsides with the world' (131).

But Margaret and Foster are well aware that many 'virtues' are required to make the Robust ideal work. To a list which begins with competence, enterprise, energy, others are added of a distinctively military nature. Neatness, decision and obedience have contributed to 'forming our civilization' thinks the narrator, and 'Margaret could not doubt it' (112). From a strictly ethical perspective, they are obviously 'virtues of the second rank'; but when in practice they are to be found linked to kindness and good humour and good manners (with or without the bonus of property), the combination is appealing to a not-so-young lady – Margaret – who one day suddenly finds herself alone and unwanted on a platform at Kings Cross station.[10] Hence, in Margaret's thoughts these qualities are most acceptable when modified by certain adjectives: Mr Wilcox's

---

[8] Note the narrator's assessment of Tibby Schlegel: 'His was the leisure without sympathy – an attitude *as fatal as the strenuous*: a little cold culture may be raised on it, *but no art*': p. 302, emphasis added.

[9] Some critics have claimed that the Schlegel sisters were somehow to blame for this unhappy state of affairs: 'The book ends with the two girls and their misbegotten heir in complete and undisputed possession of Howards End, in its real and its spiritual estate – and with all the human creatures they connected with either maimed, imprisoned or dead. Once again things had gone on until there were no more men'. See Wilfred Stone, *The Cave and the Mountain* (Stanford, CA: Stanford University Press, 1966), p. 263.

[10] Many critics have faulted Forster on the implausibility of this Schlegel-Wilcox marriage: see for example, F.R. Leavis, 'E.M. Forster', *The Common Pursuit* (London, 1952), p. 269 and H.M. Daleski, *Unities* (Athens: University of Georgia Press, 1985), p. 121.

air of '*humorous* strength' is attractive; Margaret is sure they – and this means her husband – can make Helen and Tibby 'do anything by *judicious* management'. But later, at the moment of angry confrontation, Margaret will spurn Henry's '*unweeded* kindness' and '*superficial* gentleness'. At this point, though still possessing virtues, he is now not good enough (300, 324, emphasis added).

The hybrid nature of the Robust ideal emerges in Margaret's picture of a character that is industrious, enterprising and – perhaps surprisingly – also chivalric; the latter quality still having its uses. For the fastidious, chivalry may form a defence against squalor, the code of politeness and propriety keeping vulgarity at bay. Thus the odours from the abyss associated with the appearance in their house of 'Mrs Lanoline' need never be experienced again. But Margaret's attitude to the continuing practice of protection, that is part and parcel of this chivalric code, changes once she is married from bemusement to ambivalence and finally to rejection. When she must be protected from her own sister, she feels rage but is calm: 'I deserve it; I am punished for lowering my colours' (281). There is nothing wrong of course with the desire to protect. On beginning to feel 'an interest that verged into liking' for the Wilcoxes, Margaret 'desired to protect them, and often felt that they would protect her, excelling where she was deficient' (111). It is rather that just like the practice of management it should be 'judicious'. It requires a dose of practical wisdom to determine when and in what way protection is necessary, which means a capacity for what has been called 'situational appreciation'. This faculty according to David Wiggins 'does not involve maxims or precepts ... in no case will there be a rule to which an [individual] can simply appeal to tell him what to do ... the [individual] may have no other recourse but to invent the answer to the problem'.[11]

In Forster's novel there are two characters who possess, or come to possess, the kind of enhanced perception, imagination and understanding which characterizes 'situational appreciation': the first and the second Mrs Wilcox. The second, Margaret, we are informed, is 'no barren theorist'. But she starts off 'inexperienced', and spends the novel perfecting her talent until, finally, out of the 'turmoil and horror' arising from Leonard's death, she is able to take care of both a Wilcox and a Schlegel, bringing them together in a state of mutual comprehension. Doing 'what seemed easiest', Margaret proves John Kekes's point that to be 'wise is to find simple the moral situations others find complex'.[12]

It is not by chance that the wisdom which involves realizing how to act for someone's good is attributed in this novel to characters of the female sex. Indeed

---

[11] See David Wiggins, 'Deliberation and Practical Reason', in *Needs, Values, Truth* (Oxford: Blackwell, 1987), pp. 236–7.

[12] As John Kekes observes 'while the same can be said of being foolish, there is a deep difference: the morally wise have overcome the complexities, while the foolish are not aware of them': *Moral Wisdom and Good Lives*, p. 74. Cristina Mejía notes the importance of notions of practical wisdom or moral reason in this novel: 'Moral Capacities and Other Constraints', in A. Hadfield, D. Rainsford and T. Woods (eds), *The Ethics in Literature*, (London: Palgrave, Macmillan, 1999), pp. 212–28.

the narrator himself becomes at one point an honorary female, asserting that 'pity, if one may generalize, is at the bottom of woman. When men like us, it is for our better qualities' (240). In the same way, he can generalize about the defects of the male sex when he recognizes that it is 'man's deft assertion of his superiority' (295) that initiates the tragedy of Leonard's death. Forster's novel goes along with the idea that there are certain kinds of behaviour – and it would appear even certain capacities or virtues – that for better or worse are gender-related. How far we are able to change or develop aspects of our character is then open to question. At one point Helen's conduct seems to demonstrate so rigid a pattern of response that the narrator is filled with pessimism: 'Well, it is odd and sad that our minds should be such seed-beds, and we without power to choose the seed' (273).

That one could to some extent determine one's character, that one possessed some control over one's future development, was a central tenet in John Stuart Mill's Perfectionist ethos.[13] Self-optimizing theories of the kind Mill elaborated in *On Liberty* hold that what is of immense benefit is the business of self-improvement, which involves developing the potentialities or talents that will contribute to the creation of a strong, vital and highly distinctive character.[14] For Mill this is an ongoing progress which requires that the individual do his utmost to promote 'the most harmonious development of his powers to a complete and consistent whole'. The well-developed or self-cultivated person 'must *ceaselessly* direct his efforts' towards this objective (121, emphasis added).

Forster's narrative can be seen to diffuse a similar ethos as it sketches in the salient elements of his character discourse – though we shall find, I think, that ultimately Forster sets distinct limits to Mill's exacting enterprise. Like Mill, Forster finds that the enterprise of self-perfecting is one and the same as the realization of a distinctive even 'eccentric' self. This distinctive-eccentric-authentic self is one 'whose desires and impulses should be [her] own'. Moreover, this kind of moral personality is necessarily strong, since it takes courage and resolve to create and sustain an eccentric character during the inevitable and ongoing struggle with the prevailing forces of convention and mediocrity.[15] Yet courage and resolve are clearly not enough. A true individual, one who possesses 'individual spontaneity', paradoxically it might seem, requires the exercise of 'self-government' or control: 'If, in addition to being his own, his impulses are strong and are under the government of a strong will, he has an energetic character' (124).

The issue of control returns as a significant element in John Kekes's recent account of the qualities that make for moral wisdom, which is in turn a fundamental component in his conception of a good life. But what is striking about Kekes's argument is that

---

[13] *On Liberty*, ed. Gertrude Himmelfarb (Harmondsworth: Penguin, 1974), p. 124.
[14] Thomas Hurka, *Perfectionism* (New York and Oxford: Oxford University Press: 1993), pp. 3–4.
[15] 'Eccentricity has always abounded when and where strength of character has abounded …': *On Liberty*, ed. Himmelfarb, p. 132.

the qualities which he claims are characteristic of a disposition of which wisdom might be expected, are the very same qualities that Forster's narrator discerns at times and admires in Margaret Schlegel. And these comprise imaginative resourcefulness, self-knowledge, moral depth (the attitude which makes for reasonable hope), together with the control that manifests inner strength. Thus Kekes argues that:

> The extent to which we have control is the extent to which we approximate the Socratic ideal of self-sufficiency. Total control would be to be completely self-sufficient. This is an ideal state ... It is a state in which we are *masters* of our character and our circumstances. We know what we desire; we know that it is good; and we live so as to achieve it. Our knowledge, desires, capacities, and values, in a word, our characters, are what we consciously decided they should be. Our lives, therefore, are shaped by self-direction, and not by external influences. (74, emphasis added)

To what extent is control possible? and What kind of control might one exercise over one's growth/talents/life? are questions that are central to Forster's narrative. At one point the narrator observes that Margaret (who is characterized from the beginning of the novel as 'impulsive') 'has succeeded – so far as success is yet possible. She does understand herself, she has some rudimentary control over her own growth. Whether Helen has succeeded one cannot say' (273). In the very first chapter, as we have seen, Helen's self-indulgence or loss of control at Howards End provides the Schlegels with a salutary scare. For Helen fear returns as she listens to Beethoven's Fifth Symphony: 'Panic and Emptiness! Panic and Emptiness! The goblins were right'. Without Love there is emptiness, without control there is panic or chaos. In Helen's musically induced vision heroism is foresworn and eradicated as inner instability or 'cowardice and unbelief' are cause and effect of a general dissolution, of anarchy and nihilism. But, 'as if things were going too far, Beethoven took hold of the goblins and made them do what he wanted ... Beethoven chose to make all right in the end ... But the goblins were there. They could return' (46–7, emphasis added).

Appropriately, it is the artist/genuis who functions in the novel as the paradigmatic achiever; he who has come closest to the perfectionist ideal of self-exertion and control through the accurate management of his energy and talents in the service of an ideal. Ruskin, too, provides a telling example. Of his book *The Stones of Venice*, the work that Leonard tries to model his own style upon, the narrator can enthusiastically affirm: 'How perfectly the famous chapter opens! How supreme is its *command* of admonition and of poetry!' (61, emphasis added) However, although the artist/genius has supreme command or enviable mastery of his medium, and can work a resolution if he desires, the prospect of the loss of control and instability that results in chaos is always present in Life, and with chaos comes the loss of any chance of 'splendour' or 'heroism' or 'joy' (46–7).

Forster's ideas about the possibility of control expand in the novel in various directions, but the central focus of this discourse is unmistakeably Margaret Schlegel. And it is her thoughts that define first of all what personal control is not about. Control is not about being prepared or cautious. Sometimes/often one must be willing to take risks: Margaret felt 'that those who prepare for all the emergencies of life beforehand may equip themselves at the expense of joy'. Too much planning or foresight leads inevitably to failure. Risk in this sense means openness and spontaneity of response to the possibility of all those sources of the good: 'beauty and all the other intangible gifts that are floating about the world' (86). 'I hope to risk things all my life', says Margaret (71). Forster as narrator could not agree more: concluding the first phase of the Schelgel/Wilcox story which ends with the death of Mrs Wilcox, he comments on the strength that goes to waste in the constant effort to be prepared for 'the crisis that never comes': 'The tragedy of preparedness has scarcely been handled, save by the Greeks. Life is indeed dangerous, but not in the way morality would have us believe. It is indeed unmanageable, but the essence of it is not a battle. It is unmanageable because it is a romance, and its essence is romantic beauty' (115).

Margaret hopes to be less cautious. In Forster's novel control is then not a matter of careful self-protection in the face of 'romance'. Rather control is an essential element in the exercise of practical wisdom. And the version here elaborated would appear to conform in essentials to an Aristotelian model of *phronesis*, which involves 'a form of contextually embedded and situationally sensitive judgment of particulars'.[16] Practical wisdom involves being able to work out what is good for oneself as well as others, which means finding ways of coping with adversities, of combating unfavourable forms of influence, but also of being capable of seizing or retaining the initiative when it is important for one to do so.

*

To Leonard Bast, Margaret Schlegel appears as the epitome of self-mastery, while to the first Mrs Wilcox she seems in comparison to Helen to possess 'a deeper sympathy, a sounder judgement' (75). Yet, as the narrative charts her relations with the Wilcox family, the self-assurance of the soon-to-be-wed Evie Wilcox invokes visions of her own 'futility', and Margaret begins to feel anything but wise. '[Evie's] voice was gruffer, her manner more downright, and she was inclined to patronize the more foolish virgin. Margaret was silly enough to be pained at this. Depressed at her isolation, she saw not only houses and furniture but the vessel of life itself slipping past her, with people like Evie and Mr Cahill on board' (155). It is one of those moments when 'virtue and wisdom fail us', notes the narrator. Then immediately Mr Wilcox arrives on the scene and all her feelings of loneliness and inadequacy vanish. What also happens, equally significantly, is that Mr Wilcox starts to take control of the situation. Most frivolously, this means that he won't have her eating fish pie. 'Go for something for me, then', said Margaret (156). Though what she has to say is as witty as ever, it is not only over houses that Margaret seems to be losing control: 'Gentlemen seem to mesmerize houses ... I've no control over the saucy things. Houses are alive. No?' (159). The interesting issue to emerge, then, is not whether Margaret is wise to marry Henry Wilcox – if life is a 'romance' she too will take her chance – but rather whether

---

[16] See Benhabib, *Situating the Self*, p. 25.

she is wise in the way she 'manages' her marriage to Henry Wilcox. As the narrative traces the ways in which these key characters act, react and interact, the reader will discover whether or not Margaret is able to 'manage' his influence.[17]

So – to adopt John Kekes's formulation – when is control within our control? In Kekes's discussion of the nature of both practical and moral wisdom, we find the kind of explanation that provides a rationale for Margaret's attempt to fashion a life after her own vision of the good. Kekes argues that being in control involves shaping ourselves to become the person our conception of the good life requires. And this means transforming our character from the fortuitous to the deliberate; and this, in turn, requires self-direction. For a start we need to be able to make considered choices. Thus we continue to be open – but not open to everything – we begin to discriminate between desires in order to perfect or pursue those plans we have knowingly chosen and to which we have awarded priority. The development of talents, the exercise of creativity, can only occur when assessments have been made as to what 'things' we value most.

Margaret's marriage to Henry Wilcox sees her thinking along just such lines: 'she had outgrown *stimulants*, and was passing from words to things. It was doubtless a pity not to keep up with Wedekind or John, but some closing of the gates is inevitable after thirty, if the mind itself is to become a *creative* power' (258, emphasis added). Some interests will be discarded in order to pursue others more thoroughly; pleasurable experiences will be given up for the greater satisfaction of creativity. Margaret's self-identity and the plans to which she is committed are now conceived, above all, as being bound up with her active role as Henry's wife.

But to echo a question Helen asks of Leonard: 'What kind of person is [Henry's second] wife?' Does Margaret really know? Does Henry? At one point, Henry most contentedly thinks of Margaret as 'so lively and intelligent, and yet so submissive' (255). And indeed it would seem that Margaret loses considerable control over her life even as she feels it necessary to exert more control over herself. It is notable that even before Henry Wilcox proposes to her she starts 'keeping herself in hand'. When he does propose she has great control over the control she has: 'when he said, "I am asking you to be my wife", she made herself give a little start. She must show

---

[17] C.B. Cox, like Leavis, finds that Margaret's marriage to Henry 'shocks us by its sacrifice': *The Free Spirit: A Study of Liberal Humanism in the Novels of George Eliot, Henry James, E.M. Forster, Virginia Woolf, Angus Wilson* (London and Oxford: Oxford University Press, 1963), pp. 78–9. In the view of H.M. Daleski 'It is difficult to accept the verisimilitude of the marriage on a literal level, it being hard to believe Margaret could marry a man who is so obviously lacking in the qualities she values most': *Unities*, p. 121. Born finds a cynical motive in the overriding importance of houses to Margaret's decision: 'Critics have paid too much attention to Margaret's rhetoric about connection, and not enough to this primary obsession with realty – the matter largely responsible for her marriage to a man so incompatible as Wilcox': 'Private Gardens, Public Swamps', p. 152. On the other hand, Alan Wilde maintains that 'Margaret is, after all, genuinely in love': *Art and Order: A Study of E.M. Forster* (London: Peter Owen, 1965), p. 114.

surprise if he expected it' (168). This is the kind of control which seems more akin to self-restraint than self-direction. When they talk about their future life together Henry makes all the decisions (181–2) and insists on escorting Margaret back to her hotel, despite her wishes to the contrary. Margaret gives in. Will such behaviour continue? And is it wise? Apparently it is. 'A younger woman might have resented his masterly ways, but Margaret had too firm a grip of life to make a fuss. She was, in her own way, as masterly ... And if insight were sufficient, if the inner life were the whole of life, their happiness had been assured' (185). Control over the inner life is effective self-monitoring and self-editing, and this involves improved knowledge of the self and other, greater understanding, and considered judgement. The Outer life, the life of external pressures, of adversities and the unexpected, cannot be controlled. So would Forster agree with Kekes.

But for Forster there is one circumstance that may acquire particular importance in our lives, and that is the impression we give others; their judgement of us cannot be controlled. Or can it? Forster recognizes that Margaret possesses a creative imagination, a form of 'fertility', of mental flexibility, of optimistic resourcefulness (185). This is a quality that Ruskin discerned at Torcello, where he noted that the '*fertility*' of the craftsmen can be seen in their capacity to adapt the ancient stones to the new pulpit, 'a sign of the hope of doing better things'.[18] Forster takes up the term – expecting his readers, just like Leonard Bast, to be well acquainted with Ruskin's book – and he uses it in order to define a capacity that Henry Wilcox quite fails to appreciate in his wife. For Wilcox mistakes Margaret's '*fertility* for weakness' (185, emphasis added). The important point is that Henry Wilcox cannot entirely be blamed for this mistake, for this misreading of his future wife's character. As the narrator notes: Margaret 'misled her lover much as she had misled her aunt.' Henry's reading of Margaret's 'fertility' for a form of feebleness is due then to a kind of deception on Margaret's part. Margaret has a pretty good grasp of Henry's character. She penetrated 'to the depths of his soul, and approv[ed] of what she found there' (185). But it seems not to matter to her that Henry Wilcox obtain a clearer idea of the character of the woman he has chosen to marry. The deference Margaret shows her husband contains an element of deceit.

Certainly, it would be possible to justify Margaret's 'deception' – her ability to conceal the signs of her strength – as a legitimate tactic in an accomodating strategy; one tending to the construction of a companionate marriage: she is thus compliant rather than appeasing. Nevertheless, practical wisdom, Forster suggests, may involve judging correctly how much of one's inner life or character should be disclosed or revealed fearlessly to those who matter most. It means considering whether acquiescence should be allowed to predominate within the patterns of one's responsiveness to those who matter most.

That Margaret continues to 'deceive' becomes apparent at Evie's wedding. That she desires to take more control is also increasingly apparent. During her visit to

---

[18] *The Stones of Venice* (New York, London: Garland,1979), vol. 2, p. 21.

Howards End she mentally changes the arrangement of the rooms and muses 'Would that she could deal as high-handedly with the world!' (200). As Forster focuses on the dynamics of the Wilcox-Schlegel marriage, the novel examines the relation between wisdom and control, and does so in a way that frustrates an unequivocal evaluation of Margaret's behaviour. Time and again the reader cannot help but be aware of the pressure of circumstances, the impact of personal codes and ideals, the drawbacks of strength. The question arises then of how we are to interpret Margaret's behaviour during the muddle of incidents that occur during Evie's wedding: is she wise or is she foolish? Later reflecting miserably over the events of the day, it seems to Margaret that she has assisted at a 'carnival of fools' (238).

As this crucial phase in her relationship with Henry Wilcox gets underway, Margaret, we find, becomes determined to take more control. Filled with indignation at the way the men are behaving when the cat is run over, she reasons that 'the whole system's wrong, and she must challenge it' (213). She is determined to gain control over her own movements, to exert her authority, to manage things better by providing the necessary female voice of apology and concern. However, after having jumped out of the moving car and injured her hand, she reflects during the ensuing fracas that the situation had become 'absurd' and her challenge to the male way of doing things is short-lived. By the time they have arrived at the house she has 'decided' to play the part of the foolish female – '"Oh Henry", she exclaims, "I have been so naughty"' – and so she 'prepares' the way for an image of herself which 'fitted in too well with their view of feminine nature' (214). 'Artfully', she manages to convince both Charles and Henry that her actions were uncontrollable (the result of her 'nerves'). Such actions have a precise – practical – aim in view; they are designed to protect Charles from his father's anger. And Margaret is successful. She is wise, it seems, to play at being foolish.

As if the incident had made her more aware of her own ambivalent behaviour, Margaret decides that she must endeavour 'to remain herself'. 'She must remain herself, for his sake as well as her own' (220). She must remain herself – 'a shadowy wife degrades the husband whom she accompanies' – and yet to please Henry she continues to practice a certain amount of 'kowtowing to the men'. Being herself is easier, however, when Helen appears upon the scene, bringing with her the now unemployed Leonard Bast and his wife, Jacky. Discarding the airs of a hostess, Margaret gives vent to her anger that Helen should have dragged the Basts to the wedding party. But then she 'controls' her voice, promises that she will use her influence with Henry to help the Basts, and sums up what is to her the most important issue: the happy life is the disciplined life. 'I haven't nearly done with you, though, Helen. You have been most self-indulgent. I can't get over it. You have less restraint rather than more as you grow older. Think it over and alter yourself, or we shan't have happy lives' (227). Intolerant of Helen's self-indulgence, she yet tolerates or 'side[s] with men as they are', and by adopting the skills of diplomacy, 'gives him the kind of woman that he desired' (229, 227). On this occasion this accomodating strategy seems entirely justifiable; it works: Margaret's 'tact and devotion' are rewarded, and Henry agrees to find Bast a job. We may conclude, then, that Margaret's mode of 'managing' both herself and her future husband is vindicated by her success (though some 'shame' at using the methods of the harem, is the unavoidable trade-off). With such discreet management it looks as if everything will turn out for the best. Yet circumstances conspire (in the form of Helen's carelessness in leaving Mrs Bast behind her at the party) to complicate matters, and take both plot and argument a step further.

The first major crisis of Margaret's relationship with Henry Wilcox occurs at this point, when a drunken Jacky reveals that Henry was once her lover. However, once more a controlled response seems to be the best policy. Only the words '"so that" – ' burst from her': 'She stopped herself from saying more' (230). When Margaret discovers that the act of adultery happened ten years ago, 'she left him without a word'. 'For many hours [she] did nothing; then she *controlled* herself, and wrote some letters' (237, emphasis added). Margaret reasons and reflects, and, as she does so 'her anger, her regard for the dead, her desire for a scene, all grew weak' (240). Margaret 'had determined' against a scene, but there is one anyway to please Henry. 'It was somehow imperative' (241). Highly accomplished at the practice of self-editing, Margaret again chooses 'her words carefully and so saved him from panic' (243).

It is a determined and self-disciplined Margaret, a highly controlled and yet reasonable character, one who knows a great deal and can guess the rest, who renews her commitment to her ideal of the good life. This is a life of 'comradeship', of domesticity and companionship, in which tolerance for male weakness is rationalized and redefined in a larger scheme of things – a way of seeing things/him whole. 'His actions, not his disposition, had disappointed her, and she could bear that' (246). Henry's past actions need not necessarily affect Margaret's future happiness. Managing her own responses she allows him to assume command over himself again: 'she chose her words carefully ... She played the girl ... old Henry fronted her, competent, cynical and kind' (243–4, emphasis added).

But Margaret has mismanaged elsewhere, and the question that arises is what her mistake signifies in Forster's developing discourse on the possibilities of practical wisdom. For Margaret soon finds out that she has 'mismanaged' Helen. The letters she sends her sister with their terse, even brutal, dismissal of the Basts ('The Basts are not at all the type we should trouble about', 239), are couched in Henry's language of 'types'. Clearly on this occasion Margaret has not chosen 'her words carefully' enough. Indeed she seems not to have chosen them at all, but rather slipped into Henry's idiom. And this means that Helen, like Henry, is able to misinterpret her. Helen is confirmed in her fear that Henry's influence has become so strong as to have brought about a significant change in her sister's outlook and even character.

It is a view the reader may well agree with. Yet an alternative and more complex interpretation is possible. Living up to her image as a strong character, Margaret intends to protect Henry from further contact with the Basts. While the desire common to the strong to protect those they care for is habitual to Margaret, the style of the letters is not. And the language she adopts signifies far more than Margaret intends. (She does after all also consider that 'something might be arranged for the Basts later on ...', 239.) At this dramatic moment Margaret Schlegel can be taken to be acting both in and out of character. The kind of strength she displays now exemplifies an oxymoron: it is an 'imperfect virtue', which perfectly reflects her present imperfect vision. For as Margaret mediates on her husband's character, her vision narrows as she decides what matters most: 'Henry must be forgiven, and made better by love; *nothing else mattered*' (240, emphasis added).[19]

'Oniton, like herself', thinks Margaret, 'was imperfect' (229). With its trees, meadows and mountains, for the narrator, it represents 'the earth', enduring contact with which provides a 'binding force on character'. And Margaret, gazing over the landscape with 'deep emotion', 'loves her future home' (246). However, she soon finds out that Oniton is also 'damp' and 'inconvenient', and that, without consulting her, Henry is already in the process of selling the house and grounds. Controlling her displeasure when this news is casually broken to her is hard, but she manages it. She seems to have little choice with regard to her future home and her words to Henry giving him 'a free hand' may be interpreted this time as a form of self-deception: 'If Oniton is really damp, it is impossible, and must be inhabited by little boys. Only, in the spring, let us look before we leap. I will take warning by Evie, and not hurry you. Remember that *you have a free hand this time*' (257, emphasis added). What power does Margaret have to confer on Henry? it may be asked. And an answer may be found in a specific conception of practical wisdom. We may be said to be in control even if we act according to external influences – influences which we have not created – when we act according to them because we have evaluated them and assigned them a place in our conception of a meaningful, fulfilling life. According to this way of thinking, we satisfy the requirements of practical wisdom when we identify deliberately with the desires that prompt our actions.[20] Hence Margaret may be viewed as not simply

---

[19] According to John Dewey ' Of all the habits which constitute the character of an individual, the habit of *judging* moral situations is the most important, for this is the key to the *direction* and the *remaking* of all other habits. When the act is overt, it is irretrievably launched. The agent has no more control ... It is not surprising that the Greeks, the first seriously to inquire into the nature of behavior and its end or good, should have eulogized *wisdom, insight*, as the supreme virtue and source of all the virtues': *Ethics*, vol. 5 (1908), *The Middle Works, 1899–1924*, ed. Jo Ann Boydston (Carbondale: Southern Illinois Press: 1978), p. 375.

[20] Kekes continues: 'If the occasion or the need arose, requiring us to be reflective and articulate about our favorable evaluation, we would say that we want to be, or at least that we do not mind being, the sort of person who aims to satisfy that sort of desire. We may not be consciously engaged in forming our character, nonetheless it is being formed, and we could or would say upon reflection that we approve of the way in which its formation is proceeding. This identification ... proceeding by way of our evaluation of our desires, is, of course, a second-order activity. Its aim is not to satisfy a particular desire, but to decide whether a particular desire should be satisfied. The decision is based on the evaluation of the desire in the light of the standard set by our conception of a good life. We approve or disapprove of the desire, and we act to satisfy or to suppress it, not merely because the desire is what it is, but also because the desire is aiding or hindering our development of the character we wish to have. And we wish it because our conception of a good life calls for it': *Moral Wisdom and Good Lives*, pp. 77–8.

weakly conciliating her husband, but rather as delegating her power of choice to him. Having willingly, knowingly, accepted his desires as her own, she is strong enough to trust that he will choose well on her behalf.

That some external influences or pressures will have a transformative effect would seem to be inevitable. And the narrator is quite candid in admitting that Margaret's character does change to some extent – she began to 'think conjugally': 'Marriage was to alter her fortunes rather than her character, and she was not far wrong in boasting that she understood her future husband. Yet he did alter her character – a little. There was an unforeseen surprise, a cessation of the winds and odours of life, a social pressure that would have her think conjugally' (177). But her conduct is on the whole consistent with her ideal – that of marriage as comradeship, expressing loyalty and companionship. The desires she endorses are those which are compatible with this ideal. And because Forster believes in the importance of time relativity in personal development, the starting point for the creation of a viable relationship is the time when Margaret needs it most, not some visionary time in the future when equality for women has been achieved and men cease to exploit every advantage.

Margaret Schlegel, it would appear, is well aware of the nature of her desires and of her circumstances; she has evaluated the costs and benefits and may be said to have begun to construct her life accordingly. By marrying Henry Wilcox she has taken a risk, but she has also enlarged her field of possibilities. Rejecting the romanticism of overreaction, characteristic of Helen's approach to life, she also tries to circumvent the disengagement or denial of the Wilcox way.[21] The control, she possesses is, on this view, a matter of permission and prohibition; it is the allowing and refusing of external influences to shape her responses in accordance with her own deliberation or understanding as to what is appropriate, what matters most. This awareness and evaluation of reasons explains why she lets Henry's responses, and sometimes his anger, occasionally determine the amount of control she will exert over her own responses. Margaret has considerable control over the amount of control she thinks she needs to use with Henry Wilcox. This means, for example, that she knows exactly when she will let him win an argument. In a brilliantly ironic view of male obtuseness, Forster allows us a brief insight into the mind of a happily married man. Henry interprets Margaret's behaviour on the occasions that they argue as involving a spurious 'show of fight' on her part. We know of course that her acting all goes into the losing, not the fighting, of the argument. Because she identifies with his need to win, and because this counts for a great deal to him and not very much to her, he is allowed to have the last word:

> He had only to call, and she clapped the book up and was ready to do what he wished. Then they would argue so jollily, and once or twice she had him in quite a tight corner, but as soon as he grew really serious she gave in. Man is for war, woman for the recreation of the warrior, but he does not dislike it if she makes a show of fight. She cannot win in a real battle, having no muscles only nerves. Nerves make her jump out of a moving motor-car, or refuse to be married fashionably. The warrior *may well allow* her to triumph

---

[21] See Kekes, *Moral Wisdom and Good Lives*, p. 176.

on such occasions; they move not the imperishable plinth of things that touch his peace. (255, emphasis added)

Yet this is a dangerous game. If Henry is kind and competent, he is also self-deluding. Clearly he is mistaken as to which of the two of them is doing the 'allowing'. That Margaret is mistaken in allowing him to continue in his delusion as to her weakness or 'submissiveness' is arguably not so obvious. Why shatter his/their 'peace' now over something presumably quite trivial? Yet when the time for 'plain speaking' can no longer be avoided – the moment when she requests leave for (the pregnant) Helen and herself to spend the night at Howards End – Margaret discovers that Henry is unprepared for the words of an undeceiving wife. Margaret's outraged response to his refusal is that of a now wiser wife, one who realizes that wisdom requires setting limits to the exercise of tolerance and deference.

More broadly, acknowledging the need for limits has a precise bearing on the configuration of Forster's character ideal: establishing limits means determining the contours of one's character or providing one's moral personality with an authentic shape. On this view an individual may be said to possess authenticity when she is capable of making distinctions between what she understands as her fundamental interests, cares, commitments, what she knowingly loves and will defend or protect, and what is of less value, or of little or no significance to her.[22]

The articulation of such a multi-standed discourse regarding moral limits allows Forster to tackle both the (Millian) fantasy of 'ceaseless' growth and the (traditional) notion of duty as involving a sense of indeterminate responsibility that is responsive to feelings of guilt. At Howards End, Margaret repudiates any sense of guilt while advancing her critique of a perfectionist ideal which suggests that we are capable of boundless and multifaceted growth: 'All over the world men and women are worrying because they cannot develop as they are supposed to develop. Here and there they have the matter out and it comforts them. Don't fret yourself, Helen. Develop what you have …' (327). Margaret's response to Helen's fear that 'there's something wanting in me … is it some awful, appalling criminal defect?' is at the same time a response to Ruskin's request for the honesty and sincerity that underlie authenticity in life and art.[23]

In *The Stones of Venice*, Ruskin observes that 'the modern English mind has this much in common with that of the Greek, that it intensely desires in all things, the utmost completion or perfection compatible with their nature'. However, Ruskin is convinced that 'the finer the nature, the more flaws it will show through the clearness of it; and it is the law of this universe, that the best things shall be seldomest seen in their best form' (160). 'Imperfection', claims Ruskin, 'is in some sort essential to all

---

[22] As Kekes observes 'Such commitments determine for us what we must and must not do; they limit the area of our possibilities; they set a standard for gauging the seriousness of violations; and they put certain possibilities beyond the pale': *Moral Wisdom and Good Lives*, pp. 156–7.

[23] *The Stones of Venice*, vol. 2, p. 159.

that we know of life' (171). Consequently, on one thing Ruskin is clear: 'Do what you can, and confess frankly what you are unable to do; neither let your effort be shortened for fear of failure, nor your confession silenced for fear of shame' (159). More in tune with Ruskin than Leonard Bast could ever be, during her conversation with Helen, Margaret makes her own confession in a determined bid precisely to be free of shame: 'I do *not* love children. I am thankful to have *none*. I can play with their beauty and charm, but that is all – *nothing* real, *not* one scrap of what there ought to be' (327, emphasis added). Margaret's words with their repetitive negatives (not, none, nothing, not) emphasize and confirm a positive character trait: she possesses a distinctive or authentic character, one that is committed to the cause of personal coherence that is founded upon a clear-eyed recognition of her own interests and abilities, of what she does and cannot love.

That this 'individualist' perspective possesses cogency is established very early on in the novel. At the concert (as early as Chapter 5), having decided to invite Leonard Bast to come home, Margaret cannot pretend she likes all the music on the programme, 'she is not a female of the encouraging type' and doesn't try to be one. Helen can draw people out. She shares a love of the cheaper seats. Margaret does not: 'She had been to the gallery at Covent Garden but she did *not* "attend" it, preferring the more expensive seats; still less did she love it. So she made *no* reply' (51, emphasis added). In this respect, Forster suggests, if we are lucky in our circumstances, our character will develop, will flourish, under the impetus of self-cultivation, but our character can be said to be our own only in so far as we live by certain limits; for transcending limits may not be possible or desirable given our talents, situation and conception of what belongs to a good life. In fact Margaret's attitude is well summed up in the words of Thomas Hurka as a 'pragmatic restraint of ambition' by 'facts', a rejection of the romantic desire to soar beyond evidence.[24]

The next stage in Ruskin's argument finds Forster in agreement: 'And in all things that live there are certain irregularities and deficiences which are not only signs of life, but sources of beauty ... and to banish imperfection is to destroy expression, to check exertion, to paralyse vitality' (171). The somewhat paradoxical idea that forms of beauty can be born from imperfection finds confirmation in the comment on Helen's selfishness. Helen would have stopped the night at Howard's End without asking the permission of any Wilcox, and the narrator adds: 'It was the touch of selfishness, which was not enough to mar Helen's character, and even added to its beauty' (295). In life, as in art, though we may continue to strive to perfect our talents, the authenticity to be found in creative vigour partakes of the imperfect. Moreover, in Ruskin's view, the irregular feature or flaw has an essential part to play in our view of the whole; it is the deficiency that adds interest, and that through contrast throws into greater relief the beauty of the other parts.

Indubitably, some limits are due to a lack of moral imagination. Astoundingly, like the narrator, who finds the very poor 'unthinkable', Brahms and Ruskin are both

---

[24] Hurka, *Perfectionism*, p. 104.

judged to be limited by their moral imagination: Brahms has no depth, he is 'shallow'; he 'had never guessed', thinks Margaret, 'what it felt like to be suspected of stealing an umbrella' (48). While Ruskin's is the voice of one who is 'full of high purpose, full of beauty, full even of sympathy and the love of men' but who 'had never been dirty or hungry and had not guessed successfully what dirt and hunger are' (62). But for Ruskin the issue of limitations is not simply a matter of lack of vision or experience. As he glides over the lagoon on his way back from Torcello (both in *The Stones of Venice* and as imagined by the narrator of *Howards End*) Ruskin unashamedly admits that 'the power of nature cannot be shortened by the folly, nor her beauty altogether saddened by the misery of men' ('such as Leonard', Forster adds, 67). Ruskin's statement/confession here should be read together with another also made in *The Stones of Venice*, where he sanctions precisely what seems to be a transgression of conventional morality. This involves 'the relaxing of a law generally imperative, in compliance with some other imperative need'.[25] The needs of which he speaks are related to what we care greatly about, what makes life worthwhile or equally (?) important – interesting. And these belong to the category of life enhancements – nature, art, music. It is the love of these forms of life enrichment, and an opening to their 'power', which legitimate a commitment to them. They too set in place the boundaries of our moral outlook or perspective. For all his mocking attitude to the 'rich man in his gondola', to his 'piping' and 'melodious voice', Forster can see Ruskin's point.[26] It is the point that Margaret makes when she reveals that the limits of her capacity for trust are reached when her painting by Ricketts might be placed at risk. Margaret can risk losing the apostle spoons as 'rent to the ideal' that 'its better to be fooled than to be suspicious'. But, unlike Helen, and in tune with Aunt Juley, she affirms 'I'd rather mistrust people than lose my little Ricketts. There are limits' (55).

The goal Margaret Schlegel aims at is the moral capacity to exercise the practical wisdom that is consonant with an awareness of the value of the goods that life has put in one's way.[27] This is the ethical standpoint that holds that we reflect as to what we should do on the basis of as much self-knowledge as we can muster. It is this power which enables us to distinguish between what concerns us (the poor, to whom Margaret will give half her money) and what we care about most (husband and sister, to whom she gives herself).[28] In pursuing a meaningful vision of the good life self-knowledge works well when it involves understanding when one should get fully involved, how

---

[25] *The Stones of Venice*, vol. 1, p. 248.
[26] Born claims that 'If Forster satirizes Ruskin's ability to respond to the urban poor, he is just as damning of the Schlegel sisters themselves': 'Private Garden, Public Swamps', p. 151.
[27] On this view the demands of morality are limited by considerations pertaining to an individual's psychology and well-being; for a discussion of these points see Samuel Scheffler, 'Morality's Demands and Their Limits', *The Journal of Philosophy* 83 (1986): 531–7.
[28] The reading given here may be contrasted then with other interpretations. For example, Anne Wright finds that by the end of the novel Henry has become a 'cipher', Margaret 'platitudinous' and Helen is simply 'enthusing'. For Wright, both sisters are engaged in

to manage one's resources (when to draw on one's inner strength and self-control), when to strive for candour.

That is one way of looking at one's possibilities. But pictures fluctuate as things get ugly. Then a thoroughly encumbered self sees itself implicated in a tangled mess of relationships, caught up in the consequences of other people's actions. Thus as the novel edges towards closure, Margaret Schlegel meditates on 'natural' causes and their effects:

> Events succeeded in a logical, yet senseless, train. People lost their humanity, and took values as arbitrary as those in a pack of playing cards. It was natural that Henry should do this and cause Helen to do that, and then think her wrong for doing it; natural that she herself should think him wrong; natural that Leonard should want to know how Helen was, and come, and Charles be angry with him for coming – natural but unreal. In this jangle of causes and effects what had become of their true selves? Here Leonard lay dead in the garden, from natural causes; yet life was a deep, deep river, death a blue sky, life was a house, death a wisp of hay, a flower, a tower, life and death were anything and everything, except this ordered insanity, where the king takes the queen, and the ace the king. Ah, no; there was beauty and adventure behind, such as the man at her feet had yearned for; there was hope this side of the grave; there were truer relationships beyond the limits that fetter us now. (320)

As Margaret Schlegel meditates on a progression of judgements unfortunate, unfair and unwise, she comes round to articulating a belief in a vision that might be both comforting and inspiring: the vision of 'truer relationships beyond the limits that fetter us now'. Yet the agreeable notion that one might somehow transcend one's own story is accompanied by nothing so substantial as an intent to bring about any kind of radical change in her own circumstances. This is rather a form of wishful thinking, for clearly Margaret Schlegel has no intention of extricating herself from the all-absorbing attachments which have become firmly re-established in the course of her own narrative.

The final scene at Howards End veers yet further away from the notion of doing better, insisting instead on the idea of being well, of understanding and achieving what 'leads to comfort in the end' (328). Settling down after the turmoil brings a settling of accounts, so that Schlegels and Wilcoxes can all be comfortable in the knowledge that in the final share-out of goods each has been considered and consulted. Indeed the worthy inheritor of Howards End is the character whose worth is demonstrated most obviously in her ability to provide comfort – a talent that connects her to the spiritual heiress of *Mansfield Park*. In both novels this (limited) mode of 'doing well' is obviously conducive to the heroine's state of 'being well'.

> 'working out their salvation in their dealings with money, but neither effects much change for the better': *The Literature of Crisis*, pp. 47, 60. Calvin Bedient is of the opinion that 'as champion of Romance, Margaret fails .... But Forster does not know that she fails, or rather will not admit it. And the novel is, accordingly, false and confused': *Architects of the Self* (Berkeley and Los Angeles: University of California Press, 1972), p. 225.

At the closure of *Howards End* Margaret Schlegel acquires a new home just as she demonstrates her commitment to an old principle. '"Nothing matters," the Schlegels had said in the past, "except one's self-respect and that of one's friends"' (321–2). Now, on the very last page, when Henry Wilcox puts the question 'I didn't do wrong, did I?' Margaret gives an answer that may astound, such is its simplicity: 'You didn't darling. Nothing has been done wrong' (332). Critique and confrontation are a feature of the past that need not intrude in the present. This is a comforter for whom self-respect and self-confidence just are major features of well-being.

Afterword: *Utz*

In *Howards End* Forster's heroine has to reckon with the competing demands on her attention of morality and meaning. Meaning in this novel is connected principally to personal bonds. But things, like her little painting by Ricketts are permitted to place constraints on her responsiveness to non-intimate others, circumscribing the degree to which she is prepared to run risks (55). Indeed at one point she even announces that: 'I believe we shall come to care about people less and less ... I quite expect to end my life caring most for a place' (136–7). Remarkably, perhaps, places and things are not only starkly and unapologetically acknowledged for their life-enhancing value, they are rated very high up in a scale of importance.[1] It is not that Forster wants to reject a morality of altruism, of openness and trust, but he expresses doubts about the scope and stringency of such a moral outlook.[2] A reasonable morality is a moderate morality.

More recently the figure of a Polish collector, Kaspar Joachim Utz, has generated two diverging perspectives on the profile of meaning in a good life. Just as in *Hard Times*, however, in the world Utz inhabits the prospect of living a fulfilling life looks slim: for this is a world made ugly by the inroads of a repressive regime and an all-powerful ideology. Happiness does not seem to count for much under either system, productivity and efficiency evidently matter a great deal more. To those in charge figuring out the relationship that might obtain between ethics and ideology is anything but a priority. In the twentieth-century world of Kaspar Joachim Utz regulation, deprivation and squalor are as much in evidence as corruption and the cant of a 'progressive', rationalizing, orthodoxy. So has Utz found a solution, a means of escaping the bleakness of ordinary life? And can his way of life be justified?[3] In this afterword I shall be looking at contrasting approaches to the issues that are raised in philosophical and fictional discourses featuring the collector. On the one hand, John Kekes relies on a more or less 'bare' exemplum, which provides a succinct account of what appear as unequivocal responses to key events. Here Kekes stresses the

---

[1] On the notion of ethical importance, see Bernard Williams, 'Morality, the Peculiar Institution', in Roger Crisp and Michael Slote (eds), *Virtue Ethics* (Oxford: Oxford University Press, 1997), pp. 45–65.

[2] For a discussion of the demandingness of morality and responses to this notion see Samuel Scheffler, 'Morality's Demands and Their Limits', *The Journal of Philosophy* 83 (1986): 531–7.

[3] Garrett Cullity observes that ethics is about helping people to understand how to pursue the right questions, which include problems of justification: for an individual 'genuinely to have a *justification* for living one way rather than another means finding it, and understanding it, for myself': 'Why Live This Way', *TLS*, 25 June 1999, p. 9.

force of certain needs and their perceived implications with regard to the practice of moral evasion.[4] On the other, Bruce Chatwin has created a hybrid or experimental form of realism. This form relinquishes recourse to characteristic modes of classical realism and problematizes its representation of character, so complicating the reader's response.[5] But this mischievous work, with its wry refusal of solemnity and elusive protagonist, yet allows for the nuance and complexity that befits an account of an idiosyncratic style of life, exploring the relations between features of the psyche and appropriate or 'fertile' ways of responding to the challenges of the world. It allows for some insight into the mental states that 'do the work':[6] that are conducive to meaning, that underpin fulfilment, that may make eudaimonia a possibility. In both of these texts we discover that an entire way of life becomes susceptible to a task-oriented mentality that is grounded in an intense appreciation of fine things.

*

Whatever the goods good lives require, they are most certainly imbued with meaning. According to philosopher Susan Wolf 'a person finds meaning in her life insofar as she finds herself gripped or engaged by something she sees to have positive value and has the opportunity to interact with in a positive and fruitful way'.[7] A life without sense of purpose, a life denied meaning is – as Dickens implied in *Hard Times* – a seriously defective life. Good lives, it seems, have 'identity-conferring commitments': these basic commitments 'are our most fundamental convictions – they are the rock upon which rest our identity, self-esteem and the reasons we find the weightiest'.[8] What is given emphasis here is the notion that a good life is one that will avoid the perils of personal impoverishment.[9] But in tough situations, when hard choices must

---

[4] John Kekes, *The Morality of Pluralism* (Princeton, NJ: Princeton University Press, 1993).

[5] *Utz* (London: Vintage, 1998); all references in the text are to this edition.

[6] See Taddeus Metz for a critique of philosophical studies on what makes life meaningful 'that have not systematically addressed the issue of whether it is affection, conation, volition, cognition, or some combination that fundamentally matters, sometimes shifting unwittingly between capacities': 'Recent Work on the Meaning of Life', *Ethics* 112 (July 2002): 793.

[7] Susan Wolf, 'Meaning and Morality', *Proceedings of the Aristotelian Society* 97 (1997): 305.

[8] Kekes, *The Morality of Pluralism*, p. 81.

[9] F.H. Bradley writes: 'if the question arises, Am I to advance as a good man or a good artist? morality says, 'Of course as a good man'; but then the whole matter turns on this, What line of action, the doing of what, does make me the best man? In collision of morality with morality it does not hold that the higher the morality the more harmonious the self. You may have harmony of a sort (*not perfect* harmony) without any morality, and you may have morality with but little harmony': *Ethical Studies* (2nd edn, Oxford: Clarendon Press, 1927), p. 236.

be made, can meaning legitimately take precedence over morality?[10] Philosophers have argued that if a life denied the meaning that derives from personal projects is considered by the moral agent to be a life not worth living, then there will be cases when in any clash between the two Meaning must prevail. Morality may be judged to be just too demanding.[11]

Frequently the pursuit of what gives life meaning will be accompanied by a strong sense of purpose that makes for drivenness. Focussing on the case of the painter Paul Gauguin, who left his wife and children to pursue his vocation abroad, Bernard Williams has seemed to argue that such vital even reckless sense of purpose should indeed be allowed to flourish; that in the case of the supremely gifted artist we have a clear example of when the claims of morality are to be overruled.[12] But how we view individual cases of drivenness, from the outside, would appear to involve a crucial factor: and this relates to what the individual who privileges a personal project is trying to achieve. Activities must be deemed to be worthwhile. Thus Susan Wolf claims that *'meaning arises in a person's life when subjective attraction meets objective attractiveness'* (305). Put differently, the standard by which we are required to judge any personal project is not somebody's subjectively grounded opinions, but the objective question of whether the project offers a prospect for realizing good things.

Yet viewed from the inside, however strong our will to express our power(s), however ardent our sense of vocation, moderns will typically feel the pressure that accompanies perceptions of another's (critical) need. Thus the question of whether my own cares and concerns should take precedence over the interests of another may well be an urgent one. When is it appropriate for one set of cares to prevail? In pursuing this subject I shall be turning to what looks like a postmodern novel, though it may be best seen as a hybrid, incorporating a mixture of postmodern and realist conventions. Abiding by the notion that life is confusing, the postmodern text is eager to contribute and hence to confound. Yet with Bruce Chatwin's *Utz* we find a postmodern narrative that accepts old challenges, the serious challenges of modernity, recognizing that the issue of morality versus meaning can be both urgent and interesting. However, given its ludic propensities, how can Chatwin's text work through the issue? A comparison

---

[10] As Wolf explains, there are at least two reasons to worry. The first concerns the child molester who claims that his life would lose all meaning if he could not molest children. The second gets to the 'theoretical heart of morality' and relates to 'the fundamental fact of human equality; so that one person has no more right to a good life – including in that a meaningful life – than another .... For both these reasons, if not for others, defenders of morality have resisted [Bernard] Williams' claims': 'Meaning and Morality', pp. 300–301.

[11] Robert B. Louden discusses this 'startling tendency in recent ethical theory': 'Can We Be Too Moral', *Ethics* 98 (1988): 361–78.

[12] Bernard Williams, *Moral Luck* (Cambridge: Cambridge University Press, 1981), ch. 2, pp. 20–39.

with a philosophical study whose origins lie precisely in this novel may further our understanding of the novel's achievements. An analysis of forms of argumentation means looking at the capacities of each genre to convey crucial facets of what are often complex situations. What kind of information or contextualization will the reader require? What moral and psychological features will be relevant?

In his discussion of the many-sided problem of the function of meaning in good or good-enough lives, philosopher John Kekes has contributed to the debate by focussing not on the special case of a genius, on an ardent and greatly gifted artist, but rather on an ordinary man who happens to be an avid collector of fine porcelain. The passion experienced and dedication to the cause, the sense of compulsion, we are to presume, is of an equal intensity. According to Kekes the predicament of this individual supports the claims of those who suspect there are good reasons why on occasions we should award priority to the requirements of personal meaning rather than to those of morality: a review of the motives that determine life choices should show that the 'driven' individual sometimes has reason on his side. The charge that can be levelled against such a person was explicated by F.H. Bradley: 'common morality remains both the cradle and protecting nurse of its aspiring offspring, and if we ever forget that, we live open to the charge of ingratitude and baseness'.[13]

Kekes's endeavour reveals the kind of difficulties that may be encountered, and in particular that posed by the burden of plausibility, which is linked to the issue of comprehension, when a brief description, as opposed to a narrative, is utilized in order to bear out a complex ethical argument relating to the shape of a life. Comprehension here involves various aspects of an account of the ways in which an individual engages or fails to engage with the world. We note, for instance, the strange emptiness of a self so conceived, the hollowness of a self-conception driven entirely by the promptings of (a specific) desire and deprived of moral reasons, beliefs, or frameworks. Kekes's Utz is an individual whose nature has been bizarrely fixed, locked into one dominant and dismal style.[14] Moreover, this is a character of whom we need to hear justifications in terms of a set of reasons, if we are to judge the reasonableness of his 'judgment'.[15]

---

[13] Bradley continues, 'Some neglect is unavoidable; but open and direct outrage on the standing moral institutions which make society and human life what it is, can be justified (I do not say condoned) only on the plea of overpowering moral necessity. And the individual should remember that the will for good, if weakened in one place, runs the greatest risk of being weakened in all': *Ethical Studies*, p. 227.

[14] Daniel C. Dennett argues that 'our natures aren't fixed because we have evolved to be entities designed to change their natures in response to interactions with the rest of the world': *Freedom Evolves* (New York: Viking, 2003), p. 91.

[15] Consider Sophia R. Moreau: 'To take a second-personal point of view toward someone else's judgment about his reasons is to regard that judgment, not just as a psychological fact about him, but as a judgment that he endorses, and as a judgment that you must either endorse or [dis] agree with. For you, it is simply not an option to stand back and regard it as a brute fact about him. You, too, must treat it as a judgment that stands in need of justification ... To leave room for a distinct second-person point of view, one must be able

Comprehension prefers reasoning, a discursive activity involving what is usually a process; it prefers some indication of the mind's inner speech and logic – to the citing of a single motive.

It is furthermore somewhat ironical that the original novel on which Kekes's text is based – Bruce Chatwin's novel *Utz* – not only highlights some advantages of the narrative mode of proceeding, but also comes to the opposite conclusion: the stance the novel works towards suggests that morality has a good chance of winning in cases of conflict with the (personal) meaning that derives from the pursuit of an absorbing project, because it can embody more meaning. In *Utz* it also turns out to be a psychically healthier option: the option that curtails one form of serious self-distortion.

It is worth noting for a start that the changes Kekes has had to make to the original are far from insignificant. Kekes has managed in transcribing the story of the collector, to strip the original Utz of all that makes him Utz. What we are given in the pages of Kekes's study is simply another Bitzer, and that is someone who is little more than a caricature of a human being. If Kekes's Utz begins odd, he ends up monstrous. Like Bitzer, Dickens's character, what is strange about him – and Bitzer clearly is strange – is his view of relationships as simply serving the making of bargains. But the fact that Bitzer is strange is for Dickens very much to the point. Dickens uses Bitzer precisely to point up the impoverished conception of human nature he identifies as constituting a model – the model of the rightly named 'abstract individual' – to be found at the core of another theory – that of Benthamite Utilitarianism. Equally determined, self-interested, industrious, and calculating, Kekes's Utz is ready to ignore the needs of everyone in pursuit of his goal. And in his shrivelled state it does indeed makes sense for him to have an emaciated vision of possibilities.[16] He seems to have no reason at all to care about the world in which he lives.

In Kekes's study we are given the following account of his subject:

> He lives in Prague, and the Allied betrayal of his country, the German occupation, the Second World War, the communist takeover, the various waves of terror, the murder of the Jews, the communist purges, the bombings, the show trials, the disappearance and the rare reappearance of people around him all impinge on his life merely as potential threats to the collection or as opportunities to enlarge it by judicious purchases from those who need money and have the goods. He casually cooperates with whomever happens to be

---

to recognize judgments that are not about me, but are nevertheless judgments that *I* can be asked to justify, judgments toward which I stand not as a passive observer but as someone who must either endorse or reject them.' Moreau notes that with regard to certain kinds of facts we regard ourselves and others as being 'answerable': 'Reasons and Character', *Ethics* 115 (2005): 300–303.

[16] Most relevant here is Nicholas Rescher's observation that 'someone who exists only unto himself, without relationships of community and interrelationships with others, is enmeshed in a delusional detachment from the world's course of things that makes him a freak rather than a person': *Human Interests: Reflections on Philosophical Anthropology* (Stanford, CA: Stanford University Press, 1990), p. 12.

in power, and he is quite willing, indeed eager, to exploit the latest wave of victims. He knows that the Nazis and the communists use him to lend a facade of respectability to their vicious regimes. They exhibit him as a testimony to their sensitivity to the finer things in life and to the freedom and support they provide for connoisseurship, and they even let him travel abroad to make some purchases. He allows himself to be used because he sees it as a bargain. What he has to give in terms of collaboration, the occasional public lies, the infrequent newspaper interviews, the mouthing of words of propoganda seem insignificant to him in comparison with the protection the collection receives in exchange. (164)

John Kekes's 'character' may well be rational, but he is hardly reasonable. Thus as Nicholas Rescher has remarked:

> The life of reason is not wholly a thing of calculating, planning, striving … It goes against reason to say that rational calculation should pervade all facets of human life … What is counterproductive is not the reasonableness of rationality but the unreasonableness of an exaggerated rationalism … Given that rationality is a matter of intelligence – of the effective use of mind – it is only natural and to be expected that rationality should be congenial to and supportive of that reflective, judgmental mode of happiness over which the mind itself is the final arbiter.[17]

Kekes's Utz appears obsessional to a degree that suggests a pathological condition. Or perhaps F.H. Bradley is nearer the mark when he claims that such a one could only ever exist as a figment of a theory-driven imagination.[18] Furthermore, although we are supposed to find that his life is worthwhile to him in so far as he has a strong sense of purpose, we cannot be sure exactly what end he has in sight: what is the purpose to which his sense of purpose points? Where Bitzer, indifferent to the welfare of all around him, his mother included, resolutely pursues a path which will improve his status, financial and social – a path indicated by self-interest – Kekes's character apparently sees himself as purely instrumental:[19]

> He lives a life in service of art. He cares about himself, as he does about others, only in so far as he is instrumental to perpetuating the collection. He would readily continue to suffer and endure great hardship, as he has in the past, in the interest of the treasures. (164)

Given his apparent indifference to the whole of mankind, it is by no means clear ultimately what this collecting is intended for. Kekes's Utz cannot ponder such a question. He cannot offer an explanation that is also a justification which we

---

[17] Nicholas Rescher, *Human Interests: Reflections on Philosophical Anthropology*, pp. 192–3.

[18] 'The individual man, the man into whose essence his community with others does not enter, who does not include relation to others in his very being, is, we say, a fiction … The mere individual is a delusion of theory; and the attempt to realize it in practice is the starvation and mutilation of human nature, with total sterility or the production of monstrosities': *Ethical Studies*, pp. 168, 174.

[19] Thus he would appear to avoid the 'offence' of egoistic hedonism.

can understand and endorse.[20] Chatwin's story, on the other hand, discloses what happens to individuals when they find themselves not just in the grip of their desires and passions, but also in the grip of their beliefs. And the two, we find, are not necessarily mutually supportive. Chatwin's Utz is caught up by his desire to collect and thus to be left in peace. But equally he is caught up by History, which in the guise of a fanatical Nazi cousin, will not leave him alone. The unpredictability, the potentially self-defeating impulsion and contrariety that is part of the nature of the human psyche, and that may be manifest in such circumstances, can emerge in one phrase of Chatwin's novel.

> At dinner, Utz listened politely while his cousin crowed over the victories in France: but when the man prophesied that Germans would occupy Buckingham Palace before the end of the year, he felt, despite his better judgement, a surge of latent anglophilia.
> 'I do not believe so', *he heard himself saying*. 'You underestimate this people. I know them. I was in England myself.'
> '*Also*,' the cousin murmured, and, with a click of the heels, marched out towards his waiting staff-car'. (19, emphasis added in fifth line)

Those few words 'he heard himself saying' serve to convey the implausibility of the idea of a life that can be entirely *regulated* by the demands issuing from desire, when people at critical moments can say or do what they do not mean to – such is the power of some of their beliefs and their only too human lack of self-control. Chatwin's *Utz* suggests that however strong self-regulative desire may be, if Meaning is to be consistently effective in trumping Morality then it requires the support of a foolproof system of beliefs. Marcia Cavell has argued that 'beliefs, desires, and all other propositional attitudes form a holistic network in which they are related to each other and to material reality. For this reason, when I determine what to believe, I also affect desires, emotions and values related to this belief. I potentially affect *the whole web* that is my mind'.[21] For Cavell we typically come to acquire reflexivity, and reflexivity 'generates reflection, ordering, synthesis', and hence a much needed and often threatened state of psychic integrity. Clearly, this means that in the usual course of things negotiations go on all the time, and tensions continually arise: 'for

---

[20] Excuses, as Marcia Baron explains, are different from justifications: 'I will think that I shouldn't be held responsible for my action, and that I therefore shouldn't be faulted for what I did, but this is not to say that I think I will be justified in doing it'. The 'must' someone feels should express justification, not just psychological necessity: 'On Admirable Immorality', *Ethics* 96 (1986): 558–9.

[21] Cavell argues here for the salience of the notion of self-integration, and continues 'creatures come to be persons – to have selves – through those complex processes that give rise to self-conscious thoughts. We understand ourselves as thinking, desiring subjects only to the extent that we grasp our behaviour and our thoughts as part of a unified activity. Where this breaks down to a drastic extent so does our sense of self': 'Ordering Selves', in Edna Ullmann-Margalit (ed.), *Reasoning Practically* (New York and Oxford: Oxford University Press, 2000), pp. 90–95, emphasis added.

who we are is a complicated interaction between the contingent and the uncontingent, the given and the chosen, the not-I and the I' (89).

Chatwin's recognition of the significance of words that are at once involuntary and yet spoken with conviction, exemplifies the strange reality that is human unpredictability. This phenomenon suggests that some individuals are capable when acting spontaneously from belief to act out of character, and that this may or may not be to the good. That such blunders may be self-defeating with respect to personal aims and ambitions becomes obvious in this case, as Chatwin's Utz is hauled up before the Gestapo. He evades punishment because he has with him, and is able to use to good purpose, the medal given to his father for bravery in the field of action. But the fact that he has kept it by him is a sign of who knows what: affection, pride, shrewdness?

Where Kekes gives us a monster of singlemindedness, Chatwin allows for more complexity: Chatwin's Utz acts and reacts as Charles Taylor would express it within a 'web of interlocutors'.[22] Utz does collaborate – as Kekes suggests he would – feeding the Nazi's information about the whereabouts of works of art. But he does so in order to gain sufficient respectability to be able to hide his Jewish friends from their persecutors.

> The rumours were true. He had collaborated. He had given information: a trickle of information as to the whereabouts of certain works of art – information available to anyone who knew how to use an art library. By doing so, he had been able to protect, even to hide, a number of his Jewish friends: among them the celebrated Hebraist, Zikmund Kraus. What, after all, was the value of a Titian or a Tiepolo if one human life could be saved? (20)

In Chatwin's version of the conflict between Morality and Meaning, it is Morality that wins, though conflict seems hardly the right expression when the issue is expressed in certain terms: 'what after all was the value of a Titian ...'. This question/statement suggests that the salient facts of the matter regarding Utz's crucial initiative are simply self-evident; that the idea of there being a choice here between Morality and Meaning is irrelevant, it simply doesn't come into the picture. But this short paragraph is in other ways surprising, incorporating as it does two contrasting ways of conceiving of this moral action. What Chatwin's text suggests is first that this moral agent cannot evade, cannot separate himself from his web of friendships, and that at the level of motivation the concern and active commitment or full involvement that is inseparable from genuine intimacy constitutes a potent force whatever the circumstances. Intimacy thus envisaged involves the kind of commitment that vitally constrains or limits choice. The sentence beginning 'what, after all, was the value of a Titian ...', however,

---

[22] 'This is the sense in which one cannot be a self on one's own.' A self exists only within what I call "webs of interlocution" ... The full definition of someone's identity thus usually involves not only his stand on moral and spiritual matters but also some reference to a defining community': Taylor, *Sources of the Self*, pp. 35–6.

rather than elaborating the point, provides an altogether different kind of explanation, providing a rationale for the action which is aimed at all those who fail to understand that (true) friendship is, when it comes to the realm of action and choice, a matter of Necessity. For the language of 'human lives' and *their* 'value' is the language that pertains to a universalist point of view; it is the perspective of impersonality. The reader is left, as it were, with a choice of motivating reasons.

*

In Chatwin's *Utz* we are given a character whose disposition enables him – or so it would seem – to fulfil freely and knowingly the requirements which critical moral situations demand. Informing the early chapters is what looks very much like an ethics of decency, a form of virtue ethics. Thus, in this account of one man's attempt in difficult circumstances to live a satisfying or good-enough life, Utz claims our admiration – as opposed to our interest, for we also find him intriguing – because despite his obsession and the corrupting circumstances of his world, and quite contrary to the reputation he has gained as an 'incurable decadent', he continues to remain just that, a down-to-earth 'decent' kind of man who can respond to critical situations in a way we cannot but respect. Lacking in heroic ardour, strenuousness or flamboyance, such a virtuous character possesses the 'dull' virtues of trustworthiness, honesty and solicitude.[23] At the core of decency we find constancy, which involves both steadiness and fidelity.

Yet this view of Chatwin's hero is seemingly premature, for as we read on it becomes only too apparent that this narrative makes the reader's attempt to find a precise ethical stance within this text an arduous business. Chatwin's is, we find, a playful, a ludic form of realism, one which sets out to mystify the reader, insisting, it would seem, on the utter unknowability of the subject; implying that truth about the subject can only be incomplete, the subject ever fragmentary, elusive, perhaps even 'split'. Indeed the text itself embodies a form of splitting. Suddenly we discover that the Utz we had previously encountered is nothing but an idea: an idea in the mind of the narrator, he is a figment of the imagination. When the narrator realizes he has been mistaken, that Utz had a moustache, his whole idea of the collector's life changes: "'Of course he had a moustache!" Dr Frankfurter shook with smutty laughter. "The moustache was the clue to his personality"!'(111). The moustache assumes a weight of significance: it is the marker of a metamorphosis. It is a symbol of human vanity, the vanity which, on this view, is inseparable from both self-esteem and *joie de vivre*.

It is typical of Utz, as portrayed by Chatwin in the early part of his novel, to be sensitive, to be kind, to take serious risks when faced by the urgent needs of others – both Marta and his Jewish friends. But just change one detail, one small feature of

---

[23] See John McDowell, 'Virtue and Reason', in Crisp and Slote (eds), *Virtue Ethics*, p. 144, and also Richard Freadman, 'Decency and Its Discontents', *Philosophy and Literature* 28 (2004): 392–405.

the self, Chatwin suggests, and you open the way for selfish fantasy to enter and take hold.[24] Now achieving a state of virtue or even continence becomes a very precarious business. In the first part of the novel it seems most appropriate to conceive of this individual in terms of a characteristically virtuous manner of responding to moral situations: of his 'characteristically' acting in a certain way because he possesses certain distinctive and enduring moral *qualities*. Later, however, after the narrator's discovery of the moustache we have to think again about the nature of his subject's distinguishing 'characteristics'. The 'virtue' model is at once inappropriate. For it is no longer his virtues that impress us but rather the strength of his sexual desire. No longer shy and retiring, no longer sensitive to the distress or discomfort of Marta, Utz's desire grows boundless, and with it emerges a new and more confident outlook on life.

Our picture of Utz is then nothing if not fragmentary: what we have is both the recluse and suddenly his opposite, the bold, *l'homme moyen sensuel*. The narrator of this text cannot come up with a defining image, a final version of his subject. We realize as soon as the moustached Utz makes his appearance, that the narrative we are reading is highly unstable; constituted as it is by a mélange of viewpoints whose origins often resist clarification. At times we are led to believe that the account of an event is to be attributed to Utz himself. At other times the stories are recounted by his friend, Dr Frankfurter. But large parts of the whole fabric seem to be nothing but an imaginative reconstruction by a perplexed but ingenious reporter/narrator. What is the truth? This narrator cannot be assumed to possess privileged access to this character's mind. Yet the fundamentally unknowable Other, Chatwin suggests, may yet himself acquire the kind of knowledge that powers a credible ethic. This new Utz, we will come to realize, ultimately recognizes in an 'idealizing moment' an ethical imperative which grows out of convictions or knowledge of what at this moment in time is truly right and just, and what is wrong because corrupting and degrading.[25] It is a moment when one realizes, when one knows, what the truth implies and what it may lead us to.

---

[24] As McDowell remarks: 'ethical reality is immensely difficult to see clearly. If we are aware of how, for instance, selfish fantasy distorts our vision, we shall not be inclined to be confident that we have got things right': 'Virtue and Reason', p. 161.

[25] See Thomas A. McCarthy 'Private Irony and Public Decency: Richard Rorty's New Pragmatism', *Critical Inquiry* 16 (1990): 367–70. McCarthy gives us an acute description of the idealizing moment: 'We can and typically do make contextually conditioned and fallible claims to unconditional truth ... and it is this moment of unconditionality that opens us up to criticism from other points of view. Without the idealizing moment, there would be no foothold in our accepted beliefs and practices for the critical shocks to consensus that force us to expand our horizons and learn to see things in different ways. It is precisely this context-transcendent, 'regulative' surplus of meaning in our notion of truth that keeps us from being locked into what we happen to agree on at any particular time and place, that opens us up to the alternative possibilities lodged in otherness and difference that have been so effectively invoked by post-structuralist thinkers': p. 370.

For the time being, however, the new Utz leads a highly decadent and charged kind of existence, his thoughts directed less often to his porcelain and more often to his love life, his encounters with divas of the operetta. These women now dominate the narrative, and Marta's distress is noted by the narrator but not apparently by Usk. It is not a salient factor in this energetic and eccentric and evidently enjoyable way of life. The narrative acknowledges her discomfort, yet is more impressed by her ingenuity and resilience. She is pragmatic and this, it would seem, is the appropriate attitude to take. The moral issue is lost in the details of her accomodating strategy. To insist on its importance is, one is somehow made to feel, to blunder by dragging in considerations that are somehow not appropriate to the situation:

> She prayed and prayed. She went tirelessly to Mass ... She begged forgiveness for her husband's infidelities, and for her role in turning the bedroom ... into 'something like a Polish bordel' .... Yet she acquired a professional's skill in preparing the bedroom for ladies too proud, or too ashamed, to bring an overnight bag .... Since the queue of ladies became more, not less, pressing over the years, the number of nights she had to sleep out increased. There was never a hint of reproach on her part. Nor, on his, the least acknowledgement that she had ever been inconvenienced. She believed that, by marrying her, he had done her all the honour in the world. My impression is that, in her mind, and perhaps even in his, she played the part of the consort who is obliged to witness, with amused condescension, a succession of hysterical mistresses. After moving into the apartment, she had slept under a quilt on the narrow Mies van der Rohe daybed. But one night, while reliving in a nightmare the horrors of Utz's arrest by the Gestapo, she landed on the floor with a reverberative wallop that set the porcelains clattering on the shelves. Thereafter, she preferred a kapok-filled camping-mattress that could be rolled out in the hallway: any night intruder would have to tread on her. (112–13)

Where John Kekes seems to want us to condone the monstrous, Bruce Chatwin gives us a celebration of the odd. What is not so very odd, however, is his subject's struggle with ambivalence. If Chatwin's novel theorizes the power of the pleasure principle, meditating on the endless drive for gratification which the porcelain exists to provide, then it is equally clear that the achievement of this kind of state is no simple business. Whether returning with Marta from a joyful day mushroom gathering in the grounds of the estate which one belonged to him – when he rediscovers a shared pleasure in the enterprise of bartering – or back from his holiday in France, he would find the porcelain 're-exert its power of snobbery', reminding him of his expertise, the taste and connoisseurship that divides him from his lowly housekeeper. 'Living with lifeless porcelain' brings on 'boredom, verging on fury'. Each time before leaving for France, 'he would make a resolution, never, ever to return – while at the same time making arrangements for his return – and would set off for Switzerland in the best of spirits' (74).

The collection 'held him prisoner', it had 'ruined' his life (75), he tells the narrator. If indeed he were a prisoner of his collection, in the sense that it is *the* factor that invariably conditions his crucial choices, Utz could then be said to have consented knowingly to the loss of a fundamental good, his freedom to choose. And his acquiesence in this state of affairs could then be taken as proof of irrationality. For much of the novel the collection is indeed a major factor, conditioning or constraining this life, until in temporary exile in France and alone in his hotel room, Utz finds himself reflecting on what he misses in Prague. Suddenly, he realizes that what he cannot do without is not the collection but his relationship with Marta: the pull of intimacy exerts its power again: 'He continued to stare at the idiotic chandelier, turning over in his mind the most troublesome question of all. He was desperately homesick, yet hadn't given a thought for the porcelains. He could only think of Marta, alone, in the apartment' (67). In modern realist novels such critical moments of reflection are more often than not crises of self-evaluation, which – as with Gaskell's Margaret Hale and Forster's Margaret Schlegel – may give rise to an uncomfortable, perhaps an unbearable, acquisition of self-knowledge. Utz, however, in reflecting on his own well-being does not reflect upon himself.

Bruce Chatwin's novella abstains from showing us how his collector reasons or deliberates. It largely avoids revealing through direct or indirect thought processes how Utz stands in regard to those 'circumstances' which, according to Hume, were so 'requisite to happiness'; namely 'inward peace of mind, consciousness of integrity [and] a satisfactory review of our own conduct'.[26] When the narrator tries to piece together what happened during the last months of Utz's life he can only surmise why Utz came to the decision he did. But the narrator decides that self-image had a lot to do with his subject's incredible decision. He theorizes that the collection of Meissen figurines became a motive for self-disgust, and that with Marta's help, Utz dumped – perhaps smashed – the lot.

But clearly what needs to be factored into the final picture is a new desire, 'an expanded and complicated desire',[27] a yearning for the personal goods of integrity and independence and the social good of freedom. This is the freedom to live without constant fear of repression and imprisonment; it involves the liberty to speak openly.[28] The ethical mode of this character is thus responsive to an ideal that becomes ever more pressing under the impact of an alien and oppressive ideology and regime. And it is a responsiveness to this force which will drive him towards the unthinkable. The incredible actions of Chatwin's hero can be interpreted then as marking a commitment to the ethical project of recognizing what makes for truthful living or an authentic life and the satisfaction of genuine interests.

---

[26] *Enquiries Concerning Human Understanding and Concerning the Principles of Morals*, ed. L.A. Selby-Bigge, rev. P.H. Nidditch (Oxford: Oxford University Press, 1975), p. 283.

[27] Thus Harpham, 'Ethical actions themselves reveal that what one "wants" can include what one does "not want" – the weight of necessity, compulsion, obedience to the [moral] law': 'Language, History and Ethics', p. 141.

[28] In *The Heart of What Matters: The Role for Literature in Moral Philosophy* (Berkeley, Los Angeles, London: University of Califormia Press, 2001). Cunningham claims that 'some values will always be more fundamental than others, and at times [these] may speak with a voice that silences the rest', p. 59.

I believe that, in reviewing his life during those final months, he regretted having always played the trickster. He regretted having wheedled himself and the collection out of every tight corner. He had tried to preserve in microcosm the elegance of European court life. But the price was too high. He hated the grovelling and the compromise – and in the end the porcelain disgusted him. (125)

At this point a comment by philosopher Owen Flanagan seems particularly appropriate: 'We do best', he remarks, 'if we reflectively examine the *encumbrances* we have and judge what kind of goods, if they are goods at all, these *encumbrances* are'.[29] Flanagan's use of the term 'encumbrance', instead of the more habitual vocabulary of 'interests', 'concerns' or 'commitments', in his account of what might be considered of value to us, and hence of significance to our sense of ourselves, seems especially relevant to the revised ethical perspective articulated in the remarkable closing chapters of Chatwin's novel. The precious porcelains can be viewed as 'encumbrances', are best redescribed as encumbrances that burden the individual and compromise his dignity, integrity, and freedom of action. They are best disposed of when what is recognized as essential to a satisfactory self-image (which is an essential component in a sense of well-being) is the kind of honesty that acknowledges the primacy of the social good of liberty. What counts on an individual level is then the determination to reassert one's independence, to achieve a greater measure of self-direction by not compromising, not to giving in to a system that through control and confiscation enacts a process of confinement and repression. In Chatwin's *Utz* background is also foreground, and one individual's work of destruction paradoxically becomes a moral response to a social evil. Taking a moral stand that signifies at one and the same time commitment to personal coherence and to the greater good of liberty, Utz realizes that an ethical life cannot part company with its world; where this world is perceived as a value-filled or a value-impoverished place: a place in which one can play a part that may be concealed, that seems to lack positive value, but that is still meaningful (subjectively and objectively meaningful).[30] For a reasonable person this kind of ethics just endows a life with more meaning.[31]

---

[29] Owen Flanagan, 'Identity and Strong and Weak Evaluation', in Flanagan and Rorty (eds), *Identity, Character and Morality*, p. 60, emphasis added.

[30] See Harpham's discussion of the 'usefulness' of morality. 'Standing explicitly opposed to mere culture ... morality rescues us from circumstances where society yields no "confidence". Under these circumstances, which may mean all circumstances, morality alone provides a guide to belief or action, overriding a vicious or conflicted culture by appealing to an imperative that transcends it': 'Language, History and Ethics', pp. 135–36.

[31] For John Finnis, amongst other things reasonableness means not attributing to any particular project the overriding and unconditional significance which only basic human goods can claim: *Fundamentals of Ethics*, p. 75.

Bibliography

Aarsleff, Hans, 'Locke's Influence', in Vere Chappell (ed.), *The Cambridge Companion to Locke* (Cambridge University Press, 1994), pp. 252–89.
Adam, Ian (ed.), *This Particular Web: Essays on Middlemarch* (Toronto and Buffalo: Toronto University Press, 1975).
Adams, R.M., 'Saints', *Journal of Philosophy* 81 (1984): 392–401.
Alford, Fred C., 'Emmanuel Levinas and Iris Murdoch: Ethics as Exit?', *Philosophy and Literature* 26 (2002): 24–42.
Allen, Walter, *George Eliot* (New York: Macmillan, 1964).
Allport, G.W., 'Attitudes', in C.A. Murchison (ed.), *Handbook of Social Psychology* (Worchester, MA: Clark University Press, 1935), pp. 1–50.
Anderson, Quentin, 'George Eliot in *Middlemarch*', in Boris Ford (ed.), *From Dickens to Hardy* (Harmondsworth: Penguin, 1958), pp. 274–93.
Anscombe, G.E.M., 'Modern Moral Philosophy', in Roger Crisp and Michael Slote (eds), *Virtue Ethics* (Oxford: Oxford University Press, 1997), pp. 26–43.
Arendt, Hannah, *Between Past and Future: Six Exercises in Poltical Thought* (New York: Meridian, 1961).
Aristotle, *The Ethics of Aristotle: The Nicomachean Ethics*, ed. Jonathan Barnes, trans. J.A.K.Thomson (Harmondsworth: Penguin, 1976).
Arnold, Matthew, *Culture and Anarchy and Other Writings*, Cambridge Texts in the History of Politics, ed. Stefan Collini (Cambridge: Cambridge University Press, 1993).
Armstrong, Isobel, *Mansfield Park: Penguin Critical Studies* (Harmondsworth: Penguin, 1988).
———, *Sense and Sensibility: Penguin Critical Studies* (Harmondsworth: Penguin Books, 1994).
Ashton, Rosemary, *George Eliot: A Life* (London: Hamish Hamilton, 1996).
Auerbach, Nina, 'Jane Austen's Dangerous Charm: Feeling as One Ought about Fanny Price', in Janet Todd (ed.), *Jane Austen: New Perspectives, Women and Literature*, vol. 3 (New York and London: Holmes and Meier, 1983), pp. 208–23.
Austen, Jane, *Sense and Sensibility*, ed. Tony Tanner (Harmondsworth: Penguin, 1969).
———, *Northanger Abbey*, ed. Anne Henry Ehrenpreis (Harmondsworth: Penguin, 1972).
———, *Pride and Prejudice*, ed. Tony Tanner (Harmondsworth: Penguin, 1972).
———, *Mansfield Park*, ed. Tony Tanner (Harmondsworth:Penguin, 1966).
———, *Persuasion*, ed. D.W. Harding (Harmondsworth: Penguin, 1965).
Bagehot, Walter, *Physics and Politics* (London: F. Morgan, 1876).
Baker, William (ed.), *The George Eliot-George Henry Lewes Library: An Annotated Catalogue of their books at Dr Williams's Library, London* (New York: Garland, 1977).
Baron, Marcia, 'On the Alleged Moral Repugnance of Acting from Duty', *Journal of Philosophy* 81 (1984): 197–219.
———, On Admirable Immorality', *Ethics* 96 (1986): 557–66.
Bedient, Calvin, *Architects of the Self: George Eliot, D.H. Lawrence, and E.M. Forster* (Berkeley: California University Press, 1972).

Beer, Gillian, *Darwin's Plots: Evolutionary Narrative in Darwin, George Eliot and Nineteenth-Century Fiction* (London: Routledge and Kegan Paul, 1983).
Benhabib, Sheyla, *Situating the Self, Gender, Community and Postmodernism in Contemporary Ethics* (Oxford: Polity Press, 1992).
——, 'The Generalized and the Concrete Other: The Kohlberg-Gilligan Controversy and Moral Theory', in Eva Feder Kittay and Diana T. Meyers (eds), *Women and Moral Theory* (Totowa, NJ: Rowman and Littlefield, 1987), pp. 154–77.
Blake, Kathleen, '*Middlemarch* and the Woman Question', in Harold Bloom (ed.), *George Eliot's Middlemarch* (New York: Chelsea House, 1987), pp. 49–70.
Bloom, Harold (ed.), *George Eliot's Middlemarch* (New York: Chelsea House, 1987).
—— (ed.), *Charles Dickens* (New York: Chelsea House, 1987).
—— (ed.), *Thomas Hardy's The Return of the Native* (New York, Chelsea House, 1987).
Blum, Lawrence A., *Moral Perception and Particularity* (Cambridge: Cambridge University Press, 1994).
Bodenheimer, Rosemarie, *The Politics of Story in Victorian Social Fiction* (Ithaca and London: Cornell University Press, 1988).
Born, Daniel, 'Private Gardens, Public Swamps: *Howards End* and the Revaluation of Liberal Guilt', *Novel* 25 (1992): 141–159.
Bosanquet, Bernard (ed.), *Aspects of the Social Problem* (London: Macmillan, 1895).
Bosanquet, Helen, *The Strength of the People: A Study in Social Economics* (2nd edn, London: Macmillan, 1903).
Bouthoul, Gaston, *Les Mentalités* (Paris: Presses Universitaires de France, 1952).
Bradley, F.H., *Ethical Studies* (2nd edn, Oxford: Clarendon Press, 1927).
Brown, Julia Prewitt, *Jane Austen's Novels: Social Change and Literary Form* (Cambridge, MA: Harvard University Press, 1979).
Brudney, Daniel, 'Knowledge and Silence: *The Golden Bowl* and Moral Philosophy', *Critical Inquiry* 16 (1990): 397–437.
——, 'Marlow's Morality', *Philosophy and Literature* 27 (2003): 318–40.
Buell, Lawrence, 'What We Talk About When We Talk About Ethics', in Marjorie Garber, Beatrice Hanssen and Rebecca L. Walkowitz (eds), *The Turn to Ethics* (New York and London: Routledge, 2000), pp. 1–13.
Butler, Judith, 'Ethical Ambivalence', in Marjorie Garber, Beatrice Hanssen and Rebecca L. Walkowitz (eds), *The Turn to Ethics* (New York and London: Routledge, 2000), pp. 15–28.
Butler, Marilyn, *Jane Austen and the War of Ideas* (Oxford: Clarendon Press, 1975).
——, *Romantics, Rebels and Reactionaries* (Oxford: Oxford University Press, 1981).
Carroll, David, '*Middlemarch* and the Externality of Fact', in Ian Adam (ed.), *This Particular Web: Essays on Middlemarch* (Toronto and Buffalo: Toronto University Press, 1975), pp. 73–90.
Cavell, Marcia, 'Ordering Selves', in Edna Ullmann-Margalit (ed.), *Reasoning Practically* (New York and Oxford: Oxford University Press, 2000), pp. 85–97.
Chalier, Catherine, *What Ought I to Do?: Morality in Kant and Levinas*, trans. Jane Marie Todd (Ithaca and London: Cornell University Press, 2002).
Chatwin, Bruce, *Utz* (London: Vintage, 1998).
Christ, Carol, 'Aggression and Providential Death in George Eliot's Fiction', *Novel* 9 (1976): 130–40.
Coleman, Janet, 'MacIntyre and Aquinas', in John Horton and Susan Mendus (eds), *After MacIntyre: Critical Perspectives on the Work of Alasdair MacIntyre* (Oxford: Polity Press, 1994), pp. 65–90.

Coles, Nicholas, 'The Politics of *Hard Times*: Dickens the Novelist versus Dickens the Reformer', *Dickens Studies Annual* 15 (1986): 145–79.
Collini, Stefan, 'The Idea of 'Character' in Victorian Political Thought', *Transactions of the Royal Historical Society* 35 (1985): 29–50.
———, *Public Moralists: Political Thought and Intellectual Life in Britain, 1850–1930* (Oxford: Oxford University Press, 1991).
Connor, Steven, *Charles Dickens* (Oxford: Basil Blackwell, 1985).
Cox, C.B., *The Free Spirit: A Study of Liberal Humanism in the Novels of George Eliot, Henry James, E.M. Forster, Virginia Woolf, Angus Wilson* (London and Oxford: Oxford University Press, 1963).
Crisp, Roger and Slote, Michael (eds), *Virtue Ethics* (Oxford: Oxford University Press, 1997).
Cudworth, Ralph, *A Sermon Preached before the Honourable House of Commons at Westminster, March 31, 1647*, ed. Edward Tagart (Printed and sold by the Unitarian Association, 1843).
Cullity, Garrett, 'Why Live This Way', *TLS*, 25 June 1999: 9.
Cunningham, Anthony, *The Heart of What Matters: The Role for Literature in Moral Philosophy* (Berkeley, Los Angeles, London: University of California Press, 2001).
Daleski, H.M., *Unities* (Athens: University of Georgia Press, 1985).
Damico, Alfonso J. (ed.), *Liberals on Liberalism* (Totowa, NJ: Rowman and Littlefield, 1986).
Dancy, Jonathan, *Moral Reasons* (Oxford: Blackwell, 1993).
Dave, J.C., *The Human Predicament in Hardy's Novels* (London: Macmillan, 1985).
Davidson, Jenny, *Hypocrisy and the Politics of Politeness: Manners and Morals from Locke to Austen* (Cambridge: Cambridge University Press, 2004).
Dennett, Daniel C., *Freedom Evolves* (New York: Viking Press, 2003).
Dewey, John, *The Middle Works, 1899–1924*, ed. Jo Ann Boydston, vol. 5 (Carbondale: Southern Illinois Press, 1978).
Diamond, Cora, 'Having a Rough Story about What Moral Philosophy is', *New Literary History* 15 (1983): 155–69.
Dickens, Charles, 'On Strike', *Household Words*, 11 February 1854: 553–9.
———, *Hard Times*, ed. David Craig (Harmondsworth: Penguin, 1969).
———, *Hard Times*, Norton edition, ed. George Ford and Sylvère Monod (New York: W.W. Norton, 1966, 1990).
———, *Little Dorrit*, ed. John Holloway (Harmondsworth: Penguin, 1967).
———, *Great Expectations*, ed. Angus Calder (Harmondsworth: Penguin, 1965).
———, *The Letters*, The Pilgrim Edition, ed. Madeline House, Graham Storey and Kathleen Tillotson, vol. 3 (Oxford: Clarendon Press, 1974).
Doody, Margaret Anne, '"A Good Memory is Unpardonable": Self, Love, and the Irrational Irritation of Memory', *Eighteenth-Century Fiction* 14 (2001): 67–94.
Doris, John M., *Lack of Character: Personality and Moral Behaviour* (Cambridge: Cambridge University Press, 2002).
Eagleton, Terry, 'Thomas Hardy: Nature as Language', *Critical Quarterly* 13 (1971): 155–62.
———, *The Illusions of Postmodernism* (Oxford: Blackwell, 1996).
Eldridge, Richard, *On Moral Personhood: Philosophy, Literature, Criticism and Self-Understanding* (Chicago and London: Chicago University Press, 1989).
Eliot, George, *Middlemarch*, ed. W.J. Harvey (Harmondsworth: Penguin, 1981).

Ermath, Elizabeth, *Realism and Consensus in the English Novel* (Princeton: Princeton University Press, 1984).
Federico, Annette R., 'David Copperfield and the Pursuit of Happiness', *Victorian Studies* 46 (2003): 69–95.
Finnis, John, *Fundamentals of Ethics* (Oxford: Clarendon Press, 1983).
Flanagan, Owen, *Varieties of Moral Personality: Ethics and Psychological Realism* (Cambridge, MA: Harvard University Press, 1991).
——, 'Identity and Strong and Weak Evaluation', in Owen Flanagan and Amélie Oksenberg Rorty (eds), *Identity, Character and Morality: Essays in Moral Psychology* (Cambridge, MA and London: MIT Press, 1993), pp. 37–66.
Flanagan, Owen and Rorty, Amélie Oksenberg (eds), *Identity, Character and Morality: Essays in Moral Psychology* (Cambridge, MA and London: MIT Press, 1993).
Flathman, Richard E., 'Liberalism and the Human Good of Freedom' in Alfonso J. Damico (ed.), *Liberals on Liberalism* (Totowa, NJ: Rowman and Littlefield, 1986), pp. 67–94.
——, *Willing Liberalism: Voluntarism and Individuality in Political Theory and Practice* (Ithaca: Cornell University Press, 1992).
Fleishman, Avrom, *A Reading of Mansfield Park: An Essay in Critical Synthesis* (Minneapolis: University of Minnesota Press, 1967).
Ford, Boris (ed.), *From Dickens to Hardy* (Harmondsworth: Penguin, 1958).
Forster, E.M., *Howards End*, ed. Oliver Stallybrass (Harmondsworth: Penguin, 1973).
Fowler, Roger, 'Polyphony and Problematic in Hard Times', in Robert Gittings (ed.), *The Changing World of Charles Dickens* (Totowa: Barnes and Noble, London: Vision Press, 1983), pp. 91–108.
Frankfurt, Harry, *The Importance of What We Care About* (New York: Cambridge University Press, 1988).
——, 'On the Necessity of Ideals', in G. Noam, and Thomas E. Wren (eds), *The Moral Self: Building a Better Paradigm* (Cambridge, MA: MIT Press, 1993), pp.16–27.
Franklin, Benjamin, *Autobiography and Other Writings*, ed. Russel B. Nye (Boston: Houghton Mifflin, 1958).
Freadman, Richard, 'Decency and Its Discontents', *Philosophy and Literature* 28 (2004): 392–405.
Freeden, M., *The New Liberalism: An Ideology of Social Reform* (Oxford: Clarendon, 1978).
Friedman, M., 'Moral Integrity and the Deferential Wife', *Philosophical Studies* 47 (1985): 141–50.
Gallagher, Catherine, *The Industrial Reformation of English Fiction: Social Discourse and Narrative Form, 1832–1867* (Chicago and London: University of Chicago Press, 1985).
Ganz, Margaret, *Elizabeth Gaskell: The Artist in Conflict* (New York: Twayne, 1969).
Garber, Marjorie, Hanssen, Beatrice and Walkowitz, Rebecca L. (eds), *The Turn to Ethics* (New York and London: Routledge, 2000).
Gard, Roger, *Jane Austen's Novels: the Art of Clarity* (New Haven and London: Yale University Press, 1992).
Gaskell, Elizabeth, *North and South*, ed. Esther Alice Chadwick (London: Dent, 1914, 1975).
Gaus, Gerald F., *The Modern Liberal Theory of Man* (London: Croom Helm, 1983).
Gibson, Andrew, *Postmodernity, Ethics and the Novel from Leavis to Levinas* (London: Routledge, 1999).
Gilbert, Sandra M. and Gubar, Susan, *The Madwoman in the Attic: The Woman Writer and the Nineteenth-Century Literary Imagination* (New Haven: Yale University Press, 1979).

Gilligan, Carol, *In a Different Voice: Pyschological Theory and Women's Development* (Cambridge: Harvard University Press, 1982).

———, 'Moral Orientation and Moral Development', in Eva Feder Kittay and Diana T. Meyers (eds), *Women and Moral Theory* (Totowa, NJ: Rowman and Littlefield, 1987), pp. 19–36.

Gittings, Robert (ed.), *The Changing World of Charles Dickens* (Totowa: Barnes and Noble, London: Vision Press, 1983).

Gladstone, David (ed.), *The Philosophy of the State and the Practice of Welfare: The Writings of Bernard and Helen Bosanquet (Pioneers of Social Welfare)* (London: Routledge, 1996).

Gordon, Mary, '"Things That Can't Be Phrased": Forster and *Howards End*', *Salmagundi* 143 (2004): 89–103.

Graver, Susanne, *George Eliot and Community* (Berkeley: California University Press, 1984).

Gray, John, *Liberalisms: Essays in Political Philosophy* (London: Routledge, 1989).

———, 'Mill's Conception of Happiness and the Theory of Individuality', in John Gray and G.W. Smith (eds), *J.S. Mill, 'On Liberty' in Focus* (London: Routledge, 1991), pp. 194–207.

Gray, John, and Smith, G.W. (eds), *J.S. Mill, 'On Liberty' in Focus* (London: Routledge, 1991).

Green, Samuel, *The Working Classes of Great Britain, their Present Condition and the Means of their Improvement and Elevation* (London: J. Snow, 1850).

Gregor, Ian, *The Great Web: The Form of Hardy's Fiction* (London: Faber and Faber, 1974).

Griffin, James, *Well-Being: Its Meaning, Measurement and Moral Importance* (Oxford: Clarendon, 1986).

Gutting, Gary, *French Philosophy in the Twentieth Century* (Cambridge: Cambridge University Press, 2001).

Hadfield, A., Rainsford, D. and Woods, T. (eds), *The Ethics in Literature* (London: Palgrave, Macmillan, 1999).

Halperin, John, *Egoism and Self-Discovery in the Victorian Novel: Studies in the Ordeal of Knowledge in the Nineteenth Century* (New York: Burt Franklin, 1974).

Hardy, Barbara (ed.), *Middlemarch: Critical Approaches to the Novel* (London: Athlone Press, 1967).

———, *Charles Dickens: The Later Novels* (London: Longman, 1968).

———, '*Middlemarch* and the Passions', in Ian Adam (ed.), *This Particular Web: Essays on Middlemarch* (Toronto and Buffalo: Toronto University Press, 1975) pp. 3–21.

———, 'Public and Private Worlds', in Harold Bloom (ed.), *George Eliot's Middlemarch* (New York: Chelsea House, 1987), pp. 27–48.

Hardy, Thomas, *The Return of the Native*, ed. George Woodcock (Harmondsworth: Penguin, 1978).

Harman, Barbara Leah, *The Feminine Political Novel in Victorian England* (Charlottesville and London: Virginia University Press, 1998).

Harpham, Geoffrey Galt, 'Language, History and Ethics', *Raritan* 7 (1987): 128–46.

Helps, Arthur, *The Claims of Labour: An Essay on the Duties of the Employers to the Employed* (London: William Pickering, 1844).

Henberg, M.C., 'George Eliot's Moral Realism', *Philosophy and Literature* 3 (1979): 20–38.

Herbert, Christopher, *Culture and Anomie: Ethnographic Imagination in the Nineteenth Century* (Chicago: University of Chicago Press, 1991).

Holloway, John, *The Victorian Sage: Studies in Argument* (London: Macmillan, 1953).
Holmes, Stephen, *The Anatomy of Anti-Liberalism* (Cambridge, MA: Harvard University Press, 1993).
———, 'The Permanent Structure of Anti-liberal Thought', in Nancy L. Rosenblum (ed.), *Liberalism and the Moral Life* (Cambridge, MA: Harvard University Press, 1989), pp. 159–82.
Horton, John and Mendus, Susan (eds), *After MacIntyre: Critical Perspectives on the Work of Alasdair MacIntyre* (Oxford: Polity Press, 1994).
Hoy, Cyrus, 'Forster's Metaphysical Novel', *PMLA* 75 (1960): 126–36.
Hulme, Hilda M., 'The Language of the Novel: Imagery', in Barbara Hardy (ed.), *Middlemarch: Critical Approaches to the Novel* (London: Athlone Press, 1967), pp. 87–124.
Hume, David, *Enquiries Concerning Human Understanding and Concerning the Principles of Morals*, ed. L.A. Selby-Bigge, rev. P.H. Nidditch (Oxford: Oxford University Press, 1975).
———, *A Treatise of Human Nature*, ed. L.A. Selby-Bigge, rev. P.H. Nidditch (Oxford: Clarendon Press, 1978).
Hurka, Thomas, *Perfectionism* (New York and Oxford: Oxford University Press, 1993).
Ingram, Allan, *The Language of D.H. Lawrence* (Basingstoke: Macmillan, 1990).
Ingham, Patricia, 'Nobody's Fault: the Scope of the Negative in Little Dorrit', in John Schad (ed.), *Dickens Refigured: Bodies, Desires and Other Histories* (Manchester: Manchester University Press, 1996), pp. 98–116.
James, William, *The Varieties of Religious Experience: A Study in Human Nature* (London: Longmans, Green and Co., 1920).
———, *The Principles of Psychology* (2 vols, New York: Dover Publications, 1950).
Johnson, Bruce, 'Pastoralism and Modernity', in Harold Bloom (ed.), *Thomas Hardy's The Return of the Native* (New York, Chelsea House, 1987), pp. 111–36.
Johnson, Claudia L., *Jane Austen: Women, Politics and the Novel* (Chicago: Chicago University Press, 1988).
Jones, Karen, 'Trust as an Affective Attitude', *Ethics* 107 (1996): 4–25.
Joyce, Patrick, *Work, Society, and Politics: The Culture of the Factory in Later Victorian England* (New Brunswick, NJ: Rutgers University Press, 1980).
Kant, Immanuel, *The Metaphysics of Morals*, trans. and with an introduction by Mary J. Gregor (Philadelphia: Pennsylvania University Press, 1971; revised edition, Cambridge: Cambridge University Press, 1991).
———, *Foundations of the Metaphysics of Morals*, trans. and with an introduction by Lewis White Beck (Chicago: Chicago University Press, 1950).
Kaye-Smith, Sheila and Stern, G.B., *Speaking of Jane Austen* (New York and London: Harper, 1944).
Kekes, John, *The Morality of Pluralism* (Princeton, NJ: Princeton University Press, 1993).
———, *Moral Wisdom and Good Lives* (Ithaca and London: Cornell University Press, 1995).
———, *The Art of Life* (Ithaca and London: Cornell University Press, 2002).
Kelly, Paul, 'MacIntyre's Critique of Utilitarianism', in John Horton and Susan Mendus (eds), *After MacIntyre: Critical Perspectives on the Work of Alasdair MacIntyre* (Oxford: Polity Press, 1994), pp. 127–45.
Kettle, Arnold, 'The Early Victorian Social-Problem Novel', in Boris Ford (ed.), *From Dickens to Hardy* (Harmondsworth: Penguin, 1958), pp. 169–87.

Kierkegaard, Sören, *Purity of Heart is to Will One Thing*, trans. and with an introduction by Douglas Steere (London: Collins, 1961).
Kirkham, Margaret, 'Feminist Irony and the Priceless Heroine of *Mansfield Park*', in Janet Todd (ed.), *Jane Austen: New Perspectives, Women and Literature*, vol. 3 (New York and London: Holmes and Meier, 1983), pp. 231–47.
Kittay, Eva Feder and Meyers, Diana T. (eds), *Women and Moral Theory* (Totowa, NJ: Rowman and Littlefield, 1987).
Knoepflmacher, U.C., *Religious Humanism and the Victorian Novel: George Eliot, Walter Pater and Samuel Butler* (Princeton: Princeton University Press, 1965).
Knox-Shaw, Peter, *Jane Austen and the Enlightenment* (Cambridge: Cambridge University Press, 2004).
Kolnai, Aurel, *Ethics, Value and Reality: Selected Papers of Aurel Kolnai* (London: Athlone Press, 1977).
Kymlicka, Will, *Liberalism, Community and Culture* (Oxford: Clarendon Press, 1989).
Langbaum, Robert, *Thomas Hardy in our Time* (London: Macmillan, 1995).
Larson, Jil, *Ethics and Narrative in the English Novel, 1880–1914* (Cambridge: Cambridge University Press, 2001).
Leavis, F.R., *The Great Tradition* (London: Chatto and Windus, 1948).
———, *The Common Pursuit* (London Chatto and Windus, 1952).
———, *Thought, Words and Creativity: Art and Thought in Lawrence* (London: Chatto and Windus, 1976).
Lerner, Laurence, 'Dorothea and the Theresa-Complex', in P. Swinden (ed.), *Middlemarch* (London: Macmillan, 1972), pp. 225–247.
Levenson, Michael, *Modernism and the Fate of Individuality: Character and Novelistic Form from Conrad to Woolf* (Cambridge: Cambridge University Press, 1995).
Levine, George, '*Little Dorrit* and Three Kinds of Science', in Joanne Shattock (ed.), *Dickens and Other Victorians: Essays in Honour of Philip Collins* (London: Macmillan, 1988), pp. 3–24.
Locke, John, *An Essay Concerning Human Understanding*, ed. Peter H. Nidditch (Oxford: Clarendon Press, 1975).
Lodge, David, 'How Successsful is *Hard Times*?', in *Working with Structuralism* (Boston: Routledge and Kegan Paul, 1981), reprinted in George Ford and Sylvère Monod (eds), *Hard Times*, Norton edition (New York: W.W. Norton, 1966, 1990), pp. 381–9.
Louden, Robert B., 'Can We Be Too Moral', *Ethics* 98 (1988): 361–78.
Lukes, Steven, *Individualism* (Oxford: Basil Blackwell, 1973).
McCabe, Herbert, OP, *The Good Life: Ethics and the Pursuit of Happiness* (London and New York: Continuum, 2005).
McCarthy, Thomas A., 'Private Irony and Public Decency: Richard Rorty's New Pragmatism', *Critical Inquiry* 16 (1990): 367–70.
McDowell, John, 'Virtue and Reason', in Roger Crisp and Michael Slote (eds), *Virtue Ethics* (Oxford: Oxford University Press, 1997), pp. 141–62.
McGinn, Colin, *Ethics, Evil and Fiction* (Oxford: Clarendon Press, 1997).
Maccall, William, *The Elements of Individualism* (London: John Chapman, 1847).
MacIntyre, Alasdair, *After Virtue: A Study in Moral Theory* (London: Duckworth, 1981).
Mackie, J.L., *Hume's Moral Theory* (London: Routledge and Kegan Paul, 1980).
Medalie, David, *E.M. Forster's Modernism* (London: Palgrave Macmillan, 2002).
Mejía, Cristina, 'Moral Capacities and Other Constraints', in A. Hadfield, D. Rainsford and T. Woods (eds), *The Ethics in Literature* (London: Palgrave, Macmillan, 1999), pp. 212–28.

Metz, Taddeus, 'Recent Work on the Meaning of Life', *Ethics* 112 (2002): 781–814.
Meyers, Diana T., 'The Socialized Individual and Individual Autonomy: An Intersection between Philosophy and Psychology', in Eva Feder Kittay and Diana T. Meyers (eds), *Women and Moral Theory* (Totowa, NJ: Rowman and Littlefield, 1987), pp. 139–53.
Mill, James, *Essay on Government*, ed. and with an introduction by Currin V. Shields (Indianapolis: Bobbs-Merill, 1955).
Mill, John Stuart, *On Liberty*, ed. Gertrude Himmelfarb (Harmondsworth:Penguin, 1974).
———, *Autobiography*, ed. John M. Robson (Harmondsworth: Penguin, 1989).
———, *Principles of Political Economy*, in John M. Robson et al. (eds), *Collected Works of John Stuart Mill*, vol. 3 (Toronto: University of Toronto Press, 1963).
———, 'The Claims of Labour', in *Essays on Economics and Society*, in John M. Robson et al. (eds), *Collected Works of John Stuart Mill*, vol. 4 (Toronto: University of Toronto Press, 1967).
———, 'A System of Logic', in John M. Robson et al. (eds), *Collected Works of John Stuart Mill*, vol. 7 (Toronto: Toronto University Press, 1973).
———, 'Remarks on Bentham's Philosophy' (1833), in *Essays on Ethics, Religion, and Society*, in John M. Robson et al. (eds), *Collected Works of John Stuart Mill*, vol.10 (Toronto: University of Toronto Press, 1969).
———, 'Bentham' (1838), in *Essays on Ethics, Religion, and Society*, in John M. Robson et al. (eds), *Collected Works of John Stuart Mill*, vol. 10 (Toronto: University of Toronto Press, 1969).
———, 'Utilitarianism' (1861), in *Essays on Ethics, Religion, and Society*, in John M. Robson et al. (eds), *Collected Works of John Stuart Mill*, vol.10 (Toronto: University of Toronto Press, 1969), pp. 203–59.
Miller, D.A., *Narrative and its Discontents: Problems of Closure in the Traditional Novel* (Princeton: Princeton University Press, 1981).
———, '*George Eliot: The Wisdom of Balancing Claims (Middlemarch)*', in K.M. Newton (ed.), *George Eliot* (London: Longman, 1991), pp. 187–97.
Miller, J. Hillis, Poirier, Richard and Hardy, Barbara, '*Middlemarch*: Chapter 85: Three Commentaries', *Nineteenth-Century Fiction* 35 (1980): 432–53.
Moore, G.E., *Principia Ethica* (Cambridge: Cambridge University Press, 1922).
Moreau, Sophia R., 'Reasons and Character', *Ethics* 115 (2005): 272–305.
Morris, Herbert, *On Guilt and Innocence* (Berkeley: California University Press, 1976).
Murdoch, Iris, *The Sovereignty of Good* (London: Routledge, 1970).
Myers, William, *The Presence of Persons: Essays on Literature, Science and Philosophy in the Nineteenth Century* (Aldershot: Ashgate, 1998).
Nardin, Jane, *Trollope and Victorian Moral Philosophy* (Ohio: Ohio University Press, 1996).
Nazar, Hina, 'The Imagination Goes Visiting: Jane Austen, Judgment and the Social', *Nineteenth-Century Literature* 59 (2004): 145–78.
Neill, Edward, *The Secret Life of Thomas Hardy* (Aldershot: Ashgate, 2004).
Newey, Vincent, *Centering the Self: Subjectivity, Society and Reading from Thomas Gray to Thomas Hardy* (Aldershot: Ashgate, 1995).
———, *The Scriptures of Charles Dickens: Novels of Ideology, Novels of the Self* (Aldershot: Ashgate, 2004).
Newson, Robert, *Dickens Revisited* (New York: Twayne, 2002).
Newton, Adam Zachary, *Narrative Ethics* (Cambridge, MA: Harvard University Press, 1995).

Newton, Judith Lowder, *Women, Power and Subversion: Social Strategies in British Fiction* (Athens: University of Georgia Press, 1981).
Newton, K.M., *George Eliot, Romantic Humanist: A Study of the Philosophical Structure of her Novels* (London: Macmillan, 1981).
—— (ed.), *George Eliot* (London: Longman, 1991).
Noam, G. and Wren, Thomas E. (eds), *The Moral Self: Building a Better Paradigm* (Cambridge, MA: MIT Press, 1993).
Nokes, David, *Jane Austen, A Life* (London: Fourth Estate, 1997).
Norman, Richard, *The Moral Philosophers: An Introduction to Ethics* (Oxford: Oxford University Press, 1998).
Nussbaum, Martha C., *Love's Knowledge: Essays on Philosophy and Literature* (Oxford: Oxford University Press, 1990).
——, *Upheavals of Thought: The Intelligence of the Emotions* (New York: Cambridge, 2001).
O'Hara, Patricia, 'Narrating the Native: Victorian Anthropology and Hardy's *The Return Of the Native*', *Nineteenth-Century Contexts* 20 (1997): 147–63.
Orwell, George, 'Charles Dickens', in Sonia Orwell and Ian Angus (eds), *The Collected Essays, Journalism and Letters of George Orwell*, vol. 1 (4 vols, London: Secker and Warburg, 1968), pp. 413–60.
Paris, Bernard J., *Experiments in Life: George Eliot's Quest for Values* (Detroit: Wayne State University Press, 1965).
——, *Character and Conflict in Jane Austen's Novels: A Pyschological Approach* (Detroit: Wayne State University Press, 1978).
Parker, David, *Ethics, Theory and the Novel* (Cambridge: Cambridge University Press, 1994).
Paterson, John, *The Making of the Return of the Native*, University of California Publications: Studies in English 19 (Berkeley, 1960).
Patrides, C.A., *The Cambridge Platonists* (London: Edward Arnold, 1969).
Pecora, Vincent P., 'Ethics, Politics and the Middle Voice', *Yale French Studies* 79 (1991): 203–30.
Perkins, Pam, 'A Subdued Gaiety: The Comedy of *Mansfield Park*', *Nineteenth-Century Literature* 47 (1993): 1–25.
Pickrel, Paul, 'Lionel Trilling and *Mansfield Park*', *Studies in English Literature* 27 (1987): 609–21.
Pikoulis, John, '*North and South*: Varieties of Love and Power', *Yearbook of English Studies* 6 (1976): 176–93.
Poirier, Richard and Miller, J. Hillis, '*Middlemarch*: Chapter 85: Three Commentaries', *Nineteenth-Century Fiction* 35 (1980): 448–53.
Poovey, Mary, *The Proper Lady and the Woman Writer: Ideology as Style in the Works of Mary Wollstonecraft, Mary Shelley and Jane Austen* (Chicago: Chicago University Press, 1984).
Pope, Alexander, *Poems*, selected by Douglas Grant and introduced by Angus Ross (Harmondsworth: Penguin, 1985).
Price, Martin, *Forms of Life: Character and Moral Imagination in the Novel* (New Haven and London: Yale University Press, 1983).
Pulsford, Stephen, 'The Aesthetic and the Closed Shop: The Ideology of the Aesthetic in Dickens's *Hard Times*', *Victorian Review* 21 (1995): 145–60.

Putnam, Ruth Anna, 'The Moral Life of a Pragmatist', in Owen Flanagan and Amélie Oksenberg Rorty (eds), *Identity, Character and Morality* (Cambridge MA and London: MIT Press, 1993), pp. 67–89.
Radford, Andrew, *Thomas Hardy and the Survivals of Time* (Aldershot: Ashgate, 2003).
Rainsford, Dominic, *Authorship, Ethics and the Reader: Blake, Dickens and Joyce* (London: Macmillan, 1997).
Rawls, John, *A Theory of Justice* (Cambridge, MA: Harvard University Press, 1971).
Rescher, Nicholas, *Rationality: A Philosophical Inquiry into the Nature and the Rationale of Reason* (Oxford: Clarendon Press, 1988).
——, *Human Interests, Reflections on Philosophical Anthropology* (Stanford: Stanford University Press, 1990).
——, *A System of Pragmatic Idealism* (3 vols, Princeton: Princeton University Press, 1993).
Richardson, Samuel, *Pamela*, ed. Margaret A. Doody (Harmondsworth: Penguin Classics, 1980).
Robbins, Jill, *Altered Reading: Levinas and Literature* (Chicago: University of Chicago Press, 1999).
Roberts, David, *Paternalism in Early-Victorian England* (London: Croom Helm, 1979).
Rorty, Amélie Oksenberg, 'What It Takes To Be Good', in G. Noam, and Thomas E. Wren (eds), *The Moral Self* (Cambridge, MA: MIT Press, 1993), pp. 28–55.
—— and Wong, David, 'Aspects of Identity and Agency', in Owen Flanagan and Amélie Oksenberg Rorty (eds), *Identity, Character and Morality* (Cambridge, MA and London: MIT Press, 1993), pp. 19–36.
Rose, Nikolas, *Inventing Ourselves: Psychology, Power and Personhood* (Cambridge: Cambridge University Press, 1996).
Rosenblum, Nancy L., 'Pluralism and Self-Defence', in Nancy L. Rosenblum (ed.), *Liberalism and the Moral Life* (Cambridge, MA: Harvard University Press, 1989), pp. 207–26.
—— (ed.), *Liberalism and the Moral Life* (Cambridge, MA: Harvard University Press, 1989).
Ruskin, John, *The Stones of Venice* (3 vols, New York, London: Garland, 1979).
Sabini, John and Silver, Maury, 'Lack of Character? Situationism Critiqued', *Ethics* 115 (2005): 535–62.
Said, Edward, *Culture and Imperialism* (London: Chatto and Windus, 1993).
Samuel, Herbert Louis, *Liberalism. An Attempt to State the Principles and Proposals of Contemporary Liberalism in England*, with an introduction by the Rt Hon. H.H. Asquith (London: Grant Richards, 1902).
Schad, John (ed.), *Dickens Refigured: Bodies, Desires and Other Histories* (Manchester: Manchester University Press, 1996).
Scheffler, Samuel, 'Morality's Demands and Their Limits', *Journal of Philosophy* 83 (1986): 531–7.
Schneewind, J.B., *The Invention of Autonomy* (New York: Cambridge University Press, 1998).
Schor, Hilary M., *Scheherezade in the Marketplace* (Oxford: Oxford University Press, 1992).
Seed, John, 'Unitarianism, Political Economy and the Antinomies of Liberal Culture in Manchester, 1830–50', *Social History* 7 (1982): 1–25.
Selby-Bigge, L.A., *British Moralists; Being Selections from Writers Principally of the Eighteenth Century* (2 vols, New York: Dover, 1965).

Sen, Amartya and Williams, Bernard (eds), *Utilitarianism and Beyond* (Cambridge: Cambridge: University Press, 1982).
Shattock, Joanne (ed.), *Dickens and Other Victorians: Essays in Honour of Philip Collins* (London: Macmillan, 1988).
Shaw, Harry E., *Narrating Reality: Austen, Scott, Eliot* (Ithaca and London: Cornell University Press, 1999).
Sidgwick, Henry, *Outlines of the History of Ethics* (London: Macmillan and Co., 1906).
Simmons, G., *The Working Classes: their Moral, Social and Intellectual Condition, with Practical Suggestions for their Improvement* (London: Patridge and Oakey, 1849).
Simons, Judy (ed.), *Mansfield Park and Persuasion* (Basingstoke: Macmillan, 1997).
Singer, Peter (ed.), *Ethics* (Oxford: Oxford University Press, 1994).
Smith, Angela, M., 'Responsibility for Attitudes: Activity and Passivity in Mental Life', *Ethics* 115 (2005): 236–71.
Smith, Michael, 'Realism', in Peter Singer (ed.), *Ethics* (Oxford: Oxford University Press, 1994), pp. 170–76.
Sommer, Doris, 'Attitude, Its Rhetoric', in Marjorie Garber, Beatrice Hanssen and Rebecca L. Walkowitz (eds), *The Turn to Ethics* (New York and London: Routledge, 2000), pp. 201–20.
Southam, B.C. (ed.), *Critical Essays on Jane Austen* (London: Routledge and Kegan Paul, 1968).
Spencer, Jane, *The Rise of the Woman Novelist: From Aphra Benn to Jane Austen* (Oxford: Basil Blackwell, 1986).
Stocker, M., 'The Schizophrenia of Modern Ethical Theories', *Journal of Philosophy* 63 (1976): 453–66; reprinted in Roger Crisp and Michael Slote (eds), *Virtue Ethics* (Oxford: Oxford University Press, 1997), pp. 66–78.
Stone, Wilfred, *The Cave and the Mountain* (Stanford: Stanford University Press, 1966).
Swanton, Christine, *Virtue Ethics: A Pluralistic View* (Oxford: Oxford University Press, 2003).
Swinden, P. (ed.), *Middlemarch* (London: Macmillan, 1972).
Symons, Jelinger Cookson, *Tactics for the Times, as Regards the Condition and Treatment of the Dangerous Classes* (London: John Ollivier, 1849).
Tagart, Edward, *Locke's Writings and Philosophy Historically Considered* (London: Longman, Brown, Green and Longmans, 1855).
Tanner, Tony, *Jane Austen* (London: Macmillan, 1986).
Taylor, Charles, *Sources of the Self: The Making of the Modern Identity* (Cambridge: Cambridge University Press, 1989).
———, 'The Diversity of Goods', in Amartya Sen and Bernard Williams (eds), *Utilitarianism and Beyond* (Cambridge: Cambridge: University Press, 1982), pp. 129–44.
Thale, Jerome, *The Novels of George Eliot* (New York: Columbia University Press, 1959).
Thomas, Jeanie, *Reading Middlemarch: Reclaiming the Middle Distance* (Ann Arbor: UMI Research Press, 1987).
Tillotson, John, *The Works of the Most Reverend Dr John Tillotson*, ed. T. Birch (10 vols, London: Dove, 1820).
Todd, Janet (ed.), *Jane Austen: New Perspectives, Women and Literature*, vol. 3 (New York and London: Holmes and Meier, 1983).
Toulmin, Stephen, *Return to Reason* (Cambridge, MA: Harvard University Press, 2001).
Trilling, Lionel, *The Liberal Imagination: Essays on Literature and Society* (New York: Viking Press, 1950).

———, *The Opposing Self* (New York: Viking Press, 1955).

———, 'Preface to *Beyond Culture*' (1965), in *The Moral Obligation to be Intelligent: Selected Essays*, ed. and with an introduction by Leon Wieseltier (New York: Farrar, Straus, Giroux, 2000), pp. 549–56.

———, *Sincerity and Authenticity* (London: Oxford University Press, 1972).

Trotter, David, 'Dickens's Idle Men', in John Schad (ed.), *Dickens Refigured: Bodies, Desires and Other Histories* (Manchester: Manchester University Press, 1996), pp. 200–17.

Tylor, E.B., *Primitive Culture: Researches into the Development of Mythology, Philosophy, Religion, Language, Art and Custom* (2 vols, London: John Murray, 1871).

Uglow, Jenny, *Elizabeth Gaskell: A Habit of Stories* (London: Faber and Faber, 1993).

Ullmann-Margalit, Edna (ed.), *Reasoning Practically* (New York and Oxford: Oxford University Press, 2000).

Vickery, Amanda, *The Gentleman's Daughter: Women's Lives in Georgian England* (New Haven and London: Yale University Press, 1998).

Waldron, Mary, 'The Frailties of Fanny: *Mansfield Park* and the Evangelical Movement', *Eighteenth-Century Fiction* 6 (1994): 259–81.

Walzer, Michael, 'The Communitarian Critique of Liberalism', *Political Theory* 18 (1990): 6–23.

Webb, Beatrice, *My Apprenticeship* (London: Longmans, 1926).

Widdowson, Peter, *E.M. Forster's 'Howard's End': Fiction as History* (London: Sussex University Press, 1977).

Wiggins, David, *Needs, Values, Truth* (Oxford: Blackwell, 1987).

Wilde, Alan, *Art and Order: A Study of E.M. Forster* (New York: New York University Press, 1964).

Wilkie, Brian, 'Structure and Layering in Jane Austen's Problem Novels', *Nineteenth-Century Fiction* 46 (1992): 517–44.

Williams, Bernard, *Moral Luck* (Cambridge: Cambridge University Press, 1981).

———, 'Morality, the Peculiar Institution', in Roger Crisp and Michael Slote (eds), *Virtue Ethics* (Oxford: Oxford University Press, 1997), pp. 45–65.

Williams, Michael, *Jane Austen: Six Novels and their Methods* (London: Macmillan, 1986).

Williams, Raymond, *Culture and Society: 1780–1950* (New York: Harper and Row, 1966).

Williams, Thomas, 'Moral Vice, Cognitive Virtue: Austen on Jealousy and Envy', *Philosophy and Literature* 27 (2003): 223–30.

Wiltshire, John, *Jane Austen and the Body* (Cambridge: Cambridge University Press, 1992).

Wolf, Susan, 'Moral Saints', *Journal of Philosophy* 79 (1982): 419–39.

———, 'Meaning and Morality', *Proceedings of the Aristotelian Society* 47 (1997): 299–315.

Wollstonecraft, Mary, *A Vindication of the Rights of Woman*, ed. Miriam Kramnick (Harmondsworth: Penguin Classics, 1975).

Wright, Anne, *The Literature of Crisis, 1910–22* (London: Macmillan, 1984).

Yeazell, Ruth Bernard, 'The Boundaries of *Mansfield Park*', in Judy Simons (ed.), *Mansfield Park and Persuasion* (Basingstoke: Macmillan, 1997), pp. 67–87.

Index

affection 24, 31, 36, 38, 48, 54, 63, 65, 71, 75, 77, 106, 110, 128, 131, 135, 140, 184, 190
Alford, C. Fred 2
all-things-considered stance 3, 48, 50
Allport, G.W. 70
altruism 5, 96, 183
amiability 65
Anderson, Quentin 129–30
Anscombe, Elizabeth 134
Arendt, Hannah 100
argumentation, substantive 17
Aristotle/Aristotelianism 34, 61, 82, 83, 170, 184
Armstrong, Isobel 75, 77
Arnold, Matthew 151–3, 157–9, 163
    Culture and Anarchy 151, 158
Ashton, Rosemary 130, 136
Asquith, Herbert Henry 6
attention 4–5, 14, 15, 31, 37–9, 41, 46, 53, 66, 68, 70, 72–3, 81, 107, 113–14, 120–21, 171, 183
attitudes 10–14, 16–17, 22, 26, 33, 37, 39–41, 46–7, 55, 60–61, 65, 68–70, 73, 77, 80, 86, 90–91, 94, 98–100, 103, 107, 112, 114, 124, 131, 136–7, 140, 150–51, 157–8, 166–7, 169, 178–9, 189, 193
    dominant 14, 158
    reasonable 3, 11–14, 17, 25–6, 29, 53–5, 60–62, 68–71, 73–7, 74, 82, 94, 96, 117, 134–5, 160, 169, 174, 183, 186, 188, 195
    unreasonable 10–11, 25, 32, 52, 61, 68, 70, 74–5, 77–8, 127, 134, 138–9, 188
Auerbach, Nina 63, 67
Austen, Jane 2–5, 7, 9–12, 23–7, 29, 46–7, 53, 55–6, 59–83
    Mansfield Park 4, 7, 10–12, 23, 25–6, 42, 46–7, 50, 53–6, 59–83, 180
    Northanger Abbey 62, 83

Persuasion 5, 9, 59, 60, 80
Pride and Prejudice 12, 27, 61, 65, 76, 102
Sense and Sensibility 11, 17, 46, 75, 77
authenticity 5, 17, 28, 73, 85, 100, 101, 103, 124, 177, 178
autonomy 8–10, 23, 26, 28, 32, 33–40, 85–103
    see also independent thoughts/mind

Bagehot, Walter 156, 158, 159
    Physics and Politics 156–7, 158
Baron, Marcia 131, 189
Bedient, Calvin 126, 180
Beer, Gillian 152
belief 6, 33, 35, 50, 87, 99, 116, 118, 125, 128, 130, 132, 134–6, 158, 189, 195
    forms of 125, 135
Benhabib, Seyla 29, 94, 95, 100, 170
Blake, Kathleen 123
Bloom, Harold 118, 123, 152
Blum, Lawrence A. 114, 125
Bodenheimer, Rosemarie 49, 85, 86, 96, 101, 110
Booth, Wayne 47
Born, Daniel 161, 171, 179
Bosanquet, Bernard 14, 162
Bosanquet, Helen Dendy 14, 161–5
    The Strength of the People 161–2
Bouthoul, Gaston 36, 144, 157
Bradley, F.H. 4, 14, 34–5, 36, 144, 160, 184, 186, 188
    Ethical Studies 4, 34, 36, 144, 160, 184, 186, 188
    on language contagion 36, 144
    on the mere individual as a delusion of theory 188
    on morality 4, 184, 186
    on self-realizedness 34, 144
Brown, Julia Prewitt 4, 66, 69
Brudney, Daniel 1, 45
Buell, Lawrence 1

Butler, Judith 2
Butler, Marilyn 2, 12, 59, 64–6

Cambridge Platonists 15, 31, 115–16, 119
Carroll, David 137
Cavell, Marcia 189–90
Chalier, Catherine 31, 33
Chalmers, Thomas 162
Chatwin, Bruce 17, 184–5, 187, 189–95
 Utz 17, 183–95
Christ, Carol 129
Christian-humanitarian theorists 91
Clarke, Samuel 134–5
Coleman, Janet 41
Coles, Nicholas 105
Collini, Stefan 10, 151, 162
comfort/comforter 5, 11, 22, 24, 34, 42, 59, 63, 72, 74, 83, 102, 180, 181
commitment/s 14, 30, 37 38, 86, 107, 108, 110, 120, 163, 165, 177, 184, 195
communitarianism 110
Connor, Steven 113
constancy 61, 135, 191
control 111, 113, 115, 128, 130, 146, 148, 159, 161, 165–6, 168–73, 175–6, 195
conversion 28, 36, 48, 49, 55, 79
Cox, C.B. 171
Cudworth, Ralph 115–16, 119
 Sermon Preached, A 115
Cullity, Garrett 183
culture 1, 8, 29, 36, 39, 88, 145, 146, 149, 150, 151, 152, 153, 154, 158, 166, 195
 as categories and habits of thought 149
 as complex whole 153
 of Hebraism and Hellenism 151, 152, 153, 157, 159
 'high' 36
 practices, traditional 152, 154
 scheme, Yeobright's 34–6, 143–4, 146–52, 154–60
Cunningham, Anthony 45

Daleski, H.M. 166, 171
Dancy. Jonathan 127, 128, 130
Dave, J.C. 146
Davidson, Jenny 25
Dennett, Daniel C. 186

desire/s 24, 26, 28, 33, 40–42, 56, 59, 61, 66, 69–70, 74–7, 81, 90–92, 98–9, 114, 119–20, 125, 130, 132–3, 135, 159, 175, 178, 186, 189, 192, 194
 expanded and complicated 194
 idealized 132
 independent 130
 informed 132
 second-order 175
Dewey, John 175
Diamond, Cora 26
Dickens, Charles 2–7, 9, 14, 15, 22, 27, 29–31, 47–51, 60, 86, 105–23, 129, 184, 187
 Bleak House 113
 Great Expectations 4, 5, 8, 113
 Hard Times 6, 15, 29, 30, 31, 47, 48, 49, 50, 51, 54, 87, 105–123, 183, 184
 Little Dorrit 47, 107, 108, 110, 118
 Martin Chuzzlewit 113
 Nicholas Nickleby 113
 Tale of Two Cities, A 113
dissonance (narrative) 47, 56
Doody, Margaret Anne 61, 76
Doris, John M. 13
drivenness 17, 185
duty 11, 23, 25, 32–3, 40, 55, 69, 71, 73, 88, 95, 125–6, 131–4, 159, 177

Eagleton, Terry 1, 152
education 6, 27, 31, 54, 83, 91, 106, 150, 152, 154, 163
Eldridge, Richard 1
Eliot, George 2–5, 7, 9–10, 14, 26, 31–3, 41, 43, 60, 101, 123–37, 141, 152, 171
 Adam Bede 125
 Middlemarch 7, 9, 31, 33, 41, 43, 47, 50, 51, 52, 123–42
 Romola 130
emotions 22, 25, 33–4, 38, 40, 51, 68, 76, 85, 107, 125, 129–30, 132, 154, 189
Enlightenment, The 2–3, 10–11, 21, 61, 118
Ermath, Elizabeth 128, 136
ethics 1–6, 10–11, 13–15, 17, 23–5, 29–30, 32–3, 45–6, 48, 50–51, 53, 61–2, 68, 83, 87, 102, 113, 124–5, 131–2, 134–9, 162, 167, 175, 183–5, 187, 189, 191, 194–5

ethics and ideology 51, 183
eudaimonia/eudaimonism 3, 4, 7, 10, 17, 21, 23, 34, 53, 62, 123, 184
Evangelicalism 11, 135
evil 8–9, 50, 52, 54, 59, 65, 92, 106, 116, 140, 154–6, 162–3, 195

fairness/fair-mindedness 7, 25, 53, 55, 132, 157
Federico, Annette R. 5
Finnis, John 11, 68, 195
Flanagan, Owen 7, 13, 25, 125, 195
Flathman, Richard E. 108, 111, 115–17
Fleishman, Avrom 67
flourishing 2–4, 13, 21, 35, 63, 68, 106, 125
  see also well-being
Forster, E.M. 2–3, 6–7, 9, 12, 14, 22–3, 26, 28, 32–3, 36–8, 40–42, 126, 161–83, 194
  Howards End 6, 7, 14, 17, 33, 36, 37, 38, 41, 42, 161–83
Fowler, Roger 106
Frankfurt, Harry 15, 16, 28, 118–19
Franklin, Benjamin 26, 61
Freadman, Richard 191
Freeden, M. 87
freedom 8–9, 32–3, 37, 51, 68, 76, 89, 106, 109–11, 117, 119, 132–3, 188, 193–5
friendship 37, 39, 82–3, 90–91, 95, 97, 108, 120, 131, 191
Froude, J.A. 128

Gallagher, Catherine 49, 85–6, 97, 106–7, 110
Ganz, Margaret 85, 86, 87, 97
Gard, Roger 12, 62, 67, 81
Gaskell, Elizabeth 2–3, 5, 6, 7, 14, 22, 26–9, 39, 49, 85–104, 109–10, 123–4, 194
  Mary Barton 88
  North and South 6, 7, 9, 27, 28, 42, 85–104, 109, 123
Gaus, Gerald F. 91, 93, 97, 99
gender 168
generosity 7, 82, 102, 130, 136
Gilbert, Sandra M. 127
Gilligan, Carol 95, 96, 101
Good, the 16, 70, 113, 117, 120, 128, 134

good/goods 4–5, 9, 13, 15–17, 24, 29–32, 36–7, 39–40, 42, 45, 48, 51–2, 59, 60–62, 68, 71, 74, 80, 93, 101, 105–11, 114–16, 119, 124–5, 128–9, 132, 136, 138–9, 154, 162–3, 167, 170–71, 175, 179–80, 184–7, 190, 193–5
  constitutive 60, 106
  foundational 108, 139
  genuine 128
  greatest 30, 33, 63, 71, 74
  hypergood 109, 114
  life, the good 5–6, 17, 23–4, 28, 32, 34–7, 39, 43, 71, 87, 109, 124–5, 164, 168, 171, 174–5, 178–9, 183–5
  key 51, 62, 106, 110, 134, 163–4, 175
  partial 128–9
  personal 194
  social 52, 194–5
Gordon, Mary 14
gratitude 76–7, 79, 92, 102, 134
Graver, Susanne 127
Gray, John 99, 103
Green, Samuel G. 86, 89, 92–3
Green, T.H. 162
Gregor, Ian 143, 152
Griffin, James 37
Gubar, Susan 127
guilt 4, 41–2, 137, 143, 147, 153, 156, 158, 160–61, 177
Gutting, Gary 8

Hadfield, A. 167
Halperin, John 126
Hardy, Barbara 107, 123, 128–9
Hardy, Thomas 2–5, 7, 14–15, 26, 33–6, 86, 143–7, 149–56, 159
  Far From the Madding Crowd 143
  Return of the Native, The 4, 7, 34, 143–60
Harman, Barbara Leah 86
Harpham, Geoffrey Galt 102
health 32, 82, 132
Helps, Arthur 86, 89, 91, 93
Henberg, M.C. 129
Herbert, Christopher 156
Hobhouse, L.T. 91
Holmes, Stephen 108, 110
Hume, David 32, 34, 65, 102, 117, 135, 194
Hurka, Thomas 168, 178

identification 39, 41, 89, 175
identity 7, 13, 30–32, 41–2, 95, 101, 103, 108–10, 119, 128, 131, 138, 157, 184, 190
ideology and ethics 6, 9, 27–8, 48–51, 93, 96, 183, 194
impartiality 30, 53, 64, 68
implied author 3, 47–8, 51, 56, 71
independence 8, 28, 39, 40, 54, 86, 90, 95, 100, 103, 106, 117, 194–5
independent thoughts, mind 38–40, 209
individuality/individualist 27–9, 87–8, 97, 103, 110–11, 117, 124, 159, 178
influence management 9
Ingham, Patricia 47, 107, 110
Ingram, Allan 17
integrity 5, 17, 41, 81, 101, 127, 129, 137–8, 189, 194–5
intentions 17, 25, 43, 47, 55, 68, 73–4, 108, 144, 147
interests 3, 5, 10, 14, 21–4, 29–30, 50, 53, 69, 72, 76, 86, 88, 92–5, 107, 116, 124, 161–4, 171, 177–8, 185, 194–5
intimacy 42, 110, 139–41, 190, 194
irony/ironic vision 46, 56, 63, 67, 69, 71–3, 135, 158

James, William 7, 23–4, 40, 137, 162
   character 162
   Principles of Psychology, The 24, 40
   on the overtrust of saints 137, 138
Johnson, Claudia 60
Johnson, Dr 69, 77
Jones, Karen 136
Joyce, Patrick 85, 86
justice 12, 17, 33, 61, 89, 92, 93, 94, 97, 99, 116–17, 129, 132, 134, 136
justification 17, 49, 51, 90, 101, 154, 183, 186, 188–9

Kant, Immanuel 14, 31, 32, 130–34
   Kantianism 31–3, 130–34
Kekes, John 14, 23–4, 35, 38, 167–9, 171–2, 175–7, 183–4, 186–8, 190, 193
Kelly, Paul 16
Kettle, Arnold 86
Kierkegaard, Sören 128
Kirkham, Margaret 62

Kittay, Eva Feder 94, 95, 101
Knoepflmacher, U.C. 126
Knox-Shaw, Peter 2, 4, 10, 11
Kolnai, Aurel 137–8
Kymlicka, Will 110

Langbaum, Robert 143
language inheritance 36
Larson. Jil 4, 15
Lawrence, D.H. 16, 17, 159
Leavis, F.R. 1, 107, 159, 166
Lerner, Laurence 138
Levenson, Michael 164
Levine, George 108
liberal/s 6, 27, 29, 49, 51, 86–8, 90, 93, 95, 102, 105–6, 108–11, 116–17, 164–5
liberal humanism 105
liberal ideals 86, 109, 165
liberal virtues 105, 117
liberalism 6, 27–9, 49, 87–8, 93, 105–6, 108–10, 116–17
   classical 27, 28, 49, 93, 95, 110
   new 6, 87–8, 99, 162
life enhancements 179
Locke, John 10, 12, 25–6, 76, 115–16
   Essay Concerning Human Understanding, An 10, 12, 76
   on memory 76
   on probability 10
   on reason, reasonableness and unreasonableness 10, 25
Lodge, David 112
Louden, Robert B. 185
love 31, 38, 69, 75–6, 85, 97–9, 101–2, 111, 119, 121, 131, 133, 143, 155, 158–60, 171, 175, 178–9, 193
loyalty 31, 33, 48–9, 111, 134–5, 176
luck 163, 166

Maccall, William 88
   The Elements of Individualism 88
MacIntyre, Alasdair 3, 16, 41, 61, 108, 110, 117
Mackie, J.L. 135
Mantel, Hilary 26
Marmontel 22
   Memoirs 22

marriage 33, 37, 40, 52, 54, 75, 87, 106, 109, 111, 124, 126–7, 136, 140, 147, 171–3, 176
  as companionship, comradeship 90, 174, 176
  as passionate and enterprising alliance 140
Marshall, Alfred 162
Masterman, C.F.G. 161, 162
maturity 96, 100–102, 113, 213
McCabe, Herbert 13
McCarthy, Thomas A. 192
McDowell, John 191, 192
McGinn, Colin 45
meaning 5, 7, 16–17, 22, 24, 30–31, 34, 37–8, 48, 127, 129, 133, 135, 144–7, 150, 153–4, 158–60, 163, 183–7, 189–90, 192, 195
  determination of 147
  in (good) lives 7, 23–4, 26, 29, 38, 63, 184
Medalie, David 6, 162
Mejía, Cristina 167
Metz, Taddeus 184
Meyers, Diana T. 94, 95, 101
Mill, James 116
Mill, John Stuart 6, 8–9, 14–15, 17, 21, 22, 27, 28–30, 49, 50, 85–93, 97–9, 103, 110, 116, 121, 124, 162, 165, 168, 177
  Autobiography 6, 9, 17, 21, 22, 26, 27, 61, 62, 88
  'Bentham' 30
  on (Benthamite) Utilitarianism 29, 30, 93, 106
  on character 8, 22, 98, 116, 168
  on the Christian ideal 121
  and individuality and well-being 27–8, 87–8, 99, 103
  on making choices 97
  on moral influences 27, 30
  On Liberty 6, 8, 28, 87, 97, 98, 99, 121, 168
  Principles of Political Economy 89, 99, 103
  on protection and the patriarchal system 89–92
  'Remarks on Bentham's Philosophy' 50
  and self-cohesion 92
  and self-development 88, 89, 98, 177
  System of Logic, A 98, 116
  on the will 99, 101, 116, 177
Miller, D.A. 51, 65, 80, 141
Miller, J. Hillis 125
modern consciousness 151
modernity 2, 5, 6, 8, 109, 152, 185
Moore, G.E. 36–7
moral
  agency 7, 107, 108, 113, 121, 131, 133
  competence 120, 144
  conversation 29, 100
  dilemma/predicament/quandary 2, 35, 53, 127, 132, 159
  endeavour 42, 124
  excellence 33, 123, 124
  maturity 96, 100–102
  motivation 130, 133–4
  obligation 149
  omission 159
  paralysis 22
  personality 15, 31, 65, 107–8, 120–21, 128–9, 131, 168, 177
  phenomenology 23
  philosophy 1, 13, 15–16, 23, 26, 45, 117, 134, 194
  progress 97, 100, 101
  psychology 15, 23, 25. 42
  radical 9
  responsiveness 114–15
  righteousness 4, 23, 43
  saintliness 33, 125–6, 138
  steadfastness 23
morality 2–5, 7, 11, 17, 23–5, 28, 30–34, 37–9, 43, 49, 61, 63, 65, 88, 95–6, 101, 113, 121, 125–6, 129, 131, 133–5, 137–8, 170, 179, 183–7, 189, 190, 195
  of altruism 5, 96, 183
  Christian 121
  demands of 179, 185
  of interdependence 96
  and meaning 7, 38, 183
  puritanical 126
  a reasonable 183
  of righteousness with significant 43
  as strict adherence to principle 55
  teleological 35, 53
Moreau, Sophia R. 186

Morris, Herbert 137
motivation/motives 4, 10, 13, 26, 43, 70, 72, 91, 107, 112, 117, 120, 125–31, 133–4, 186, 190
Murdoch, Iris 70, 113, 114, 117, 120
Myers, William 15

Nardin, Jane 23
narrative disjunction 3, 53, 138
narrative voice 4, 17, 46, 47, 50, 51, 62, 72, 125, 141
  agenda 47
  attitudes 47
  functions 72
  persuasion 46
narrator, the 32–3, 35–6, 42, 47–8, 50–56, 64, 69, 71, 73, 75, 79–80, 83, 106, 120, 123, 125, 127, 130, 135, 138–9, 141, 146–7, 149, 150, 153–4, 159, 164–6, 168–70, 172, 175–6, 178–9, 191–4
  as author 42, 47, 48, 53
  as character 48
  partisan 55
  presence of 48
  as source of tension 47
  as subscriber 48, 50
narrator's gap or evasion 55
Nazar, Hina 2, 4
Necessity 28, 118, 119, 191
Neill, Edward 144
Newey, Vincent 6, 7, 145
Newton, Adam Zackary 46, 113
Newton, Judith Lowder 96
Newton, K.M. 127, 129, 141
Nidditch, P.H. 10, 12, 25, 32, 65, 76, 194
Nietzsche, F.W. 2, 3, 21
non-conformity, non-conformists 9, 97
Norman, Richard 5, 31, 53
Nussbaum, Martha C. 1, 15, 26, 45, 47

O'Hara, Patricia 152
Orwell, George 105

Paris, Bernard J. 60, 129
Parker, David 1
paternalism 6, 48–9, 86, 89–90, 96, 108
Paterson, John 149, 150
Pecora, Vincent P. 50

perception 31, 41, 46–7, 51, 76, 97, 107–8, 112–14, 120, 123, 134, 152, 167
perfectionism, perfectionist ethos 53, 124
peripeteia 46, 112
Perkins, Pam 56, 64, 67
perspective, all-things-considered 3, 48, 50
Pickrel, Paul 67, 71
Pikoulis, John 97
Poovey, Mary 66, 69
postmodernism 1, 17, 29, 185
Power, David 89
practical reason, reasoning 31, 38, 56, 70, 130, 133, 167
practical wisdom, wisdom 4, 46, 100, 102, 151, 167–75, 177, 179
pride 12, 36, 102, 159, 190
psychological defence mechanisms/psyche, defence mechanisms of 60, 69–70
psychological maturity 96
psychological realism 70
Pulsford, Stephen 105

Radford, Andrew 146, 153, 154
Rainsford, Dominic 48, 167
rationality 29, 33, 62, 71–3, 78, 152, 188
  cognitive 73
  imaginative 78
Rawls, John 97
realism 9, 10, 70, 125, 128, 129, 132, 136, 184, 191
reason 5, 10, 12, 17, 25, 29, 31, 38, 49, 55, 62, 66–9, 71, 72, 74, 76–7, 82, 88, 91, 97, 99, 109, 114, 118, 130, 132–3, 136, 167, 186, 188, 191–2
  epistemic 72
  instrumental 29, 109
  normative 25, 72, 108
  order 29
reasonableness 11, 12, 14, 25–6, 29, 53, 55, 61–2, 68–71, 74, 96, 160, 169, 186, 188, 195
Rescher, Nicholas 22, 41, 68, 71, 78, 187, 188
Reid, Thomas 23
respect 5, 12, 17, 34, 51–2, 67, 79, 91, 101–2, 109, 114, 117, 119, 131, 134, 138–9, 160, 165, 178

responsibility 7, 11, 14, 35, 41, 54–5, 90, 93–7, 101, 117, 144, 147, 149, 150, 159, 177
  code of 93, 95, 97
  personal 54, 90, 93
Richardson, Samuel 60, 61, 65, 66
  Pamela 61, 65–6
rights 7, 27, 38, 88, 90, 93–5, 103, 117
Roberts, David 85, 86, 97
Rorty, Amélie Oksenberg 7, 13, 16, 25, 43, 195
Rose, Nikolas 8, 27
Rousseau, Jean Jacques 99
Ruskin, John 161, 163, 169, 172, 177–9
  Stones of Venice, The 169, 172, 177, 179

Sabini, John 13
Samuel, Herbert Louis 6
Sandel, Michael 117
Scheffler, Samuel 179,183
Schneewind, J.B. 9, 10, 23
Schor, Hilary M. 86, 93
Seed, John 88
self-
  abnegation, sacrifice 32, 101, 108
  absorption, indulgence 136, 159, 164–5, 169, 173
  abuse, distortion, deception 3, 56, 70, 72, 148, 175, 187
  assurance 42, 102, 170
  awareness, knowledge 25, 42, 70, 72, 101, 169, 179, 194
  coherence 7
  conception, image, representation 22, 31–2, 40–42, 53, 101–2, 107, 127–8, 186, 194–5
  control 25, 89, 98, 134, 164, 180, 189
  creation, cultivation 8, 152, 178
  defence mechanisms 60
  determination, direction, mastery 5, 7, 8, 49, 27, 81, 144, 147, 159, 169, 170–72, 195
  esteem, respect 22, 32, 52–3, 101–2, 109, 136, 138, 181, 184, 191
  fulfilment, realization 3, 6, 21, 24, 28, 34, 71, 107, 125, 144, 163
  improvement 25, 28, 88, 116, 139, 168
  interest 29, 49, 71, 106–8, 116, 188
  love 3
  perfection 24, 125
  persuasion 55, 64, 74
  reliance, sufficiency 49, 88, 89, 90, 169
  responsibility 35
  scrutiny, monitoring 172
  understanding 5, 7, 35, 70, 73, 116
  worth 41, 101
self as construct 15, 111, 158, 190
Shaw, Harry E. 10, 47
Sidgwick, Henry 23
Silver, Maury 13
Simmons, G. 89, 93
  The Working Classes 93
sin, sinfulness 76, 82, 135, 151, 153, 157–9
situationism 13
Smith, Angela M. 14
Smith, John 31
Smith, Michael 132
speech-acts 144
Spencer, Jane 67
Spinoza, Baruch 128–9
Stephen, Leslie 12
Stocker, Michael 125, 131
Stone, Wilfred 166
strength of character/inner strength 42, 135, 162, 163–6, 167, 168–9, 175, 180
Swanton, Christine 3, 32
Symons, Jelinger Cookson 86, 89, 91, 92
  Tactics for the Times 91, 92

Tagart, Edward 14, 15, 31, 115–16
  Locke's Writings and Philosophy Historically Considered 116
Tanner, Tony 11, 12, 53, 59, 61, 62, 75
Taylor, Charles 2, 10, 15, 16, 29, 30, 45, 109, 190
Thale, Jerome 123
Thomas, Jeanie 126
Tillotson, the Most Reverend Dr John 3
  Sermons 3
toleration 14, 38, 51, 88, 165, 174, 177
Toulmin, Stephen 17
traits, of character or identity 13, 61, 126
Trilling, Lionel 28–9, 67, 70–73, 118, 149
Trotter, David 113
trust 33, 95, 98, 111, 125, 135–8, 176, 179, 183

truth 1, 10, 12, 17, 70, 73, 77, 91, 101–2, 128, 134, 138, 145, 156, 162, 167, 191–2
Tylor, E.B. 153, 154, 156, 158
Primitive Culture 153, 154, 156

Uglow, Jenny 85, 98
Unitarianism/Unitarians' Domestic Home Mission 14, 88, 115, 116
Utilitarianism 16, 29, 30, 31, 93, 106, 109, 187

values 4, 9, 13, 24, 28, 36, 41, 51, 53, 62, 70, 72, 103, 105–6, 109–10, 111, 117, 125, 164, 169, 171, 180, 189, 194
 liberal 109, 165
 and motives 125
Vickery, Amanda 141
virtues 7, 13, 33, 49, 61, 62, 67–8, 82, 95, 105, 110–11, 117, 135, 160, 166–8, 175, 191–2
 liberal 117
 social 7
von Humboldt, W. 88, 154

Waldron, Mary 11
Walzer, Michael 110
Webb, Beatrice 29
well-being 2, 4, 6, 23–5, 29, 34–5, 48, 50, 53, 59–60, 63, 72, 87, 89–90, 95, 101–2, 105, 109–10, 124, 128–9, 133, 138–9, 146–7, 159, 163, 179, 181, 194–5
 see also eudaimonia, flourishing
wholeness 124, 129, 137
Wiggins, David 167
Wilde, Alan 171
Wilkie, Brian 62, 63
will, the 31, 60, 99, 108, 112, 115, 116, 117, 118, 119, 120, 132, 133, 134, 159, 186
 conscientious 99
 good, the 5, 9, 13, 15–16, 23–4, 31–2, 35–7, 42, 45, 51, 59, 61–3, 71, 80, 87, 101, 106, 108, 115–16, 119, 125, 128, 139, 162, 166, 170–71, 174, 179, 190
 self- 115, 116, 118
 strong 99, 108, 168
 wanton 117, 119
Williams, Bernard 30, 109, 183, 185
Williams, Michael 64
Williams, Raymond 107
Wiltshire, John 67
wisdom and control 173
Wolf, Susan 16, 34, 124–5, 184–5
Wollstonecraft, Mary 61, 66
 Vindication of the Rights of Woman, A 61
Wordsworth, William 158
 The Prelude 158

Yeazell, Ruth Bernard 66, 71